MANAGING
FOR INNOVATION

Leading Technical People

Watts S. Humphrey

IBM Corporation

PRENTICE-HALL

Englewood Cliffs, New Jersey 07632

Library of Congress Cataloging-in-Publication Data

Humphrey, Watts S., (date)
  Managing for innovation.

  Includes bibliographies and index.
  1. High technology industries—Management.
  2. Organizational change.   3. Professional employees.
  4. International Business Machines Corporation—
  Management.   I. Title.
  HD62.37.H85 1987   620'.0068   86-11262
  ISBN 0-13-550302-7

Editorial/production supervision and
  interior design: Richard Woods
Cover design: Lundgren Graphics, Ltd.
Manufacturing buyer: Carol Bystrom

Printed in the United States of America

10 9 8 7 6 5 4 3 2 1

ISBN 0-13-550302-7   025

PRENTICE-HALL INTERNATIONAL (UK) LIMITED, London
PRENTICE-HALL OF AUSTRALIA PTY. LIMITED, Sydney
PRENTICE-HALL CANADA INC., Toronto
PRENTICE-HALL HISPANOAMERICANA, S.A., Mexico
PRENTICE-HALL OF INDIA PRIVATE LIMITED, New Delhi
PRENTICE-HALL OF JAPAN, INC., Tokyo
PRENTICE-HALL OF SOUTHEAST ASIA PTE. LTD., Singapore
EDITORA PRENTICE-HALL DO BRASIL, LTDA., Rio de Janeiro

To Barbara

Contents

Part II   Managing Technical and Professional People

Part IV   Innovation

Part VI   The Organization

Part V   Innovative Teams

Part VII   Managing Change

21   TECHNICAL ASSESSMENT   167

22   STRUCTURAL CHANGE   176

23   THE CHANGE PROCESS   184

Preface

It has long been recognized that the dedication which produces superior performance is best obtained through deep personal commitment. It is through such commitments to specific goals that truly outstanding achievements are made. An effective commitment is based on both the intellectual belief in the goal and the emotional desire to achieve it. When people want to accomplish something so deeply that they put everything else aside, they will perform not only at their very best but often far beyond what even they thought was possible. That is the kind of dedication which breaks the four-minute mile, produces a program like Lotus 1-2-3, or deciphers the structure of the DNA molecule. Such things are not done casually or by people who don't care. They come from hard work and from the undiluted dedication of people who are deeply and personally committed. Commitment is thus the first essential management step in achieving superior performance in modern technology.

Suppose, for example, that you needed a new program written. You would want your programmers to give it high priority and to dedicate their energies to the project. Although there is no simple procedure to insure that they will do this, there are a number of methods which have been shown to work with reasonable consistency. Many managers are able to achieve such results occasionally, and some managers seem able to do so almost at will. The key is to both understand the professionals and to follow the right set of management principles. This knowledge and these principles are the subjects of this book.

THE IBM PERSONAL COMPUTER

In every organization, some groups always do the best work. They are separated from the rest by an energy and a spirit that seem to carry them over every obstacle. The group that developed the IBM PC had this character. Don Estridge, their leader, was told by IBM's top management to use any resources he needed and to break any rules within reason that got in his way to bring out an IBM personal computer at flank speed.

None of the individual things that Don did seem terribly remarkable, but the results he produced certainly were. His first step was to move the entire development group to a dedicated location where they could work as a closely integrated team. He then involved them in project planning and had every professional use a personal computer in his work. These were not IBM machines, but they were vivid daily reminders of the competition. This small hard-driving team made many innovations and broke many previously sacred IBM traditions to bring out a new machine in only one year. In just three years, they took IBM from ground zero to the undisputed leadership of the industry.

This success was not due to the IBM name, for other IBM teams had struggled with this same problem with little success. Even the unique charter of the PC team itself was not the answer, for this same group had only mixed results with the PC junior a few years later. This group's performance, however, did not happen by accident. It took the right kind of management actions—actions which any manager of professionals can and should use with his people.

There are an enormous number of factors which can improve professional performance. They include such items as confidence, skill, and respect. There are also many potential negatives, such as boredom, resentment, or simple misunderstanding. Some items are complex, while others are positive at one point and negative at another. Some teams will even perform well at one time and later, when faced with seemingly identical circumstances, not be productive at all. The complexity of this subject comes from the inherent complexity of the professionals themselves. Every professional has talents, desires, and fears, and these are the levers the manager must understand and use to obtain the dedication which produces superior performance.

THE BOOK'S STRUCTURE

Employee commitment can only be obtained by leadership. The leader must establish the goals and convince his people to accept them as their own. Part One deals with the elements of leadership and those leadership standards which sustain dedication and enthusiasm. The manager's leadership ability largely determines his organization's performance. Starting with leadership principles in Chapter 1, the key standards of commitment, professionalism, and respect for the individual are respectively treated in Chapters 2, 3, and 4.

Part Two deals with the motivation and development of those individual professionals who form the foundation of every technical organization. The goals of engineers and scientists are addressed in Chapter 5, Chapter 6 describes the way professionals' attitudes change throughout their careers, and Chapter 7 outlines the application of situational leadership to the management of technical and professional people.

Part Three deals with the identification of those technical and managerial leaders who will be responsible for the future of the organization. The effort spent in their career development is the most important investment any management can make. The identification of talented people is described in Chapter 8 while Chapters 9 and 10 discuss the development of high-potential technical professionals and future executives.

To be successful, most organizations must innovate. Part Four describes the innovation process and those techniques which help insure its effectiveness. Innovation is a structured process which involves creative professionals, resources, and opportunity. The key, however, is the skill and competence with which the management combines these elements into an overall effective process. Chapter 11 discusses the importance of innovation in modern technology, and Chapter 12 describes the innovation process as well as the key innovative roles of inventor, champion, and sponsor.

Since most modern technical work is too massive to be handled by an individual, the basic working unit is the technical team. Part Five examines technical teams. Chapter 13 describes their structure and behavior, and Chapter 14 outlines some useful principles for managing them. Chapter 15 then summarizes the key environmental needs of innovative teams, while Chapter 16 discusses reward and recognition programs. Chapter 17 outlines the special characteristics of the most important team in the organization: the management team.

Major technical projects often involve hundreds or even thousands of professionals working in many separate teams. Such work is supported by large administrative staffs and complex organizational structures. If these structures are properly designed, they will assist the manager in controlling the work while inappropriate structures will be a serious impediment. Part Six deals with organizational structures. Chapter 18 summarizes the basic principles of technical organizations and the general need for some kind of integration mechanism. Chapter 19 discusses the changes in management style with organization growth and the consequent impact on innovative performance. Chapter 20 reviews the political nature of the technical manager's job and the relationship between power and bureaucratic behavior.

The technical manager's job is to introduce new products, develop better processes, or solve new problems. While this invariably involves change, each change in advancing technology is progressively more difficult. The most effective answer is to build the organization itself to handle the more challenging problems of the future. Part Seven deals with this vital dimension of modern technical management. In Chapter 21 a process is outlined for assessing the organization, identifying its problems, and defining needed changes. These problems are often structural and can be readily addressed through organizational change, as described in Chapter 22. When the problems are deeper, however, a more formal process is required to modify the attitudes and practices of the professionals themselves. This proces is outlined in Chapter 23. Finally, as described in Chapter 24, modern technological processes generally require the discipline of managing continuous change.

Acknowledgments

IBM is a leading example of corporate technological success. It has demonstrated a remarkable ability both to make the right decisions and to make its decisions right. In large measure, this facility comes from the combination of IBM's enormous technical talents and the responsible attitudes of its people. A strong commitment to delegation allows IBM's local managers to make their own decisions within a common business and strategic framework. This enhances both technical and managerial creativity and provides an enormously rich environment in which to learn and observe all facets of technical management. I am intensely grateful to IBM for 27 rewarding years.

The chain of events which led to this book started with a luncheon conversation I had with Dr. Arthur Anderson at IBM's headquarters in Armonk, New York, in the fall of 1979. He had just been named Group Vice President of IBM's Data Processing Product Group and had asked me to work with him in assessing the effectiveness of his organization. This group of 20 laboratories and manufacturing plants employed about 100,000 people developing and manufacturing IBM's large scale computing machines and programming systems. These products are among the most advanced in the world and this represented a marvelous opportunity to observe at first hand the management methods which these organizations had found to be most effective. After I had worked with Art for several months, he suggested that I write a book about our work. This volume is the result. I am much indebted to Art for the opportunity to work with him and for his encouragement, support, and guidance in writing this book.

I also thank my friends and associates who have generously taken the time to review the various drafts and to give helpful comments and suggestions, particularly Dick Case, Ted Lux, Janet Perna, Bill Timlake, and Bill Weimer. I am also most grateful for IBM's willingness to release the previously company-confidential material which I have found so useful for illustrating many of the points made in the book.

Professor Dave Rodgers of the New York University Graduate School of Business has also been enormously helpful in guiding me through the large body of relevant management literature. His broad academic background has helped to balance my practical experience and to suggest references to put this work in proper prespective. I am much indebted for Dave's invaluable guidance and informed criticism.

I also give particular thanks to my secretaries, Vicci Paluszek and Marge Mozdzierz who have been generous with their help as well as to Mike Dvorocsik and Paul Nelson who were most helpful in clearing this material through IBM in advance of publication.

The highly professional staff at Prentice-Hall has made the completion of this book far easier than I had thought possible. I am particularly grateful to Jeff Krames and Rich Woods for their invaluable guidance and generous support.

A word of very special appreciation is also due my family. My brother Phil, a professor and a scientist, has offered many invaluable comments and my daughters Sarah and Katharine have provided enormously helpful suggestions on style and format. My wife Barbara also deserves recognition for her patience and understanding during the many months of writing and rewriting and rewriting.

Finally, I should point out that, although this book draws from many IBM sources and uses a number of examples from my years with IBM, it does not represent company opinion or policy; I speak entirely for myself.

Watts S. Humphrey
Chappaqua, New York

1

Technical Leadership

When John Keffer took over as manager of the printer group in IBM's Endicott laboratory, his main products were old and increasingly exposed to competition. He knew his team needed technical stimulation, so he purchased several of the leading competitors' products and installed them in his laboratory. He then challenged his engineers to find all the ways these machines were superior to theirs.

In the next six months, his people took these competitors' machines apart, estimated their costs, and learned their strengths and weaknesses. They soon saw how to make even better machines of their own, and they eagerly proposed plans for several attractive new products. They now faced a challenge they could really understand and were raring to tackle it.

By presenting the problem to his people in this way, John made them understand and accept the vital importance of his goals. This kind of imaginative leadership is a key part of successful technical management.

THE LEADER'S GOALS

The technical leader's most important role is to set goals and drive unswervingly to meet them. One of the best examples of this is the way Bob Evans handled the introduction of IBM's 370 computers. After Bob directed the development of the earlier IBM 360 machines he was sent to Washington to head IBM's military products division. He came back to computer development some five years later when the time had come to replace these 360 systems. Competition was increasing, and new technical improvements made it likely that even better machines would soon be available. To meet this threat, a new IBM system had been under development for several years and the time for announcement was drawing near.

During this same period a new concept called virtual memory had excited the interest of university experts and leading computer users. Machines using this design would have the advantage of seeming to have more memory than was actually there. This would greatly simplify the customer's programming job, and many people argued that the new 370 machines should have this capability. There was, however, an opposing faction who argued that virtual memory was inefficient and that the rapid reduction in memory costs would allow the same result to be achieved more economically with larger memories. This did not convince the virtual memory advocates, however, so the debate raged on. The issue was complicated by the high cost of the needed changes to the 370 design and the resulting one year's delay in the new system's announcement.

Bob Evans saw that virtual memory was important and realized that a decision must be made. The marketing people and the leading engineers, programmers, and scientists, were all asked for their views. Unfortunately, there was no hard evidence to support either side, so Bob had to rely upon his intuition. As the debates raged, however, he became increasingly convinced that this new direction, though unproven, was the way of the future. So within a few months of taking over IBM's systems development, he stopped several years of work, redirected thousands of engineers and programmers, and launched the virtual memory IBM 370 systems. This act of technical leadership not only changed the IBM product line but it set a new direction for the data processing industry.

Bob Evans's 370 decision was an act of leadership because he used technical judgment when the stakes were high and there were no clear answers. The natural course would have been to wait and see if the situation would clear up by itself, but here delay would have made the decision by default. The prior design would have been completed and the 370 systems would not have included virtual memory. The issues were faced, risks were taken, and a complex decision was made rather than letting events unfold. After the fact such acts of leadership seem so right that the uncertainty and contention are forgotten. The right course was not obvious, however, and the leader's role was therefore decisive.

THE CONVICTION OF THE LEADER

In addition to setting the direction, the leader must have the courage to stick with it. James MacGregor Burns points out that "Leadership . . . is grounded in the seedbed of conflict.'"[1] Once the leader makes his decision, he must drive to overcome all obstacles, and when his people are ready to give up, he must rally them for another try. This is the way General David Sarnoff of RCA acted when he shaped the future of color television.[2] In 1950 RCA and CBS disagreed over the way color television should be broadcast in the United States. The RCA design used an advanced three-color picture tube which they had under development. CBS advocated a mechanical system using a readily available technology which spun colored disks in front of the picture, much like the synchronized shutters on a movie projector. Although the CBS system seemed complex, it was felt by many to be less risky than the unknown RCA tube.

In 1950 the Federal Communications Commission approved the CBS proposal. At the time, Sarnoff said, ''We may have lost the battle, but we'll win the war.'' He was convinced that the RCA system was superior, and he accelerated development of the tricolor tube. On December 17, 1953, after RCA had demonstrated their system, the FCC recognized its technical advantages and reversed itself, thus making the RCA design the industry standard.

With all the resources of RCA at his command, Sarnoff originally had not been able to convince the FCC. They had the final authority, and they had spoken; consequently everyone but Sarnoff thought the tricolor system was dead. Sarnoff, however, kept his people working on the tube, and when they succeeded, the television industry was revolutionized. The engineers did a remarkable job, but it was Sarnoff's conviction which carried the day.

LEADERS AND THEIR FOLLOWERS

Leaders' drive and spirit provide the focus and energy for their organization, but they must first attract followers to their cause. Without them no leader has the power to perform. Leaders' power thus stems from their ability to attract willing followers, while managers' direction limits freedom of choice. The power to control is not the same as the power to lead, for leadership is a mutual relationship, and as Burns says, ''All leaders are actual or potential power holders, but not all power holders are leaders.''[3] Fred Brooks put it best when he said, ''Even the most rabid revolutionary must have a few loyal troops.''[4]

TRANSFORMATIONAL LEADERSHIP

One way to excite people's imagination is to build on their dreams and ambitions. Most engineers and scientists secretly aspire to greatness and long to participate in the excitement of some grand venture. Tracy Kidder captures this attitude in his description of Tom West's team building for his Eagle computer project at Data General. There was a rumor that Tom was building a ''cludge'' or a patched-up machine but he countered this by portraying his project as an effort ''to try to build the unattainable, the perfect computer.''[5] West talked for weeks to engineers about his plans and how important they were to Data General. He described the competition, the problems in the marketplace, and the kind of exciting new machine he planned to build. West put together a dedicated technical team that worked incredible hours to design the best computer they could imagine. They were in a tough competitive race with another Data General project, and their tremendous effort paid off with a successful new Data General machine.

By convincing their followers to dedicate themselves to their goal, leaders are practicing what Burns calls transformational leadership.[6] Such leadership is rewarding for everybody involved. The engineers and programmers gain enormous personal satisfaction, and the company gets a superior product. This excitement is typical of such projects as the RCA tricolor tube or the IBM 370 computers. Not all technical projects have this character, however, and none of them can be this rewarding all the time. Every engineer faces months of routine for every day of excitement, and the typical scientist spends years of preparation for each discovery. This mundane preparatory work must be done well, however, or it will not produce the foundation required. As Henry Kissinger once said, leadership comes from "the subtle accumulation of nuances, a hundred things done a little better."[7]

TRANSACTIONAL LEADERSHIP

Every manager has what is called legitimate power. It is the official power of a manager's position, and he or she assumes it instantly upon taking office. It includes such key rewards as salary increases, job assignments, and promotions. Managers have wide latitude in deciding who works on what project, who is recognized, and who is promoted. Employees know that their manager's opinion is important, and they work hard to earn and to keep their manager's favor. While managers rarely use this reward and punishment power overtly, it lurks behind everything they do.

Leadership based on legitimate power is called transactional leadership.[8] It can motivate action, but it also has limitations. For example, when an employee is concerned about his salary or the next promotion, he is more likely to focus on what the boss wants rather than on what the job needs. He is thus unlikely to be as creative or to hotly debate a controversial technical issue.

On the other hand, engineers and scientists have professional pride and are anxious to do a good job even if it is not exciting. One example of this is the way a product manager saved an important printer project. The engineers had proposed a new printer to replace an earlier machine. The older printers, however, were so profitable that the financial people questioned the need for a replacement project. The engineers struggled with these business issues but soon gave up and went to the product manager to get his agreement to cancel the program. To their surprise, he was not sympathetic. He told them their job was to get this better technical product out the door, and if the financial people weren't convinced, they must convince them. He expected them to succeed. The engineers went back to work and ultimately showed the businessmen how their machine's technical advantages made financial sense as well. The program was completed and the result was a very successful new product.

Although this product manager clearly provided leadership, it was not the traditional kind. He had not threatened his people, offered a reward, or asserted his official position. He had not even appealed to their loyalty or suggested a better way to do the job. What he did was to point out that they had not tried as hard as they might. By giving up before exhausting all possibilities, they had not measured up to their own standards. Dedicated professionals feel ashamed when it is clear they have failed to perform as they know they should, and a challenge to try again can be a great stimulus.

One wonders why these engineers didn't do the job right in the first place. Why did the product manager have to give them a lecture and send them back to try again? The reason is that most people need periodic encouragement to do their best. They need to be charged up and reminded that the goal is important and achievable. In technology, there are many failures for every success, and it is easy to become discouraged. Engineers and scientists are constantly struggling against adversity: the first cost estimates are always too high, initial schedules are invariably too late, and market projections are never adequate. The developer who gives up too easily will never complete a product, and his manager must sense this and urge him to try harder. The manager should guide, support, and help, but above all, he must not let his people quit too soon.

LEADING FROM BELOW

It is tempting to view leadership as something that "someone up there" does, but every manager can behave like a leader, whether he runs a corporation or a two-man department. The stakes, of course, are dramatically different in the small organization, but that does not reduce the importance of leadership. In fact, no technical organization can do superior work unless its junior managers take charge of their jobs and energize their people. Even the most dynamic corporate executive can accomplish little unless he inspires his subordinate managers to act as leaders themselves.

In principle, there is little difference in the leader's role, whether he or she is at the top of the organization or somewhere down in its bowels. In practice, however, there is one enormous difference. The senior executive typically knows that he or she must take action, while the junior manager is often immersed in a sea of bureaucratic attitudes and routine responsibilities.

The way Peggy handled her job is a good example of subordinate leadership. After carrying out several assignments very well, she was considered ready for a management promotion. The three plant stockrooms were being consolidated under a single new department, but several candidates had already turned the job down. When they offered it to Peggy, she saw it as an opportunity and jumped at the chance.

This was Peggy's first management assignment, and she resolved to do it the very best way she could. She took pains to learn the details of each of her operations and then started looking around to see how the other plants operated their stockrooms. She soon found that no one had any good measures for stockroom performance and that the established procedures had generally been in place for many years.

She also found that her stockrooms did not share inventory with each other and that there were no backup procedures.

With this background, she met with her people and asked them what they thought. They all believed that the procedures were outmoded and could be greatly improved. After reviewing her plans with her manager, she then organized her own people into a series of study teams for analyzing operations and proposing new methods. Her enthusiasm excited her team, and they willingly did this work in addition to their regular jobs. After several months work, they produced a streamlined procedure and a proposal to consolidate the three stockrooms into two. The result was both an inventory cost reduction and better stockroom service.

By leading her people, Peggy ended up leading the entire organization. Her work was soon recognized as an example by all the plants. By attacking a routine job in a creative way, she both helped her organization and gained the visibility needed for further promotion.

LEADING TECHNICAL PROFESSIONALS

Since no organization can consistently outperform its leadership, the leader carries an enormous responsibility. There are, however, few simple formulas to guide leaders. Lee Iacocca suggests that "when you're in a crisis, there's no time to run a study. You've got to put down on a piece of paper the ten things that you absolutely have to do. That's what you concentrate on. Everything else—forget it. The spectre of dying has a way of focusing your attention in a big hurry.'"[9] This, of course, states the need for clearly understood goals which the entire organization knows and accepts.

Leaders also set the pace for their organization, for, to again quote Iacocca, "the speed of the boss is the speed of the team."[10] You can't give every project a breakneck pace, but when the boss is relaxed about a day or two's delay, the organization will go to sleep. As Fred Brooks has said, "Schedules slip a day at a time."[11] The boss must insist on meeting commitments and hold his people to them, even if it means working late or through a weekend.

Finally, no important success is ever easy. Charles Kettering once said that if you "keep going . . . the chances are you will stumble on something, perhaps when you are least expecting it. I never heard of anyone stumbling on something sitting down."[12]

When people are discouraged and ready to quit, there are usually some avenues they haven't explored. What untried alternatives are there and has anyone else faced this problem before? Who are the leading experts and have they been contacted? It is surprising how often technical people find a creative answer after the boss has urged them to try one more time. The championship fighter James J. Corbett said it in the most compelling way:

> Fight one more round. When your feet are so tired that you have to shuffle back to the center of the ring, fight one more round. When your arms are so tired that you can hardly

lift your hands to come on guard, fight one more round. When your nose is bleeding and your eyes are black and you are so tired you wish your opponent would crack you one in the jaw and put you to sleep, fight one more round—remembering that the man who always fights one more round is never whipped.[13]

NOTES CHAPTER 1

1. James MacGregor Burns, *Leadership* (New York: Harper and Row, Publishers, Inc., 1978), p. 38.

2. *RCA Executive Biography: David Sarnoff* (New York: RCA Corporation, 1970).

3. Burns, *Leadership*, p. 18.

4. F. P. Brooks, private communication.

5. Tracy Kidder, *The Soul of a New Machine* (Boston: Little, Brown & Company, 1981), p. 67.

6. Burns, *Leadership*, p. 425.

7. Thomas J. Peters and Robert H. Waterman, Jr., *In Search of Excellence: Lessons from America's Best-Run Companies* (New York: Harper and Row, Publishers, Inc., 1982), p. 82.

8. Burns, *Leadership*, p. 425.

9. Lee Iacocca and William Novak, *Iacocca: An Autobiography* (New York: Bantam Books, 1984), p. 186.

10. Ibid., p. 95.

11. F. P. Brooks, *The Mythical Man-Month* (Reading, Mass.: Addison-Wesley Publishing Co., Inc., 1975), p. 154.

12. Michael LeBoeuf, *Imagineering: How to Profit from Your Creative Powers* (New York: McGraw-Hill Book Company, 1980), p. 238.

13. Ibid.

2

The Commitment Ethic

I learned an important lesson the day I first carried an IBM product through to final announcement. The machine was almost completely developed and there was no question it would work. We had detailed parts lists, and the manufacturing, testing, and service plans were fully documented. The cost estimates and schedules had also been completed and signed off by everyone involved. I expected the approval for manufacturing release and announcement to be a formality and was surprised to have the review meeting drag on interminably. The questions were so detailed that it seemed everyone was looking for reasons to object.

By the afternoon of the first day, my annoyance must have shown, for one of the older and more experienced engineers pulled me aside and asked if I had ever been through one of these reviews before. I had not, of course, so he explained that these people weren't just nit-picking; they were getting ready to make a commitment. ''And when they do,'' he said, ''they will move heaven and earth to do what they say. Give them time to get comfortable; it will pay off in the long run.'' It did.

The discipline of commitment is hard to live with, but it can be a great comfort. When technical groups must coordinate their efforts to produce a coherent result, schedules are needed and must be based on mutual agreements or commitments. Unfortunately, people rarely make accurate estimates, and something unexpected always comes up which causes delay. Then everyone has to scramble to meet the schedule. But why does everyone scramble instead of accepting the delay and blaming bad luck? The difference is the attitude of commitment.

THE ELEMENTS OF COMMITMENT

When one person makes a pact with another and they both expect it to be kept, that is a commitment. Gerald Salancik defines a commitment as the way to ''sustain action in the face of difficulties.''[1] In technology there is rarely the comfort of familiar ground.

8

Just about everything engineers and scientists do is a first of some kind. When people work together in this surprise environment, they must support each other; and this support must be based on a commitment discipline.

In one case a programming project was threatened by a change in an engineering schedule. The programmers were completing the control program for a special-purpose machine when the engineering manager called to say the first test machine would be delayed by two months. Since they were about to start testing, the programmers were in a panic. The programming manager had been an engineer, however, and he knew what to do. He called the engineering manager and told him the programming schedule was totally dependent on delivery of the test machine, and if it didn't arrive on time, he would call an immediate meeting with the president to tell him the cause of the delay.

In the turmoil that followed, the engineers found they could keep the date for the test machine after all. They had needed an additional machine for the service department and thought they could divert the programming machine to solve the problem. When forced to take responsibility for the delay, they found another answer. Engineering had committed the current schedule to the president and they were proud of always meeting their commitments.

The motivation to meet commitments is largely the result of the way the commitments are made. First, the commitment must be freely assumed. Although in the practical laboratory or manufacturing environments the degree of commitment flexibility is often limited, the person or persons who have to deliver should feel they had some choice. Even if they are only given a brief opportunity to speak up, to object, or to propose changes, they will feel bound by the promise only if they feel they undertook it willingly.

Commitment visibility is equally important, for only then is the professional's credibility at stake. Gerald Salancik points out that "acts that are in secret or unobserved lack the force to commit because an act that has not been seen cannot be linked clearly to an individual."[2] This, of course, is the key. The professional has personally made the commitment and his credibility is on the line. Credibility is essential, for without it the professional is on his own. Lee Iacocca summed it up when he said that "credibility is something you can earn only over time. And if you haven't earned it, you can't use it."[3]

Another programming example shows what can happen when these conditions are not met. The development project was seriously behind schedule, and it was clear that the original delivery date could no longer be made. Marketing was very concerned and threatened to escalate the issue to corporate headquarters if the schedule slipped any further. The project manager knew something had to be done, so he negotiated with the marketing managers and finally got their agreement to a schedule slip of three months. Even though this was the best he could do without a big corporate investigation, the programmers were not at all happy when they heard about it. As one of them said: "That's his date; I wish him luck."

The project manager had honestly tried to do his best, but he should not have acted entirely on his own. Since none of the programmers were involved in setting the new schedule, they did not feel personally committed to it, and not surprisingly, it was missed as well. Although the corporate escalation had been delayed, the manager had a tough time explaining why the schedule had slipped twice in three months.

MAKING RESPONSIBLE COMMITMENTS

Another important element in making responsible commitments is preparation. The commitment must first be explicitly defined and estimated. If several people are involved, they should all participate, and their views should be carefully considered. It takes time to make everyone familiar with the job and what they are expected to do, but this is the only way to establish a solid commitment foundation.

Next comes the actual agreement. In the simplest case, two people are involved: one who wants the work done and another who is expected to do it. They both want prompt and economical performance, but their interests are opposed. One wants an aggressive commitment to insure the fastest possible completion, and the other wants a comfortable buffer to allow for unexpected problems. The result is a negotiation where the skill and relative power of the two parties determines the outcome.

The third commitment step is performance. When all goes according to plan, there is no problem; but this is rarely the case. There are always surprises, and in technology there is an unwritten law that all surprises involve more work. With experience, technical people learn to allow for this, but their plans can never be entirely accurate. A final crash effort is thus invariably needed to meet the agreed deadline.

When the smoke has cleared, the work should be reassessed to understand what went wrong and how to make a better commitment next time. The estimates should be reviewed to see what was overlooked, and the contingencies should be revised to include the new experiences. By comparing actual performance with the estimates, the professionals learn to make better estimates. This is why the people who will do the work should make their own plans: to learn how to make commitments they can meet.

COMMITMENTS OR CRUSADES?

Although the commitment attitude is vital, it can be carried too far. In one case a low-cost printer was needed for a banking machine, and the plan was to use a special print-wheel mechanism. A small rotating plastic wheel was to be embossed with the print characters, and when the right character was in position, it would be hit by a hammer and driven into the ribbon to print the character on the paper. The first models were simple and inexpensive and worked quite well, so the concept seemed promising.

As development progressed, however, one problem came up after another, and the project was soon in serious trouble. First, the print-wheel plastic was too soft to make a clear impression, so small metal type slugs were inserted. Next, the plastic held the type slugs too tightly together, so that adjacent characters smeared on the paper. This was fixed by using metal fingers to hold the slugs, but then the fingers started to break. Spring steel was next substituted, but the springs vibrated and sometimes made multiple characters. This final problem was solved by using a compound spring which damped the oscillations. While the end result was a working printer, the original simple concept had become so complex and expensive that the design was no longer practical.

These engineers had become so dedicated to solving each problem that they lost sight of the original goal. With each change costs increased and the original simple concept was gradually destroyed. As the problems compounded, they should have called for an overall reassessment or asked for expert assistance. While their dedication was laudable, they lost their perspective in a blind drive to meet the original commitment.

Commitment hypnosis is a relatively common problem. Festinger, for example, points out that people convince themselves that what they want to happen must happen.[4] For example, when shown undeniable evidence that their design won't work, engineers frequently redouble their efforts. They are somehow convinced that a little more time and one more attempt will solve this last problem.

OVERCOMMITMENT

One trick of the optimist is to get his management so committed to the project that it can't be canceled. This is one reason why development engineers, for example, rush to get their product announced in the belief they will then be insured against a change of plans. An extreme example of this came up early in the development of the Concorde supersonic aircraft.[5] In the negotiations between Britain and France, a clause was inserted to the effect that a partner who withdrew would have to pay the entire costs of both parties up to that point. This clause made it impractical for either side to back out, regardless of the subsequent problems, since the costs of withdrawing grew progressively greater as the program progressed. Few organizations can afford such technological crusades. Internal commitments are essential, but management should suspect a development team which urges them to make an irrevocable commitment. Often, the engineers smell a problem and are trying to insure their project against cancellation.

Usually it makes sense to relentlessly drive through every obstacle, but sometimes this only adds to the costs of a hopeless venture. Not all technical projects can succeed, and those most intimately involved are generally the last ones to face reality. This is when a more senior manager can be most helpful. By remaining objective, he can sense when a new problem is a portent of failure and call for a technical review, get research help, or hire a leading consultant. Independent advice is often needed to balance the enthusiasts, for a technical team that has gotten itself into trouble will rarely get itself out without help.

MANAGING COMMITMENTS

One special-equipment proposal illustrates a common commitment problem. The engineers had worked hard to come up with a superior technical proposal, but their development schedules and manufacturing cost estimates were not competitive. The customer had called for a nine month delivery and the sales department insisted that several competitors would meet this schedule at a much lower price. Try as they might, however, the engineers could not see how to responsibly deliver in less than twelve months, and even that was risky. Their estimated costs were also 25 percent above the expected competition, and they could find no way to cut them further.

This was an important proposal, and the debate reached the top of the business. The sales manager was convinced the schedule and price would lose the order, while the engineers hoped the customer would recognize their proposal's technical superiority. After much debate senior management backed the engineers, and a discouraged marketing team was told to do their best to sell the proposal. To everyone's surprise the customer was so impressed with their design that he chose it in spite of its longer schedule and higher price.

There is always the fear that a competitor will have a lower price or a better schedule. Management's drive to beat the competition accounts for much of the pressure on engineers and programmers. Schedules are always too long and costs are invariably too high. The more important the stakes, the greater the pressure to cut and to take a greater risk.

In these circumstances, it is hard for managers to know how hard to push their people. This is when a commitment discipline is particularly important. Responsible professionals will search for every way they can think of to improve the program, but when they have no more ideas, that is the best they can commit. If management wants to gamble on something better, the professionals will do their best, but they cannot commit. Technical managers should support their people when they reach this point.

CHANGING COMMITMENTS

The other side of this coin is the problem of deciding when to change an existing plan. Every plan is a commitment, but it must also be a basis for managing the work. With a realistic plan the technical people can coordinate with their co-workers, but when the plan is unrealistic, coordination is practically impossible. People will make extraordinary efforts to meet a plan they believe in, but when the schedule is ridiculous, motivation is lost and performance suffers.

Managers must sense when a tight commitment ceases to motivate their people. There are no infallible signals, but it is usually easy to tell when they lose heart and begin to slack off. Progress reviews become nervous affairs where nobody wants to speak first. Status is suddenly hard to define, and none of the checkpoints seem very crisp. The reason is that everybody knows the project is in trouble, but nobody wants to be the first to say so and risk taking the blame. This is when the manager must call for a comprehensive review to find out just where things really stand. Without a clear understanding of the current situation, there is no point in making a new plan.

DOING A THOROUGH JOB

Judy, a development manager, did everything right, but her project ran into unexpected problems. She then met with all her people to review status and to understand exactly where things stood. Everyone was given a chance to speak up, to describe their concerns, and to make suggestions. She next met with her three first-line managers to agree on a new schedule, and then she went to the laboratory director and vice president to get agreement. When she told them about the new schedule, they were not pleased, but they recognized the problems and agreed that it was probably the best she could do.

Within a week, one of the first-line managers shamefacedly came to Judy to tell her that one critical function had been overlooked and that more time would be needed than the new schedule allowed. She was staggered because the function was clearly called for, and the additional work would certainly require a schedule change. Rather than go forward immediately, however, she called her managers together and told them to inventory every key project function to insure that nothing else was overlooked. In the process, they found two more items and the schedule was adjusted accordingly. When she took this story to the senior managers, they were highly critical of this new change, but when she explained the problem and what she had done, they agreed she had taken the proper action.

BUILDING THE COMMITMENT ETHIC

A commitment is a mutual agreement between two or more people who trust each other to perform. Dr. Kenneth Haughton, who was then manager of the "Winchester" file development program in the IBM laboratory in San Jose, California, found that his managers were not working together as effectively as he felt they should. The problem, he believed, was one of mutual trust, so he asked the department heads to define and document their mutual interdependencies. This was followed by weekly meetings to discuss these and any new interdependencies. The entire management team thus developed a thorough understanding of their working relationships and were better able to communicate. This built the trust needed for an effective commitment discipline.

Ken had realized that an effective management team must communicate openly and freely. Without such frequent contact small disagreements will inevitably fester, and mistrust will soon develop. These interdepartmental agreements opened up management communications, and after they served this purpose, they were quickly forgotten.

COMMITMENT OWNERSHIP

The person making a commitment should feel responsible to meet it. The case of one staff department shows how this works. This group was responsible for issuing periodic quality reports, and the data they needed was distributed over many files which had to be manually assembled and analyzed each month. Frequent special studies were called for, and every one turned into a crash manual effort to rework this same material. Because the tasks were so repetitive, the people were discouraged and morale was almost nonexistent.

The group manager knew that a computerized data base would be more efficient, so he had his people work out a proposal. No additional staff resources were available, so they planned to defer some of their regular work and to fit the rest into their tight work load. When they took their plan to the director, the job was expected to take a full year. The director, however, would need a new operating plan the following summer and knew this data base system would be enormously helpful in producing it. Unfortunately, summer was only nine months away, and he was reluctant to direct this overworked team to arbitrarily shorten their schedule. He told them why he needed this system in nine months and asked them to do their best.

The entire department worked hard for the next several months, and after much searching, they figured out a way to do the job much faster. They found an existing program that did much of the job, so that they could save three month's work. The entire department came to the next status review meeting. They were proud to meet the director's request and wanted him to know it.

This is a fine example of commitment. The director made sure his people understood the problem, and he asked them to do their utmost to solve it. Had he insisted that they do the job in nine months, it would have been his date and not theirs. By outlining the need and asking for their help, however, he put them in control. They thus felt personally committed to do their best.

NOTES CHAPTER 2

1. Michael Tushman and William Moore have included an article by Gerald R. Salancik in their book *Readings in the Management of Innovation* (Boston: Pitman, 1982). On page 208, he discusses the commitment process and why it is important in innovative work.

2. Jeffrey Pfeffer, in his book *Organizations and Organization Theory* (Marshfield, Mass.: Pitman, 1982), quotes Gerald Salancik on page 291.

3. Lee Iacocca, and William Novak, *Iacocca: An Autobiography* (New York: Bantam Books, Inc., 1984), p. 267.

4. Pfeffer, in *Organizations*, quotes Festinger, Riecken, and Schacter on page 294.

5. Gerald Salancik discusses this subject on page 210 in Tushman and Moore, *Readings*.

3

The Importance

of Professionalism

Harlan Mills, an IBM Fellow and a professor of computer science at the University of Maryland, tells his students that his standard is perfection. He has concluded that with the right knowledge and discipline, error-free programs can be written by almost any competent professional. He therefore insists that for their class project they each produce a program which is defect-free the very first time it is run on a computer.

In Harlan's view many programmers simply do not understand the importance of doing perfect work well enough to make the necessary effort. Learning to write perfect programs, however, is not easy. Special techniques are needed, so Harlan shows his students how programs should be structured and what tools, languages, and practices to use. He believes, however, that the key requirement is the personal commitment to do error-free work. The techniques are important, but Harlan is convinced that error-free results can only be produced by programmers who are dedicated to excellence.

This is a tough lesson. The students are initially staggered by the discipline of writing a simple error-free program. They struggle, through, however, and soon find that they can actually do it. What is more, they discover that it is more rewarding and easier to work this way. They used to start with a general idea of what the program should do and immediately plunge into writing the code, but they now think through the design completely before starting. When the design is done, they write the code, and then they rigorously inspect it before doing any testing. Changes used to be a serious problem, but now they are practically eliminated, and this saving more than compensates for the added work of design and inspection.

Harlan's technique is more than just a classroom exercise. Paul Friday, one of his students, took a job with the U.S. Bureau of the Census, and his assignment was to write a complex real-time program to control a nationwide network of twenty computers. He completed the twenty-five thousand instruction program on time, and it was used in processing the entire 1980 U.S. census without making a single error. This was such an important achievement that Paul was given a gold medal, the highest award of the U.S. Department of Commerce.

This is an example of professionalism at its best. Professor Mills's students had to learn the best technical methods, and they had to develop the discipline to rigorously use them. Harlan, as their leader, taught them how, and he spent many hours building their dedication to excellence. He exemplifies the kind of professional commitment which produces superior performance.

THE ELEMENTS OF PROFESSIONALISM

The two key elements of professionalism are the knowledge of what to do and the discipline to do it. Technical knowledge is the true mark of the professional, for it sets him above his less learned fellows. In historic terms, however, it is only recently that humankind has learned to pass this knowledge from one generation to the next. Early word-of-mouth communication was totally inadequate for technical material, and it was not until Gutenberg developed his printing press in A.D. 1440 that volume communication of technical material was practical.

In the century after Gutenberg, scientific development began in earnest. Leonardo da Vinci, Nicolaus Copernicus, Sir Francis Bacon, Galileo Galilei, and Johannes Kepler were all born in this period. The reason for this remarkable explosion of talent was best explained by Sir Isaac Newton when he said, "If I have seen farther it is by standing on the shoulders of giants."[1] This is the most fundamental principle of professionalism: the knowledge of what others have learned and the discipline to build upon it.

REINVENTING THE WHEEL

William Norris, the chairman of Control Data Corporation, has said that "the technological wheel is being wastefully reinvented everyday."[2] Technical blindness has many costs, but one of the most important is legal. When a product is improperly designed or constructed, there is a risk that somebody will get hurt. With the increasing uses of technology this risk has now grown to where just about every engineer and scientist should be concerned. James Henderson estimates that 25 percent of all new product litigation alleges engineering negligence, and Frank Fowler points out that most technical negligence is due to the designer's failure to use readily available information.[3] He cites the example of a mechanical engineer who did not consider the fatigue properties of steel in designing an automobile bumper. Since bumpers are frequently stressed, even an uninformed jury would likely view such an oversight as negligence.

Products get used in many ways, and each new application creates added liabilities. To be reasonably safe, professionals should be aware of the latest work in their fields and use this knowledge in their work. If they don't, their work, when viewed in hindsight, may be deemed incompetent, and that could be very expensive. It is both safer and cheaper to know the subject and use this knowledge than to face the indefinite risk of product liability.

THE BENEFITS OF AWARENESS

In addition to legal protection, technical awareness also has important benefits. Dick Daugherty, the manager of IBM Raleigh manufacturing, faced a major expansion program to handle the growing volume of orders for a family of new IBM communications products. In a few months, manufacturing capacity had to double, and then volume would continue to increase for several more years. Such problems as handling waste paper reached crisis proportions, and materials handling, inspection, shipping, and packing were all under intense pressure. Dick and his people solved each problem as it came up, but these enormous volumes were a new experience, and they had trouble anticipating the next crisis.

During a review with the vice president, Dick was asked what he planned to do about this problem. The executive was satisfied with his answer that he was getting help from some IBM experts, but the question started Dick thinking about other sources of experience. In the next six months he and his team met with production experts from several parts of the United States and Japan, and they found many ideas they could use. Although these companies were in different industries and had different problems, the interchange of information stimulated their thinking and helped steer them from several blind alleys. Some time later, Dick estimated that more than half the new ideas introduced in his plant during this period were traceable to these outside meetings.

The cost of technical blindness can be severe. If an engineer or scientist is not aware of current technology, the product he designs will likely not be competitive. New concepts generally appear almost simultaneously in several places, and alert professionals will quickly pick them up. Robert K. Merton says that "great ideas are in the air, and several scholars simultaneously wave their nets.''[4] If one such new idea can replace or improve a key product, it is essential to learn about it before the competition. Informed professionals provide the only practical protection against this risk.

MANAGING AWARENESS

Awareness is so obviously important that it seems unnecessary to spend much time on it. Unfortunately, most professionals make little effort to stay technically current. They don't read the technical literature, go to conferences, or take available technical courses. In 1981 IBM ran a survey of nearly two hundred programmers to find out what they were doing to stay up to date. The key findings were as follows:[5]

1. 72 percent read trade magazines, but less than 19 percent read technical journals on a regular basis.
2. 42 percent had attended company-sponsored symposia, workshops, or seminars, but only 8 percent had been to external professional conferences.
3. 71 percent spent five hours or less per month of personal or job time in keeping informed of the latest technical events in their fields.
4. 87 percent had never published any external (to IBM) paper.

Even though most of these professionals had college degrees and had worked an average of more than ten years, they were obviously not keeping up with their professional fields. IBM recognized that this was a serious problem and established a Software Engineering Institute to help its programmers stay abreast of the latest technical developments.

Technical currency, however, is not just a problem for programmers. The Engineering Index continuously assembles and classifies abstracts from some two thousand technical periodicals and fifteen hundred conferences from all over the world. These are made available to any of the seventy thousand engineers and one hundred thousand technical organizations in the United States that want to subscribe. A study some years ago showed that from this large technical population there were only 694 monthly subscribers.[6]

The Engineering Index is now run by a private organization which treats such subscriber data as confidential, but public records show their annual revenue growth to be about 15 percent. Although the number of users is presumably still small, this rate of growth is a hopeful sign.

Keeping current used to be an almost impossible job, and the doubling of the volume of technical information every ten years has now rendered manual search methods totally inadequate.[7] Today, however, abstracting services can make computer searches for a modest fee, and technical societies publish journals and hold conferences on a host of special topics. Many employers have libraries and abstracting services of their own, and local universities also provide valuable assistance. With all these available facilities, there is no reason for technical professionals to be unaware of the latest work in their field.

Reading is the most effective way to stay current, but technical meetings are also helpful. The formal papers are one source of input, but the informal exchange of ideas with the other attendees is often even more valuable. One IBM study asked a group of engineers and programmers their views about internal technical conferences, and their responses are shown in Table 3.1.[8] Clearly, 75 percent felt they gained useful information from the meetings, and one in five felt they had learned something important to their current work.

Managers can help their people by emphasizing the value of technical awareness. They should, for example, ask them who is doing the best work in the field or if they have retained the leading experts as technical consultants. What do they know about competition, are they aware of pertinent work at the local university, and what

TABLE 3.1   Survey of Eighty-Five Attendees at IBM Conferences

Had a good time 8%
Stimulating discussion .... .17%
Got valuable general information .... .36%
Got specific information for my project .... .15%
Got very important information for my project 6%
Got specific information for a colleague's project .... .18%

relevant technical articles or books have they read? When professionals are consistently asked such questions, they make a greater effort to stay technically aware.

KNOWLEDGE IS ONLY THE BEGINNING

All the knowledge in the world, however, is useless without the will to use it. There is a story about a county agent who called on an old farmer. "Lem," he said, "How would you like to farm twice as well as you do today?" "Shucks," said Lem, "I only farm half as good as I know how already."

Few people do their jobs as well as they know they could. Abraham Lincoln expressed the proper attitude when he said that "I do the very best I know how—the very best I can; and I mean to keep doing so until the end. If the end brings me out alright, what is said against me won't amount to anything. If the end brings me out wrong, ten angels swearing I was right would make no difference.⁹

Engineers and programmers almost always have good ideas about how their jobs could be improved, but when asked why they don't do it that way, they invariably have several excuses. They are either too busy, they don't believe their management will support them, or they are too far into the current project to change. They insist they will do it that way the next time, but unfortunately these "next times" rarely happen.

One programming department had a dismal history of missed commitments, and George, the new manager, believed that documented cost estimates and detailed schedules were essential for good project control. When he asked his project managers to show him such documents, however, none of them could. They had informal notes or general ideas, but no one had formal documentation. When George asked their views on the best way to manage their projects, however, they all said that such documents would be very helpful. They rationalized not having them because their best people would have to do the work, and they simply could not afford to use them this way.

George had expected this reaction, but he was convinced that such control was the only way to meet commitments. Since his people were obviously not going to do this work on their own, he decided to review every project personally and not approve any that did not have documented schedules and estimates. When he found a project that wasn't properly managed, he would not let it proceed until it was. Soon, everybody knew that documented schedules and estimates were essential, if only to satisfy George.

There was some initial grumbling about such hard-fisted management, but pretty soon the programmers found that these detailed project plans actually helped them do their work. They had previously missed every schedule, and costs were always out of control; but now commitments were being met. Instead of making excuses, they were being praised and the experience was exhilarating.

Good work has many benefits. When the professionals thoughtfully decide on the best way to do a job, it is probably the easiest, fastest, and most economical way as well. Few people go through this thought process, however, and fewer still really do their jobs the way they know they should. The true professional, however, has the competence to find the best way and the discipline to do it just that way.

THE DANGER OF SLOPPY WORK

In this increasingly complex world, people have come to depend on technology. On November 21, 1980, for example, a group of lobstermen set out from Cape Cod for a week of fishing on the Georges Bank. They had relied on the National Weather Service's forecast of fair weather, but within one day they were hit by 100 mile an hour winds and 60 foot waves. All but one of the fishermen were drowned, and the courts subsequently awarded their families multimillion-dollar damages from the federal government. The judge ruled that the National Oceanic and Atmospheric Administration had for three months negligently failed to repair a weather buoy that could have helped forecast the storm.[10] With the increasing public dependence on technology, such acts of negligence can be both dangerous and expensive.

THE DISCIPLINE OF VISIBILITY

It is hard to do superior work, and it is almost impossible to do it in secret. When a professional's work will not be publicly exposed, he faces a terrible temptation to cut corners. It is not often that one sees the dedication of the ancient cathedral craftsmen who carefully carved the backs of the angels' heads. While they knew that no human would admire their work, they firmly believed that the Almighty would. I once knew a technician who had this same attitude. Once, we had to delve deep into the system's innards to correct a problem we hit in system test. We found carefully color-coded wiring that was squared off and neatly wrapped, and we knew that this technician had done it. Sure enough, his work was OK.

Visibility gives a professional an extra motivation to do thorough work. He thinks more logically about the alternatives and makes an extra effort to find the key references. One example of this visibility effect came up at the IBM Systems

Research Institute.[11] SRI teaches IBM engineers and programmers the latest system concepts, and distributed processing was just emerging as an important new systems idea. When the SRI advisory board suggested that they teach a course on distributed processing, the faculty said the field was too ill structured to teach. Under questioning, however, they agreed that someone would have to structure the material for the first time and that they could probably do it.

The three faculty members who were selected to develop and teach this course investigated all the available IBM and competitive products, talked to several university professors, and read all the relevant technical papers. They were surprised at how much material was available and how quickly they reached the limits of available knowledge. When the course was offered, it was an immediate success.

This example shows the power of visibility. These instructors knew their students would be experienced engineers and programmers and that some of them would be working on distributed systems. If the material were superficial, they could expect loud criticism. They were thus highly motivated to learn the subject completely and to present it logically.

VISIBILITY IS HARD WORK

When people don't want to write papers or give talks, there are always plenty of excuses. The best work is often proprietary, and management is understandably reluctant to publish an article that will help the competition. Confidentiality, however, is not an insoluble problem. There are often nonconfidential ways to describe important work, and no security classification lasts forever.

When good people publish, the competition learns their names and may try to recruit them. This is also a serious concern, but it makes no sense to try to conceal outstanding people. An engineer or programmer who seeks visibility will distrust his management if they try to hide him. It is better to treat them so that they will want to stay than to deny them the technical credit they deserve.

Writing a paper, presenting a talk, or teaching a course does, however, take a lot of work. Engineers, scientists, and programmers generally are very busy, and once they get past the excuse stage, they must somehow give such work high enough priority to get it done. Busy people never do their lowest priority tasks, and for something to get done, it must get to the top of the list for the time it takes to do it. Many busy people do this kind of work on their own time, and it is surprising how many of them will make this extra effort when asked.

An example of this is the IBM System 38. When it was announced, the project manager felt that some technical papers should be published on the machine's key features. Announcement was clearly the best time to publish, but everybody was very busy resolving the many final engineering and programming details. Because of these pressures Brian Utley didn't expect many responses but decided to ask for volunteers anyway. His people surprised him, however, for they wanted to publish their work, and they were willing to put in the needed extra time. A total of twenty-nine papers were bound together and published in the book *IBM System/38 Technical Developments*.[12]

In retrospect, this response is not too surprising. Everyone likes to be recognized, and anyone who has published knows the thrill of seeing his own name in print. Many first-time authors seriously doubt that they could produce a publishable paper, and the simple act of asking them is a compliment. They are flattered to be recognized as having something to say that is worth publication, so when faced with a real opportunity to publish, they will generally find the time to do the work.

THE BENEFITS OF VISIBILITY

One advantage of having a professionally visible organization is the pride and self-confidence it generates. Self-confident people are more willing to fight for their beliefs and to take the personal risks of creative work. It takes conviction and self-reliance to defend a new idea or propose a change. As John Gardner has said, "Excellence is not an achievement of demoralized or hopeless individuals."[13]

A professionally well-known group is also more attractive as a place to work. The best candidates want to join a leadership team, and the employees are more inclined to stay. A reputation for technical excellence is also a big help in the marketplace, for customers feel more comfortable when dealing with a recognized leader.

When Jack Kuehler ran IBM's technology division, the semiconductor operation in Burlington, Vermont, had been doing excellent technical work but was not properly recognized as a leader in the industry. Jack decided to do something about this. The semiconductor industry was then in volume production on 64K memory chips, and development was just beginning on 256K chips. The Burlington laboratory, however, already had a 288,000-bit chip in pilot production. This 288K chip was four times larger than the best units then in volume production.

At about that time, Jack was invited to talk to an electronics show in Boston, and his people told the press that he had an important announcement to make. This attracted a lot of attention, and when he described the new 288K units, IBM Burlington made the front page of *The Wall Street Journal*. This was more than just an exercise in public relations, however, for it helped to build the pride and spirit of the Burlington team. They have since been the first in the industry to announce almost every new computer memory advance, and their leadership is recognized by all.

PROFESSIONALISM AFFECTS PERFORMANCE

IEEE Spectrum recently ran a survey to find out how managers and professional nonmanagers felt about professionalism. An astounding 81 percent of those replying to the survey felt that it was either "essential" or "strongly helpful" for engineers to keep technically up to date.[14]

An RCA study compared the job performance of two hundred engineers from four RCA laboratories with their professional behavior.[15] They selected nonmanagers who were between thirty and sixty years of age and divided them into categories according to their manager's judgment of their performance. These engineers were then asked to fill out a questionnaire on their professional activities. The results showed a strong correlation between job performance and professional activity in presentations, patents, awards, and technical currency. They attributed the lack of correlation in publications to the fact that most of their people were too busy to write papers. Since at least some engineers who publish do so because they are not very busy, the value of such work is hard to demonstrate statistically.

A study by Crook also shows a significant correlation between professional activity and job performance.[16] He studied eight technical teams of between twenty and sixty professionals in two development and two manufacturing locations. To determine the performance of each team, he interviewed five senior managers and averaged their ratings. In sum, he found that more members of the high-performing teams belonged to technical societies and that they spent more than twice as much time in technical reading. They also attended more conferences, published twice as many papers, and had more than twice the patent activity.

THE MANAGER'S ROLE IN PROFESSIONALISM

There are many things a manager can do to set a professional example for his people. Engineers and scientists who have never searched the literature or written papers don't appreciate the benefits of such work, and since they invariably have more to do than they can handle, they won't make the effort unless encouraged. If they are asked the right questions, however, they are more likely to give this subject the priority it deserves. Some steps which will help to build and maintain this professional attitude are the following:

1. When reviewing a project, ask the people what they know about the work of others. If someone has a better product, why is it better, who is doing the leading work in the field, and what experts have they contacted?
2. The manager should read technical journals and send copies of interesting articles to his people with comments and questions.
3. At promotion reviews, the professional histories of each candidate should be explored. Has he given talks, published papers, filed patents, or taught courses?
4. Such professional accomplishments as talks, articles, and patents should be highlighted in promotional announcements.
5. Outstanding contributors should be celebrated at a recognition dinner or other special event.
6. The key people should be invited to give occasional talks or papers at technical society meetings, and they should get special recognition when they do.

7. Above all, the managers set the professional tone for the organization. If they behave professionally, their people are more likely to as well.

NOTES CHAPTER 3

1. Stephen Jay Gould, *The Panda's Thumb* (New York: W. W. Norton & Co., 1980), p. 47.
2. Ernest J. Breton, "Reinventing the Wheel," *Mechanical Engineering*, March 1981, p. 54.
3. Ibid.
4. Gould, *The Panda's Thumb*, p. 47.
5. This data came from a survey of 163 IBM programmers from several development laboratories which was conducted in early 1981. It concentrated on experienced programmers, although some recent computer science graduates were included. While the sample was small, little or no correlation was found between experience, degree level, educational specialty, and professional behavior.
6. Breton, "Reinventing the Wheel."
7. Ibid.
8. This information came from a survey of 150 IBM professionals who attended interdivisional technical liaison conferences. They were asked what benefits they had gained from such meetings in the previous three years. Eighty-five provided complete responses.
9. Michael LeBoeuf, *Imagineering: How to Profit from Your Creative Powers* (New York: McGraw-Hill, 1980), p. 170.
10. *The New York Times*, December 22, 1984, sec. 1.1 and May 15, 1986, p. A-22.
11. IBM established the Systems Research Institute (SRI) in 1960 to provide advanced systems education to technical employees. It has a permanent faculty, offers many courses and symposia, and conducts limited systems research. The courses are at the graduate level and several universities have granted graduate credit for SRI attendance.
12. *IBM System/38 Technical Developments* (Armonk, N.Y.: IBM Corporation, 1978).
13. John W. Gardner, *Excellence* (New York: Harper & Row, Publishers, Inc., 1961), p. 104.
14. John Adams, "Survey Finds Different Views Held by Managers, EEs, on Education," *The Institute*, vol. 8, no. 10 (October 1984).
15. W. J. Underwood and M. A. Keating, "RCA Study Links Professional Success with Job Performance," *The Institute*, vol. 8, no. 10 (October 1984).
16. Robert Anthony Crook, "Factors Affecting Technical Productivity and Creativity of Engineers," Master of Science Thesis in Management of Technology, MIT, May 1984.

4

Respect

for the Individual

Informed and motivated professionals do the best work. Take the case of an experienced engineer who was looking into the problem of circuit card damage during shipment. This was not a new problem, and the previous investigations had always stopped when the losses were found to be within estimates. This time, however, the engineer doing the study looked more deeply and found that major cost savings were possible. The current shipping packages, for example, gave only limited physical protection and no protection from electrostatic damage. These delicate circuit boards were very expensive, and it was apparent that a special shipping case would more than pay for itself. It took months to get approval to build some sample packing boxes and get them tested. Agreement for a larger pilot test took even more time. After these tests were successful, the OK for full-scale production came more quickly.

Although this change was ultimately accepted, there were many times when this engineer could easily have given up. Often, he seemed to be the only person trying to solve the problem. Engineering, for example, spent weeks debating the costs and how they should be covered; manufacturing didn't want to change their shipping and inventory procedures, and service objected to grounding the case before opening it. Since electrostatic damage was the major issue, this grounding step was an essential part of the cost justification; so he stuck to his guns. The full scale field test proved him right.

Professionals often must choose between the easy answer and a much more difficult thorough analysis. There is invariably some superficial solution which permits unmotivated professionals to get by, but this rarely solves the tough problems. Major advances are made by professionals who are motivated to do a thorough job and don't give up under pressure. As H. L. Mencken once said, "For every complex question there is a simple answer, and it is wrong."[1]

THE STANDARD OF RESPECT

To do such dedicated work, the professional must be interested in his job, motivated to succeed, and confident of his role in the organization. If not, he will likely wonder about his next assignment, complain about not getting a raise, or worry about the boss's opinion. When a professional spends his time this way, he cannot deal objectively with his management or think creatively about his assignment.

An employee's attitudes are affected by many things which are unrelated to his work. The manager's behavior, however, is the single most important work-related factor. There are several things managers should do to enhance their people's attitudes, but the essential first step is to respect their need for personal value. John Gardner defines happiness as striving for meaningful goals,[2] and unhappy professionals rarely do their best work. This means that the people should have clearly defined goals and a manager who respects their role in achieving them.

If a manager does not show that he respects his people, they will not trust him, and then even the most challenging work can become a chore. To strive to meet the organization's goals, the employees must feel their interests parallel those of their manager. When this mutually trusting relationship is coupled with challenging work, that is when jobs become truly exciting. Motivational studies show that both the employees' work and a trusting relationship with their manager are paramount. If either is lacking, nothing else can compensate.

THE ELEMENTS OF RESPECT

Respect for the individual rests on an attitude of fairness. Each person must be valued as an individual and treated according to his personal wants and needs. Merit salary scales and job evaluation programs help insure that those doing the best work earn the greatest rewards. Of necessity, promotions must be infrequent, and they should be granted according to performance. Clearly, some will be unhappy when they are passed over, but even they will grudgingly respect a fair and objective program.

William A. Cohen describes what happens when the people don't trust their management.*   .

> Several years ago during the recession, an engineering organization in a California division of a company went from twenty engineers to just seven in less than three weeks due to a rumor. What happened was this: A major contract was lost. One engineer overheard the president of the company tell the director of engineering to wind up the in-house work that was being done, and he heard the president say, ''That's the last time we'll have to bid one like that.'' The engineer spread the word that in-house work would

*Reprinted, by permission of the publisher, from PRINCIPLES OF TECH-NICAL MANAGEMENT, by William A. Cohen, pp. 198–99 © 1980, AMACOM, a division of American Management Associations, New York. All rights reserved.

cease and that he had heard the president say they were getting out of this area of business. He added that no doubt they would all be laid off. This word got around the engineering group but was not fully believed until a written communication came down ordering all in-house projects to be closed out. That was all that was needed to start a panic and a mass exodus. What the engineers didn't know was that another division in the company, also in California, had taken on a major project that would last for an indefinite period. Even before hearing of the contract loss, top management had been planning to close down the in-house programs and put all twenty engineers on this other project.[3]

Cohen's conclusion from this is an excellent prescription for the respecting environment:

> The best answers to rumor are open communications with your subordinates and timely truthfulness. By timely truthfulness I mean that you should keep your subordinates informed on a regular basis and be frank and honest when dealing with them. If you keep communication channels with your people open . . . a situation like the one described above cannot happen to you. You'll get to the members of your organization first, before rumors can get started. And if a rumor or two does slip by, your people will go where they should for the truth—to you—and you will be trusted and believed.

A Spectrum-Lou Harris survey of four thousand engineers reinforces this view:

> When asked what factors contribute to productivity and satisfaction in the work place, those surveyed indicated human relations above all other factors. These included getting more and better information from their managers about decisions that affect engineers, having more to say in decisions that affect them, and having a greater chance for recognition and promotion.[4]

These all depend on every manager's belief that each individual who works for him is important.

THE OPEN DOOR POLICY

Although the standard of respect necessarily starts at the top of the organization, it will not be generally followed unless there is some kind of independent appeal process. When a manager is not fair to one of his people, the employee needs some way to get help. Skip-level interviews and speak-up programs can be valuable, but they do not usually have the discipline required. An open door policy, as practiced by several leading corporations, insures every employee the right to communicate with senior management through a channel which is independent of his immediate supervisor. Although this sounds counter to the need for a close and respecting relationship between the manager and each of his people, its purpose is not to circumvent the good managers but to provide a safety valve to protect against occasional management mistakes or incompetence. Further, when every manager knows that each of his actions can be appealed, he will take greater pains in his dealings with his people.

Open door policies typically allow any employees to appeal to any person of greater authority at any time about any issue the company can help with, even to the chairman of the board. Of Delta's program, Peters says that "what makes it work is that something happens when the Open Door is used."[5] Every single complaint is viewed as important, and a rigorous administrative process is established to insure rapid and objective handling.

The guidelines for the IBM Open Door Policy show how such programs work:

1. Employees who have a problem are encouraged to first resolve it with their immediate manager. If they cannot do so to their satisfaction or if they do not want to discuss it with their manager, they may go to higher management. If they are still not satisfied or if they choose not to use any of these intermediate avenues, they can appeal to the personnel department or go all the way to the chairman of the board.

2. In the case of appeals to senior executives, an impartial investigator is promptly assigned who is a relatively senior manager and is organizationally separated from the employee. This investigator should have no prior awareness of the case and no prior or current relationship with any of the parties involved.

3. The investigator contacts the employee within twenty-four hours of being assigned and meets with the employee before talking with anyone else. This insures that the investigator starts with an open mind. The investigator then does the fact gathering as the employee's advocate.

4. At the initial employee meeting, the investigator explains the Open Door process, listens to the employee's concerns, and ask questions about the issues and the people involved. The investigator then personally interviews everyone who has an important bearing on the case.

5. The investigation is kept confidential and strictly confined to the issues raised. If, however, the investigator finds other topics which should be addressed, he or she can expand the investigation at his or her discretion or initiate a separate investigation.

6. At the conclusion, the investigator prepares a final report, then reviews his or her findings, including the recommendations, with the employee.

7. The investigator reviews this report with the executive who received the original complaint. The executive makes the final decision and writes a letter to the employee thanking him or her for using the Open Door and summarizing his or her conclusions.

8. Management must never take any action which could appear as retaliation for an employee's Open Door appeal, and all records of the appeal are kept in a separate file which is not available to line management. This file is retained for a maximum of three years. In no case is any mention of the Open Door or any material relating to it put in the employee's personnel file.[6]

PEER REVIEW PROGRAMS

In 1983, Control Data established a peer review program to achieve much the same objectives as the open door process.[7] Here, employees should talk first to their manager, then, if necessary, to the personnel department. Personnel will then assist them in escalating the issue to the right executive level for prompt decision. If still dissatisfied, employees can call for a peer review, and the case is referred to the Employee Advisory Resource Ombudsman, who assists them. A three-member committee is formed with one executive and two peer members, who then hear the case and reach a majority decision.

In their first case, a lower-level department manager in a manufacturing plant had a personality clash with his plant manager. He felt he was being unfairly blamed for cost overruns and other problems, so he refused to sign his next performance plan. The plant manager took this as further evidence of his uncooperative attitude and fired him. On appeal, line management supported the plant manager but the peer review board reversed the decision and ordered the junior manager reinstated.

Of the first eleven peer review cases, only four were decided in favor of the grievant, in two the peer members outvoted the executive, and eight of the eleven decisions were unanimous. CDC finds that management has accepted this process and that local managers are doing more aggressive problem solving. They report that the employees feel an increased sense of fairness and more protection against arbitrary management decisions.

These programs directly affect employee attitudes both by providing them personal safety and by improving management behavior. When the people trust their management to be fair with them, they think more constructively about their jobs, are more willing to take risks, and are far more inclined to fight for what they believe in.

ESTABLISHING A RESPECTING ENVIRONMENT

Jim, the laboratory manager, made a practice of seeing anyone who asked for an appointment. His secretary was instructed to interrupt him whenever someone not on his immediate staff asked if he was available. One day a veteran machine shop employee stopped by to see if the boss would see him for a few minutes. Although he said it wasn't important, the secretary called Jim out of a meeting, and within two minutes, they were talking in his office. The employee soon got over the shock and started to tell his story.

It seems the machine shop had a lot of long-term company men who proudly arrived on time every morning and frequently worked well past quitting time. Tardiness was greeted with a loud rapping of hand tools, so few had the temerity to arrive late. A young design engineer had recently started to hang his coat on the machine shop rack so that he could sneak into his department without his lateness being noticed. He left every day promptly at quitting time. After a few occasions of this, the machine shop was in an uproar, and the veteran felt he had to do something.

He hadn't really expected the boss to be available, but he felt obliged to make a token effort. If Jim hadn't seen him right then, he would probably not have had the nerve to make an appointment, and the problem might have continued to fester.

Nothing can be more disruptive than to have some people in the organization openly getting away with something. Lee Iacocca calls this equality of sacrifice: "If everybody is suffering equally, you can move a mountain. But the first time you find someone goofing off or not carrying his share of the load, the whole thing can come unraveled."[8] Some of the steps which help establish such an evenhanded and respecting environment are the following:

1. Every decision should be carefully explained so that the people involved can see why it is fair and reasonable.
2. Senior managers should demonstrate interest in their people's concerns and publicly urge them to come to them or the personnel department for help.
3. Several ways should be provided for the people to voice their concerns to senior management.
4. The open door principles should be used in handling appeals, and the employees should be thanked for speaking out.

Although such attitudes should be reflected at the division and corporate level, any manager can follow these principles in his own department.

NOTES CHAPTER 4

1. *Business Week,* April 21, 1980, p. 25.
2. John Gardner, *Excellence* (New York: Harper and Row, Publishers, Inc., 1961), p. 103.
3. William A. Cohen, *Principles of Technical Management* (New York: AMACOM, a division of American Management Associations, 1980).
4. Fred Guterl, "Spectrum/Harris poll—The job," *IEEE Spectrum,* June 1984, vol. 21, no. 6, p. 38.
5. Thomas J. Peters and Robert H. Waterman, Jr., *In Search of Excellence: Lessons from America's Best-Run Companies* (New York: Harper and Row, Publishers, Inc., 1982), p. 253.
6. This is a paraphrase of the material IBM provides to all its managers on the Open Door Policy.
7. Fred C. Olson, "How Peer Review Works at Control Data," *Harvard Business Review,* November–December 1984, p. 7.
8. Lee Iacocca and William Novak, *Iacocca: An Autobiography,* (New York: Bantam Books, Inc., 1984), p. 230.

5

The Goals of Engineers

and Scientists

The great scientist Helmholtz once said that "scientists with an inner drive to knowledge acquire a higher understanding of their relation to humanity. They experience the whole world of thought as a developing entity, which is infinite in comparison with the brief life of a scientist."[1] The scientist strives for knowledge and personal meaning. He sees himself as a discoverer searching for hidden order and simplicity behind nature's apparent complexity. The Würzburg physics professor Wilhelm Wien once compared theoretical physics to mountain climbing:

> When I was a young physicist, I took on problems because they interested me. I didn't solve many, gave them up, didn't care. As when I climbed in these mountains, in physics I climbed quickly with no thought to the route, and I couldn't reach the top. I often remember my teacher, Helmholtz, who likened himself to a mountain climber who doesn't know the way, who climbs slowly, who reverses frequently and has to find another way up, and who sees the best way to the top only too late. Like Helmholtz, I no longer expect to find the royal road at once. I don't hurry but spend most of my time choosing problems that I and my students can solve. It pays off in physics, I've learned, and it pays off in the mountains too.[2]

Scientists search for the meanings and relationships in nature, but engineers seek to create their own monument. George Eastman pointed out a common thread between engineers and scientists when he said that "with an ideal, the journey's end is never reached; there is always the experiment—the hazard of going beyond where anyone else has gone."[3] Charles Eames, the designer of beautifully functional products, expressed the designer's attitude when he said, "We need to design for ourselves, but deeply for ourselves. Then we're likely to discover that the result satisfies other people."

Both engineers and scientists share a basic drive to accomplish something they can point to as their own unique achievement. Tracy Kidder captures this attitude in the words of Rasala, one of the Data General engineers who helped to design and build the Eagle computer:

> "I was looking for"—he ticked the items off on his fingers—"opportunity, responsibility, visibility."
> What did those words mean to him though?
> Rasala shrugged his shoulders. "I wanted to see what I was worth," he explained."[4]

The best engineers and scientists don't work for a company, a university, or a laboratory; they really work for themselves.

THE WORK ASSIGNMENT

Because of the professional's need for unique achievement, managers need to match carefully people and work assignments. This involves more than technical issues, however, for the individual's interpersonal skills and abilities are often just as relevant. In research and advanced development, for example, the objective, in W. O. Baker's words, is "a compact, highly motivated community of scholars who interact with one another."[5] Baker was chairman of the Bell Telephone Laboratories, and he produced a highly creative environment by mixing talented people from many disciplines in an integrated community where they could stimulate each other.

In manufacturing and product development the objectives are more pragmatic, such as developing a machine or improving a production process. Here, success is measured not only in technical terms but in schedules and dollars as well. Most large projects start with a highly technical design phase, but the work gradually shifts to such business questions as manufacturing scale-up, parts costs, and change control. Some engineers are only interested in advanced technical work, and they view these later phases as pure drudgery. This work, however, is essential in the final phase of every product development. On the Eagle computer, for example, each machine had to be rewired after every test session:

> Making the changes was slow, routine labor, but it required great concentration, for a careless mistake in rewiring could cost them precious time and was the more maddening because it was unnecessary. Figuring that the debuggers were likely to be more careful than technicians with no emotional stake in Eagle, Rasala insisted that his Hardy Boys [engineers] do the rewiring themselves.[6]

All development projects have occasional moments of excitement, but these are separated by days or even months of dogged hard work. The engineer who resents this routine should consider the example of the Leakeys, who have devoted two generations to archaeological research. Another example is Dr. Salk, who dedicated many years to preparation and clinical testing before he could introduce his polio vaccine.

Thomas A. Edison once described genius as "one percent inspiration and ninety-nine percent perspiration."[7]

Part of the satisfaction of development work is the thrill of seeing the working result. This is enhanced by the development team's growing excitement as it surmounts every obstacle to get the machine out the door. In this final crash effort, senior designers check wiring harnesses, technical managers compile parts lists, and everybody watches the test results. No one complains about drudgery or thinks about quitting time. This is the thrill they have worked for, and wild horses couldn't drag them away.

Some people like to solve technical puzzles, but others seek team excitement. The lone scientist is at one extreme, and the engineering team member is at the other. Most professionals intuitively understand their own talents and seek work which best suits them, and managers who can sense this match can generally make the best job assignments. They must always, however, get them to "sign up."

THE HIERARCHY OF NEEDS

Professionals' technical skill and native ability are important, but their state of mind is, if anything, more important. The late Abraham Maslow's five-level hierarchy of needs can help managers understand their people's emotional status.[8] The most fundamental needs are for food and shelter, closely followed by personal safety. These are rarely at stake in the working professional world, but just about everyone needs the support of friends and the reinforcement of membership in a social group. After a person has gained the security of membership, his or her needs then escalate to the fourth level: the desire for recognition and status. Finally, the apex of Maslow's hierarchy is self-actualization, where the individual seeks the personal satisfaction of accomplishing a difficult task. It is this highest need which is satisfied when a professional single-handedly overcomes all obstacles to achieve a creative success. This is the motivation level which all technical managers seek for their people, and it is only possible after all of the lower level needs have been satisfied.

HYGIENE FACTORS

Dr. Frederick Herzberg has combined Maslow's hierarchy with a priority structure which divides motivational factors into two classes.[9] The first class, the motivators, provide a positive drive for accomplishment; the second are "dissatisfiers" which "demotivate" by their absence. If, for example, someone has achieved membership in a group, his or her next concern is with esteem and recognition. Now that the need for membership is satisfied, however, further memberships will provide little additional drive. Similarly, salary satisfies a basic need for food and shelter and provides very important motivation up to a point. Beyond this, however, it is called a hygiene factor since it only provides superficial value as a further incentive.

Engineers and scientists spend many years building their knowledge and skill, and they naturally seek an opportunity to apply these talents. This motivation can be very selective, however, for an electronics engineer who wants to design logic circuits will often have no interest in designing power supply circuits. Similarly, circuit design may be interesting at one point in an engineer's career but hold no attraction at a later time. Needs change with experience, and when an engineer has proven to himself that he can do something, further performance of that same task is of little interest. Personal factors are also important, for working with one team or one particular manager may be exciting, but membership in another group with another manager may be totally uninteresting.

Individual needs can change very quickly, and the most effective managers appreciate the unique circumstances of each of their people and intuitively sense the challenges which will most effectively motivate them.

LOCALS AND COSMOPOLITANS

Professor R. Richard Ritti, of New York University, has studied engineers and scientists in large organizations, and he finds an important difference in their attitudes.[10] He applies the term "locals" to those with traditional engineering attitudes and he calls the scientists "cosmopolitans." Locals' careers are a succession of assignments where they dedicate themselves to solving the organization's problems. In a sense, they are model employees, for they seek satisfaction through achieving the objectives of the organization that employs them. Rasala, for example, expressed this local attitude when he said,

> . . . I guess the reason I do it fundamentally is that there's a certain satisfaction in building a machine like this, which is important to the company, which is on its way to becoming a billion-dollar company. There aren't that many opportunities in this world to be where the action is, making an impact.[11]

Scientists, on the other hand, measure their success in terms of the boundaries of science and often become so engrossed that they ignore the practical world around them. Russell McCormmach captures this attitude in his description of a chance meeting on a walk in Heidelberg, where

> Kirchhoff asked Helmholtz if he had noticed the peculiar light reflected from a rough sea at sunset, and then for half an hour the two physicists stood thinking about that while Helmholtz's wife stood thinking about those peculiar creatures, physicists, all three standing for half an hour in soaking rain.[12]

Scientists want to learn, to understand, and to teach. They seek the company of their peers in seminars, technical meetings, and conferences, and their loyalties extend beyond the confines of their job and organization. The focus for their career is their special field of interest, and their current job is merely a convenience which permits them to pursue it.

Ritti found that these seemingly opposed attitudes of engineers and scientists are not so much products of their education and background as of their working environment. Engineers who work in research laboratories, for example, behave much like scientists and seek to publish papers and attend conferences. Similarly, scientists in product development laboratories are much more cost and schedule conscious.

Maslow's hierarchy explains this seeming contradiction in terms of the needs for membership and recognition. These can best be satisfied by the organization where the professional works, and he must conform to its values to be fully rewarded. Research laboratories thus breed cosmopolitans because they value cosmopolitan behavior, but engineering environments reinforce the more pragmatic local attitudes. The organization and its management can thus have a profound effect on the behavior of its members.

THE NEED FOR INFLUENCE

In spite of this great pressure to conform, people have differing interests and abilities. They want work that appeals to them and fits their unique talents. Unfortunately, many professionals find they have little influence over the selection of their assignments. The junior scientist has to set up the experiments, gather the data, clean the equipment, or calibrate the instruments. In product development, the more junior engineers end up building the breadboard models, expediting parts, or maintaining test records. On their very first assignments, young engineers and scientists are often saddled with these routine chores while their more influential co-workers get the more interesting jobs. They soon realize that influence is an important part of job selection. Most professionals thus seek job advancement so that they can have a greater say in what they will do.

Another reason for advancement is self-protection. Engineers and scientists quickly find that if they do not manage their own work, somebody else will. In an interview with IEEE Spectrum, Dr. Parker, an MIT scientist, described what happens then: "If you don't take responsibility for supervising others or for going after the money, doing all the things that you could care less about," he argues, "then somebody else will do it, and you will be directed by that person."[13]

This pursuit of influence is generally motivated by professionals' desire to work on projects that appeal to them. As Peter Drucker has said, "The focus has to be on the job. . . . The job is not everything, but it comes first. . . . If a job itself is not achieving, nothing else will provide achievement."[14]

Although few professionals can expect a steady diet of exciting and stimulating work, they all want their fair share. When they are assigned work that does not use their technical skills, they feel underutilized, even though they may be very busy.

Ritti found that "if his work assignment is blocking performance, blocking goal achievement, the engineer will feel both underutilized and relatively powerless to do anything about it."[15] This leads to dissatisfaction. Rensis Likert has said that satisfaction goes with challenge, and "for professional work, there is a positive relationship between job satisfaction and performance."[16]

Professional people want to be productive; therefore they seek the satisfaction of accomplishment and the rewards of recognition. These, however, only come with some of the jobs, and they quickly discover that they must get the right assignments in order to make progress. This one fact explains why so many engineers and scientists move into management: to have more control over their own destiny.

NOTES CHAPTER 5

1. Russell McCormmach, *Night Thoughts of a Classical Physicist* (Cambridge: Harvard University Press, 1982), p. 138.

2. Ibid., p. 120.

3. This George Eastman quotation is engraved on a plaque in the lobby of Eastman Kodak's headquarters building in Rochester, New York.

4. Tracy Kidder, *The Soul of a New Machine* (Boston: Little, Brown & Company, 1981), p. 143.

5. Michael Wolf, "Managing Large Egos," *Research Management*, July 1982, p. 7.

6. Tracy Kidder, "The Microkids and the Hardy Boys," *IEEE Spectrum*, September 1981, vol. 18, no. 9, p. 48.

7. Bergen Evans, *Dictionary of Quotations (New York: Bonanza Books, 1966), p. 266:17*.

8. Abraham Maslow, *Motivation and Personality* (New York: Harper and Row, Publishers, Inc., 1954).

9. Frederick Herzberg, B. Mausner, and Barbara Snyderman, *The Motivation to Work*, 2nd ed. (New York: John Wiley & Sons, Inc., 1959).

10. R. Richard Ritti, *The Engineer in the Industrial Corporation* (New York: Columbia University Press, 1971).

11. Kidder, "Microkids," p. 52.

12. McCormmach, *Night Thoughts*, p. 12.

13. Gadi Kaplan, "We Look at Ourselves: The Researcher," *IEEE Spectrum*, August 1981, vol. 18, no. 8, p. 46.

14. Peter F. Drucker, *Management, Tasks, Responsibilities, Practices* (New York: Harper & Row, Publishers, Inc., 1974), p. 266.

15. Ritti, *The Engineer*, p. 124.

16. Rensis Likert, *New Patterns of Management* (New York: McGraw-Hill Book Company, 1961), p. 15.

6

The Changing

Professional Career

As people mature, they gain a better understanding of themselves and learn to appreciate their own strengths and weaknesses. They are then able to set more realistic goals and adjust their career objectives to better fit their potentialities.

One talented young scientist is a good example of the way a professional's attitudes change during his career. He was enormously concerned about status and job titles and made a big fuss about the size of his office and the style of his furniture. At the time, office space was extremely tight, and his entire department was moved to temporary quarters in a nearby shopping center. The entrance was at the back of the building by the trash cans, and only one of the offices had a window. The manager's office didn't have a carpet, his furniture was scratched and dented, and no one's office even had a door. The young scientist saw this as a personal affront, and although the manager tried to convince him that these conditions were only temporary, he soon quit to join another company. In spite of this early immaturity, however, he was highly competent, and soon gained considerable fame in his specialty. Years later, he was entirely happy with a cluttered office in a university department and felt no concern about the lack of carpets or expensive furniture.

EVOLVING PROFESSIONAL GOALS

Throughout their careers, professionals learn from their successes and failures. The successes build self-confidence, and the defeats often provide graphic evidence of shortcomings and limitations. When they learn from these experiences to realistically accept themselves, they are better able to establish rewarding career goals.

All professionals, of course, are different, and some will mature quickly; but others may never face the typical late-life problems of discouragement or resignation. Any generalizations must be misleading in detail, but it is useful to think of career stages in terms of decades in a professional's life.

While professionals in their twenties and early thirties frequently dream of great achievements, they often lack the dedication to accomplish them. Time seems limitless, and they rarely recognize the enormous effort required to overcome any personal limitation. Frequently, they are disappointed when they discover that their first job makes little use of their hard-earned technical knowledge, and it takes them some time to recognize that the toughest problems aren't technical after all. The professional's early needs are to understand professional work, to build a foundation of self-confidence, and to learn the value of personal discipline. Although these will all generally come with experience, young professionals can be enormously helped by supportive managers and senior associates. At this stage, their greatest need is sufficient self-confidence to try things on their own, and the manager can help in this regard by recognizing and encouraging good work.

The professional who has turned thirty has few doubts about his own ability, but he is also beginning to realize that a working lifetime is not so long after all. Thirty is half way to sixty, and this distant milestone suddenly seems uncomfortably close. The thirty-year-old professional has generally gained a realistic appreciation of his own abilities and thrives on difficult and challenging work. Those that have not yet faced reverses, however, are often too cocky to seek help, and an understanding manager can be enormously valuable by urging more care and tempering their optimism. Although few realize it, the thirties are the make-or-break years, for this is when those destined for success will reach their full stride; and the greatest risk is a disaster which will tarnish their reputations.

By the end of their thirties the most successful engineers and scientists need little management guidance, but the less fortunate face new problems. Many talented and ambitious professionals somehow lack the luck, skill, or support to achieve the success they had dreamed of. For them, time is now running out, and they often feel compelled to make a last frantic drive for the promotion they are convinced they deserve. At this point, their greatest need is for a sympathetic and helpful manager who can assist them to reassess their own ambitions. For some, it is wise to break out of their current job rut and make a new start, while others should come to terms with their limited potential. The professional must make this call for himself or herself, but an understanding manager can be an enormous help.

By their late forties most professionals have a realistic view of their prospects, but their need for personal reinforcement is probably greatest. It is easy for young engineers or scientists on their way up to feel self-confident, but those who have passed their peak often face serious problems. This is when managers should take the greatest pains to assign challenging work and to be generous in their recognition of superior performance.

The late career extends from the late forties through the fifties and beyond. Here, professionals have generally accepted their fate and dismissed their dreams for what they were. While they may still think fondly of what might have been, they find comfort in their position as respected elders. They like to help their younger colleagues and are no longer so concerned with the boss's favor. They will generally speak their mind, and managers should learn to listen to them and use their experience. This is the highly rewarding career phase which Gail Sheehy entitles "no more bullshit."[1]

HOW AGE AFFECTS CREATIVITY

Enrico Fermi, when he was a professor in the physics department at the University of Chicago, created quite a stir among the graduate students when he said that those who had not made a significant scientific contribution by the age of twenty-one never would. He never gave the basis for his opinion, but it worried a lot of promising young scientists. There is a popular myth that productivity declines with age, but in spite of Fermi's opinion there is an increasing body of evidence which points the other way.

In 1951 Donald Pelz of the Survey Research Center at the University of Michigan started a multiyear study of the attitudes, environmental circumstances, and performance of the scientists and engineers at the National Institutes of Health. This research ultimately expanded to encompass some fifteen hundred engineers and scientists at a number of university, corporate, and government laboratories. They did find that performance peaked at an early age but that it declined very slightly thereafter. The precise point at which this peak occurred depended on the technical field: it was earlier in the more abstract fields of mathematics and theoretical physics and later in such pragmatic specialties as biology and geology. The initial peak generally fell in the mid thirties, but they also found a late peak in the mid to late fifties. This double-peak phenomenon occurred in all the groups of engineers and scientists that they studied, and the dip between these two peaks was not very significant.[2]

A 1979 UNESCO study of several European research institutions also found that the productivity of academic scientists declined toward the end of their careers. There was, however, a late peak after about thirty working years. Surprisingly, the scientists in industry showed a less severe decline throughout their careers and had an earlier late-life performance peak after about twenty-five years of industrial experience.[3]

Although there is little data on the effect of age on the creativity of engineers and scientists, Donal Henahan has studied the late-life creativity of such artists as Rossini, Sibelius, Ives, Elgar, and Copland, who gave up composing at the height of their careers. He also notes that some artists, like Verdi and Milton, remained creative well into old age, but that Copland and Stravinsky stopped composing and continued in new careers as conductors of their own music well past their eighties.[4]

Levinson cites several examples of late-life creativity. Sophocles wrote *Oedipus Rex* at seventy-five and *Oedipus et Colonus* at eighty-nine. Titian completed a major masterpiece at ninety-five and started another at ninety-seven. Benjamin Franklin invented bifocal lenses when he was seventy-eight, and Pablo Casals was still music's greatest cellist at ninety. Santayana and Sandburg composed major works in their seventies, and Sigmund Freud remained active into his eighties.[5]

Age does have an unquestioned impact on creativity. Gail Sheehy talks about the "unanticipated crucible" that occurs around the age of forty.[6] This is the most stressful age and one in which creative people undergo an important change. She cites the examples of Beethoven, Goethe, Ibsen, and Voltaire, who had important crises in their mid to late thirties. Gauguin, for example, left his wife at thirty-five and became a leading postimpressionist painter by the age of forty-one. For such artists as Chopin, Mozart, Raphael, Rimbaud, Purcell, Baudelaire, and Watteau, the crisis at this point in their lives was fatal. The London psychoanalyst Elliot Jaques studied the life histories of a random selection of 310 outstanding artists and found that their death rate took a sudden jump between the ages of thirty-five and thirty-nine and then fell below normal shortly after their early forties.[7]

The mid-life crises of highly creative artists are well documented. One suspects that the age effect on the creativity of technical people is similar, though this has not been verified. While its nature and degree can be highly personal, it is clear that, for creative people, the late thirties and early forties is a highly stressful period. Once they pass this hurdle, however, many engineers and scientists will continue their creative work for many years. Alexander Graham Bell, for example, invented the telephone when he was twenty-seven, but he continued to invent for another forty-five years. Albert Einstein was working energetically on modifications and extensions to his Unified Field Theory well into his seventies, and many of Thomas Edison's eleven hundred inventions were produced late in his eighty-four-year life.

HOW AGE AFFECTS PERFORMANCE

In spite of this encouraging data on the continued creativity of older people, age undoubtedly does affect performance. In 1980 Richard L. Sprott edited a series of studies on this subject which provide clear evidence of declining ability with advancing years.[8] This decline was largely related to performance speed, however, and not to intellectual ability. One of these papers gives the results of the Wechsler Adult Intelligence Test (WAITS) for a series of people in different age groups. There were six nonspeeded verbal tests and five nonverbal performance tests.[9] As shown in Table 6.1, verbal performance remained essentially flat, while speeded performance declined. Most of the declines were less than the standard test deviation of 3, however.

An interesting counter example was described by Szafran, who tested a large number of airplane pilots between the ages of twenty and sixty.[10] His findings indicate "no age-associated differences in performance even under very demanding overload conditions." Although there are many possible explanations for this surprising finding, Szafran himself concluded that this was a highly practiced sample from which the poor performers had been eliminated by natural selection. It appears, therefore, that not everyone's performance declines with age and that health, practice, and occupation can play an important role.

TABLE 6.1   Means WAIS Scores by Age during Middle Adulthood*

TEST	AGE RANGE				
	20—24	25–34	35–44	45–54	55–64
Verbal					
Information	9.8	10.3	10.3	9.9	9.9
Comprehension	10.0	10.2	10.2	9.9	9.6
Arithmetic	10.0	10.1	10.2	9.8	9.4
Similarities	10.2	10.1	9.2	9.0	8.4
Digit span	9.9	10.0	9.6	9.0	8.4
Vocabulary	9.6	10.3	10.4	10.1	10.1
Performance					
Digit symbol	10.1	9.9	8.5	7.5	6.3
Picture complete	10.1	10.0	9.8	8.6	8.0
Block design	9.9	10.0	9.4	8.5	7.7
Picture arrange	10.5	9.7	9.1	8.0	7.3
Object assembly	10.1	10.0	9.3	8.5	7.8

*Adapted from Wechsler's Measurement and Appraisal of Adult Intelligence by Joseph D. Matarazzo, 5th and enlarged edition. Copyright © 1939, 1941, 1944, 1958 by David Wechsler; 1972 by Oxford University Press, Inc. Reprinted by permission of Oxford University Press, Inc.

A further series of tests addressed the effect of age on reasoning ability.[11] A large number of men were tested on intellectual performance in two series of tests six years apart. While the proportion of men who solved the problems declined with age, there was no deterioration in reasoning ability for any of the groups under the age of seventy. Again, a natural selection process screened out those men who could not solve the problems twice, but the intellectual performance of the remainder did not decline in the six-year interval between tests except for this oldest group.

Many complex factors determine the effect of age on performance. Health, generational differences, intelligence, and continued activity all have a role. For those who remain physically and mentally competent, however, there is no statistically significant evidence of a decline in intellectual performance until well after the normal working years. Speed of performance, however, does generally deteriorate, but not to any disabling degree before the age of sixty-five.

HOW AGE AFFECTS MOTIVATION

AT&T made a twenty-year study of the changing attitudes of managers to see if they could better identify future senior executives.[12] They found a high correlation between job attitudes and career progress and identified the single most important difference to be the high priority the future executives placed on their work. Their jobs were increasingly important to them as they advanced, but those who limited their efforts to the traditional forty hours did not advance as fast or as far. Career success clearly depended on the manager's willingness to do more than the minimum required by the job.

Priorities understandably change with age, and one's willingness to strive for a promotion is always balanced against the demands of private life. Most employees intuitively sense their potential and limit their efforts accordingly. Although the most ambitious may choose career over home, few people are willing to make the personal sacrifices that senior executive positions require. For the rest, the heavy personal investment is not balanced by the questionable odds of continued advancement. With age and experience, this career trade-off gradually but steadily swings toward the home.

The management pyramid inexorably narrows at the top, and promotional progress is increasingly competitive. Since every promotion has only one winner and many losers, most employees regularly face vivid reminders of their approaching career limits. This reality can be highly traumatic, as demonstrated by the frequency of such mid-life problems as alcoholism, divorce, heart attack, and ulcers. Many topped-out employees are still ambitious, however, and can only preserve their health and sanity by withdrawing from active job involvement.

BURNOUT

This job withdrawal phenomenon is called burnout. A study by the University of Chicago found that burnout is generally caused by an employee's feeling of being helplessly trapped in a meaningless job.[13] It is not caused by age, overwork, or exhaustion but is more of a defense against the loss of self-esteem caused by an apparent lack of personal value.

As an IBM experience demonstrates, even burned-out employees can be reenergized when they are given a meaningful assignment. A major project had gotten into trouble, and a crash effort was needed. A new manager was named, and he started looking for half a dozen engineers. The only people available were some older hands who had been out of the mainstream for many years, and he reluctantly selected them because he had no alternative. Jerrier A. Haddad, a retired IBM vice president, said of this project that

> these six . . . did a crackerjack job. Somewhere along the line in their careers they had been allowed to drift. Younger people had been given the newer, more challenging assignments, and these six just went along as before. But when someone offered them a challenge, they leaped at it.[14]

When people are out of action for a long time, they get a bad reputation. Routine jobs with little challenge evoke reduced performance, one dull job inexorably follows another. All departments have top and bottom performers, and those labeled as losers rarely are able to break out of their deepening rut. If the manager assigns all the stimulating work to his stars, they will shine brighter and those at the bottom will only look worse.

An example of this self-fulfilling process is a manager who told his vice president he could get rid of the bottom 15 percent of his department and still get his job done. The boss surprised him by demanding the names of these people so he could reassign them. After several weeks, the manager admitted that he could not come up with a list. All his people were performing useful work, but some were less effective than others. By looking more closely, he had found that the poor performers had been given the dull work, and no matter how hard they tried, they could not perform up to his expectations. In looking for people he could get rid of, he had focused his attention on his poorer performers and found that they were all capable of better work.

The way a routine assignment affects an employee is illustrated by the case of Craig, an experienced programmer. After he had worked for the data processing department for several years, he was given a semiclerical task as a filler between assignments. The job of keeping track of computer usage and producing the weekly reports was so dull, however, that he lost all interest in his work. He only did the bare minimum needed to get by, and his performance rapidly deteriorated to where he was considered incapable of a more challenging job.

At this point, the manager was asked to provide a new data processing service, and since no one else was available, he reluctantly asked Craig to handle it until he could find someone else. To everyone's surprise, Craig took the job and got right to work. He quickly identified and ordered the needed equipment, arranged for new space, and worked out introduction plans for all the departments. He started getting to work early and often stayed well past quitting time. When the service was installed on schedule, it had few problems and everyone was so impressed that Craig soon had several offers of a next assignment.

THE MANAGEMENT—EMPLOYEE PARTNERSHIP

There is, of course, the risk that the employees will use their dull assignments as an excuse for poor performance. They might reason that if they had challenging jobs, they could perform. They thus view their ''burned-out'' attitudes as the fault of management for not challenging them. The second, and perhaps more insidious, risk is the propensity of managers to underestimate some of their people, stimulating the best ones while ignoring the rest.

There is no commandment or bill of rights that guarantees every employee an interesting and challenging job. In fact, it is often just the reverse. With the right attitude, almost any job can become rewarding. Challenges are largely self-made, and most jobs contain some kernel of opportunity which can be developed into an exciting task.

Again, take the case of Craig. He could, for example, have used the routine nature of his reports to his advantage. By reexamining the way the computer work was accounted for, he could have devised a system for automatically recording usage. This would have led to automating the reports, while providing a personal challenge for him and a service to his department.

The be fully effective, managers and their people should form a partnership. By striving to do their jobs in the best way, professionals help their organization while they stimulate themselves. Managers can help this process by assigning meaningful work to each of their people and helping them see how the tasks that must be done can be approached in a creative way.

CAREER RISKS INCREASE WITH AGE

As engineers and scientists age, they have fewer career options and less time to recover from mistakes. Every employee builds a reputation, and unfortunately, his defects are remembered more vividly than his successes. With the passing years fewer doors are open to the professional with a mixed history. He soon realizes that he is no longer considered when new assignments open up and that his current job is all there is left. With such limited options, he loses self-confidence and increasingly plays it safe so as not to risk this one remaining assignment.

Superior technical work, however, involves risk, and technical people who play it safe can rarely excel. One example of the problems this can cause was the evaluation done of a new testing method proposed by research. The proposal was highly controversial because costly new test equipment had recently been installed, and the new methods would not use it. The laboratory manager had been outspoken in his push to control budgets, so the person doing the evaluation suspected that he wanted the expensive research proposal rejected. He was so nervous about the likely reaction that he only focused on the proposal's problems and overlooked its many advantages. When he recommended no change, the lab manager was pleased, but research escalated him to higher management and insisted on a more thorough study. When this concluded in research's favor, it was clear that the attempt to play it safe had caused a six-month delay and an increase in total project costs.

MANAGING THE OLDER PROFESSIONAL

As Helmholtz said on his seventieth birthday, "The first seventy years are the best."[15] Age is a relative matter, and most older employees couple experience and wisdom with surprising vigor. Old age, however, can also accentuate attitudes and habits. When some people have lived with issues for a long time, they see them as immutable facts. Harry Levinson has said,

> Too many people accept what is for what will be. They most often say, "I can't do anything about it." What they really mean is that they won't do anything. . . . There are indeed alternatives in most situations. Our traps are largely self-made.[16]

In these cases, however, age is rarely the problem. With few exceptions, healthy employees, regardless of their age, are capable of imaginative and energetic work. Job tenure, however, is a different matter. Employees who have been in the same job for extended periods tend to think in constrained patterns and to see fewer options and alternatives. Although these are often the older people, the manager should recognize that age is not the problem and insist on stimulating them with a move to a new assignment.

NOTES CHAPTER 6

1. Gail Sheehy, *Passages* (New York: E.P. Dutton & Co., Inc., 1976), p. 46.

2. Donald C. Pelz and Frank M. Andrews, *Scientists in Organizations: Productive Climates for Research and Development* (New York: John Wiley and Sons, Inc., 1966), p. 177.

3. Richard Stankiewicz, "The Size and Age of Swedish Academic Research Groups and their Scientific Performance," included in *Scientific Productivity: The Effectiveness of Research Groups in Six Countries,* ed. Frank M. Andrews (Cambridge: Cambridge University Press, 1979).

4. Donal Henahan, "The Mystery of the Dropout Composer," *The New York Times,* March 14, 1982.

5. Harry Levinson, "On Being a Middle-aged Manager," *Harvard Business Review,* July/August 1969, p. 82.

6. Sheehy, *Passages,* p. 36.

7. Ibid.

8. Richard L. Sprott, *Age, Learning Ability, and Intelligence* (New York: Van Nostrand Reinhold Co., 1980), p. 51.

9. Ibid., p. 55.

10. Ibid., p. 104.

11. Ibid., p. 146.

12. Ann Howard and Douglass W. Bray, *The New York Times,* March 21, 1982, sec. 3, p. 2.

13. Patricia Brooks, "Burnout," *Think,* vol. 48, no. 1 (Armonk, N.Y.: IBM Corporation, January/February 1982), p. 26.

14. Ibid., p. 26.

15. Russell McCormmach, *Night Thoughts of a Classical Physicist* (Cambridge: Harvard University Press, 1982), p. 139.

16. Levinson, "Middle-aged Manager," p. 89.

7

Motivating Technical and Professional People

As Lee Iacocca once said, "When it comes to making the place run, motivation is everything."[1] Motivation, it turns out, not only makes the place run; it is also what makes the people run. Highly motivated people drive themselves to overachieve, while many of their brighter and more capable associates accomplish far less. The basic reason is the difference in their motivation.

Some people are incredibly motivated and overcome great personal disadvantages to achieve impressive success. Dave Schwartzkopf is both an outstanding example of what motivated people can accomplish and one of the most impressive people I have ever met. He has been nearly blind since birth and suffers from a speech impediment which caused him to be treated as mentally retarded until he was nearly sixteen years old. One of his teachers then recognized his exceptional talents and had him moved to a more appropriate school. This completely changed Dave's life, and he rapidly worked through school and college to become an engineer. He then joined IBM, and when I met him, he had progressed through several technical assignments to become manager of a technical education group. His enormous drive and motivation have earned him both a successful technical career and the respect of all those who have known him.

Motivation is what makes people persist when they run into serious roadblocks. Success in almost any field is governed by both knowledge and perseverance, and those who give up too easily rarely succeed. In modern technology ideas are cheap, and the crucial factor is the ability to couple these ideas with the right combination of skill and perseverance. It is not as important to have the right ideas as it is to have the drive and motivation to make your ideas right.

David C. McClelland has studied the characteristics of achievement-motivated people and found that they share certain traits: "the capacity to set high but obtainable goals, the concern for personal achievement rather than the rewards of success, and the desire for task-oriented feedback (how well am I doing?) rather than for attitudinal feedback (how well do you like me?)."[2] Motivated employees set their own goals and are their own toughest taskmasters. The highest level of motivation is when people seek challenges and strive to overcome obstacles, not because they want any external reward or benefit, but because they find satisfaction in their own achievements. As A. Ray McCord, the executive vice president of Texas Instruments, has said, "the employees will set tougher goals for themselves than any manager would dare to set alone."[3]

THE POWER OF MOTIVATION

One remarkable example of the power of motivation was the work of George Judson, an IBM Fellow. He was working in the Endicott laboratory when he learned his son had leukemia. This was some years ago, and leukemia was generally considered fatal. George was deeply concerned and spent much of his time at the hospital talking to the doctors and trying to understand what they could do to cure this disease. He found that there was an urgent need to separate the blood into its major components, or fractions, for treatment while it was circulating in the patient's body. Since many of the component cells of human blood are extremely fragile, however, building a machine to do this was quite a challenge.

George thought about this problem and then began to putter around the laboratory to try out some of his ideas. He soon put together some parts and began to see how such a machine could be made to work. He then got permission to build an experimental blood cell separator and arranged for cooperative clinical testing with the National Cancer Institute. Within a year, the completed unit worked so well that the institute contracted with IBM for further development work on machine improvements. Interest in the device grew so quickly in the cancer research community in the United States and Europe that a small production line had to be set up to meet the demand. Although his son did not live to benefit from his work, George went on to make many contributions to medical instrumentation, and the company recognized his achievements by making him an IBM Fellow.

MOTIVATION AND TECHNICAL COMPETENCE

It is commonly felt that technical talent applies only within a narrow field of specialty but that motivation is universally useful. While this is true to some degree, it is far too simplistic a view. Technical competence generally grows throughout a professional's career and is a constantly expanding asset. It is also more widely applicable than generally realized, for a professional with skills in one field can generally contribute in another. The basic concepts of science and engineering apply to all technology; therefore the knowledge and intuition gained in one area will be helpful in many others.

Motivation, however, is a totally different story. As a professional gains competence, he does not necessarily gain motivation. Often, in fact, an employee's motivation will decline as he gains experience in a given area. This is because a creative engineer or scientist who has learned how to accomplish something has little interest in doing it again. This motivational characteristic explains why engineers with many general interests may be fascinated by a particular problem. They will then reject all other opportunities to continue with this one absorbing interest until they have satisfied themselves. They may then, however, abruptly lose interest in this subject and seek an immediate change.

Motivation is thus fragile. It depends on the person, the task, the environment, and the professional's immediate associates. The technical factors are important, but so is the way employees feel about their job and their management. Almost all the nontechnical elements of employee motivation are directly controllable by the professional's immediate manager.

THE EVOLUTION OF MANAGEMENT

A dramatic change in management thinking started at the beginning of the twentieth century. Early management methods were based on Frederick Winslow Taylor's *Principles of Scientific Management*.[4] This pioneering work was published in 1911, and it proposed that employees be treated essentially like machines. Work was to be subdivided into well-structured elements, and each worker, assigned to a single repetitive task. Since they were assumed to have no feelings, unique abilities, or motivations, workers were told precisely how to do their job and paid on a piece-work basis. Taylor's mechanistic approach to management has been called "Theory X."[5]

Although Taylor's theories took an essentially negative view of employees, they were generally accepted until Elton Mayo of Harvard University started his famous productivity studies at Western Electric's Hawthorne, Illinois, plant in 1924.[6] These studies were intended to find the mix of lighting and other physical conditions which would produce the highest worker productivity. By the end of the studies nearly ten years later, they had started a revolution in management thinking which continues to this day.

Mayo started by adjusting the lighting level in the Western Electric factory to see how it affected worker productivity. His team divided the employees into control and test groups, with one continuing to work under normal conditions, while the lighting for the other was changed. Over a year and a half, the test group's productivity improved in step with the brighter lighting, exactly as expected. Unexpectedly, however, the control group's productivity increased at the same time. To understand what was happening, Mayo decided to return all the conditions to exactly the way they had been at the beginning of the study. They reduced the lighting and also eliminated some newly introduced benefits, such as flexible rest breaks and longer lunch periods. Instead of the expected sharp drop in productivity, however, the output of both the test and the control groups reached a new all-time high.

These results were so unexpected that Mayo broadened his studies to include interviews which probed the workers' opinions about their jobs and the company. They found that the mere existence of the study showed management interest in the workers and their conditions. Being asked what they thought made them feel more important, and they felt that the study was the best thing the company had ever done. Since they felt better about the company, they not surprisingly did better work. These results of Mayo's were the first to demonstrate that the attitudes of employees are a crucial factor in determining their performance.

From this beginning, Mayo launched his "Human Relations Movement" in industrial management. These ideas ultimately attracted broad support, and in 1960 Douglass McGregor characterized the new approach as "Theory Y."[7] Its basic premise is that people are psychologically motivated to work, and management should help and support them rather than coerce them. This is the basic concept behind much of modern management thinking.

Theory X and Theory Y are diametrically opposed. While Theory X assumes the worst about the employees, Theory Y assumes the best. Not surprisingly, the truth generally falls somewhere in between. If managers always treat all of their people the same way, they will be wrong at least some of the time because only some people are highly motivated, and no one is uniformly energetic and hardworking. A more balanced approach, which recognizes this highly individual nature of people management, is called situational leadership.[8] It states that managers should change their approach depending on the situation and the current needs of each of their people.

Situational leadership can be very helpful in improving the motivation of professional employees. With skill and understanding, managers can decide when to direct their people and when to delegate to them. New employees, for example, may need detailed instructions, while more experienced professionals can be given more leeway. They must naturally be told what is wanted, but they need not be instructed on how to do it. Ultimately, as employees' ability and initiative increase, managers can delegate increasing amounts of decision making to them. The proper use of such flexible management styles will steadily improve professionals' motivation and result in their doing correspondingly better work.

BUILDING TASK MATURITY

Situational leadership concerns two different dimensions of employee performance: task maturity and relationship maturity. Task maturity deals with technical competence, while relationship maturity considers employees' attitudes toward their job and their management. Task maturity is built throughout the employees' education and working career, and as it develops the manager should progressively increase the complexity and challenge of his or her assignments. The professional's abilities are thus continually taxed, thus progressively improving his or her technical competence and task maturity.

The advantages of such an approach were demonstrated by a sales training experiment run by a large insurance company shortly after the second world war. New sales recruits were divided into three groups, and each was given a different kind of training. One group received comprehensive instruction on how to sell insurance, including specific guidance on how to act and what to say in every anticipated situation. The second group was given minimal training and then assigned to work with an experienced salesperson who acted as an on-the-job tutor. After accompanying their tutors on sales calls for several months, this second set of trainees was then set out on their own. The third group was given minimal training and then immediately sent out to make solo sales calls. After several months of selling, they were brought back to headquarters for comprehensive instruction.

The long-term performance of these three groups varied considerably. The first group not only had the worst initial sales record but their performance lagged the others for the duration of the study. The experimenters secretly observed them and found that these salespeople were not thinking for themselves. Most of their efforts were devoted to remembering their canned sales pitches, and they were lost in unexpected situations. Although the second group did better, the third group performed best, both initially and throughout their entire sales careers. These latter trainees clearly learned most effectively from an education program which directly related to their experience. When they first made sales calls on their own, they made mistakes; but they also quickly learned how to rely on their own judgment. This experience then provided them a vivid appreciation of the selling process and the best possible foundation for their later educational program.

Learning is most effective when the trainee can see its direct relevance to his needs. Whether in the laboratory or in the classroom, real problems provide a motivation which is hard to duplicate. This same principle applies to new engineers and scientists. They should be given challenging problems and just enough guidance to get them started and keep them out of serious trouble. While some will need more help than others, the general principle is the same as the solo flight: get them on their own as soon as possible. They should be encouraged to come back for help whenever they need it, but they will learn best by trying to solve their own problems and learning from their own mistakes.

BUILDING RELATIONSHIP MATURITY

When professionals have developed a reasonable level of task maturity, they should be able to work on their own. Whether they actually can, however, depends on their relationship maturity. The fact that people are technically capable of doing a job does not necessarily mean that they can, or will, do it. They may lack self-confidence, resent some management action, or have some severe personal problem. There are as many varieties of relationship problems as there are people, and just about any personal problem can severely limit employee performance. Some examples illustrate the wide variety of issues involved.

A young engineer had worked for several months before being given a project to do by himself. His progress was good, and it seemed he would finish on schedule and within budget; but then he went to the personnel department to complain about his salary and lack of promotion. On investigation, the personnel manager found no real salary or promotion problem and concluded that this engineer was really troubled by the lack of management attention. As a new employee he felt lost and unsure without the reinforcement of frequent management contact. The manager had given him too much independence before he was ready.

Another case concerns an experienced programmer who was given a new application program to design. He worked for several months with frequent management interaction, but he didn't make much progress. When his performance was reviewed, he seriously disagreed with his poor rating and complained that his direction was so specific that he felt like a flunky. He was confident he could do the job but felt he had not been given the chance. Since he was entirely capable of doing the work, his manager should have told him what was wanted and given him the independence to do it on his own.

A third situation involves an experienced engineer who was temporarily assigned to the headquarters staff. His manager asked him to develop a new training program for the entire division, but he said he didn't know any of the headquarters people and had no idea where to start. The manager took several hours to tell him what he had in mind and why the job was important, but he insisted that the engineer make his own contacts and work out the program specifics by himself. The engineer soon found several people who made some very good suggestions, and he quickly put together the outlines of the program. He got agreement from his manager, and in less than a year he had a pilot program under way. He had found his own way around headquarters, had become familiar with the other staffs, and had made many presentations to senior managers and executives. Although he had not initially known where to start, his manager threw him in and made him swim. He quickly found that he could.

Another example involves a newly hired professional with a degree in computer science. His manager did not have an immediate project available, so he asked him to temporarily coordinate departmental test activity. His shift supervisor was an old hand in the testing business who had not completed college, and Bill resented having him as boss. This upset him so much, in fact, that he did not even do his simple coordination job very well. The department manager soon realized there was a problem and discussed the situation with the supervisor. They both agreed that Bill was technically capable of very good work but that his attitude was a serious problem. The manager then talked to Bill, who complained that he should be leading the group, since his education was so much better than his supervisor's. The manager agreed he had the training to do far more challenging work but told him that his current performance was so poor that no manager would give him a better assignment. Bill was both smart and ambitious, and he realized that if he couldn't do a competent job of test coordination, he could not get promoted, regardless of his education. He buckled down, did a first-class job, and soon was given a new and better assignment.

As these examples show, relationship maturity is a complex combination of many factors. For professionals to do superior work, they must be capable of working at the self-actualizing level. This is extremely difficult for anyone, and the more severe their personal problems, the harder it is. Managers should thus focus on each of their people and look for symptoms of relationship immaturity. If employees perform below expectations, are hard to deal with, complain about lack of advancement, or constantly seek support, they likely have such concerns. Managers should then talk to them to see if they can identify the problems that lie behind this behavior. Then they can either provide the additional support themselves or get professional help.

BUILDING MOTIVATION

The process of building employees' motivation is quite different from enhancing their competence. Once employees have learned a skill, they will retain it almost indefinitely. Motivation, however, is slower to develop and can be destroyed in an instant. Highly motivated employees can be antagonized or discouraged by a manager who overlooks their achievements, assigns them uninteresting work, or unintentionally offends them. Managers should realize that, as James MacGreggor Burns said, "People need appreciation, recognition and a feeling of accomplishment, and the confidence that people who are important to them believe in them."[10]

This, of course, requires a sustained and relatively intimate level of interaction between managers and each of their people. Pelz's studies showed that the most productive scientists were those who were given a moderate degree of management freedom.[11] Those with the greatest freedom, however, tended to work by themselves and lacked the stimulation of frequent management interaction and the resulting challenge of short-term goals. The tightly managed scientists, on the other hand, were invariably well motivated, but Pelz found they were too constrained by their manager's style and thus not very creative. He found that when the manager's style was not directive, there was a strong positive correlation between professionals' performance and their frequency of management contact. Rensis Likert similarly found that total independence is rarely as productive as a reasonable level of sustained interaction.[12] In several studies he has shown that young scientists who saw their superiors at least daily performed significantly better than those who were left to operate independently.

In the final analysis professionals are potentially their own best managers, and they will be most effective when their own personal standard is superior performance. Managers can build this attitude by showing frequent interest in each of their people's work, involving them in the decisions that affect them, recognizing and respecting each of them as an individual, and giving them reasonable control over how they do their job.

MOTIVATING PROFESSIONAL PEOPLE

Although there are no simple formulas which can assure employee motivation, the following guidelines are generally helpful with technical people:

1. After professionals have gained a minimal level of experience, their manager's focus should turn to what is wanted, with the professionals given progressively more discretion on how to do it.
2. Managers should hold frequent informal meetings with each of their people and ask questions about their technical approach, who they have talked to, and what they know about others' work in the field.
3. When professionals seek advice, managers should suggest avenues to explore rather than give specific direction. Managers should certainly discuss their own ideas, but employees should have the freedom to accept them and be expected to justify their own final conclusion.
4. Managers should be enthusiastic about good work and insure that their people know it.
5. The best people should be involved in at least some nonproject activities. Since an exclusive project focus limits creativity, they should occasionally participate in relevant studies, task forces, or committees.
6. The most promising professionals should be asked to present their work to senior managers, customers, or outside professional groups. This both builds their self-confidence and motivates them to more logically structure their work.
7. Finally, professionals should make the plans and estimates for their own work. If they are too conservative, their manager should ask tough questions and probe for contingencies and soft spots. A relaxed management will rarely get the best performance, for good people thrive on hard work, especially when their managers demand it.

THE MANAGER'S STYLE

Many managers see a conflict between the need for strong leadership and the necessity of being more participative with their people. There is, however, no real conflict, because each professional wants both to do important work and to do it his own way. The strong leader reinforces the urgency and importance of the goal, while the participative manager recognizes success and provides the freedom and support his or her people need to do their work their own way. Clearly, a good manager must be able to behave both ways.

Engineers or scientists will soon become uneasy when their manager leaves them alone. They will wonder if their assignment is truly important or if they have somehow fallen into personal disfavor. They may begin to suspect some unknown change in project plans or a secret reorganization and dream up imagined problems which will both distract them and limit their creativity. The best insurance from this problem is daily management contact and the challenge of crisp and important goals.

Participation does not mean relaxation. Important work calls for urgency with aggressive schedules and a challenging pace. If the people seem to be getting comfortable and relaxed, tighter deadlines are needed. If the job is to take a week, set a meeting for that day and don't accept a delay without an explanation. The manager's style should be honest and participative, but it should also be demanding.

NOTES CHAPTER 7

1. Lee Iacocca and William Novak, *Iacocca: An Autobiography* (New York: Bantam Books, Inc., 1984), p. 56.

2. David C. McClelland's research is briefly summarized by Hersey and Blanchard in *Management of Organizational Behavior* 3rd ed. (Englewood Cliffs, N.J.: Prentice-Hall, Inc., 1977). The references they list are David C. McClelland, J. W. Atkinson, R. A. Clark, and E. L. Lowell, *The Achievement Motive* (New York: Appleton-Century-Crofts, 1953) and *The Achieving Society* (Princeton, N.J.: International Thompson Organization Inc., Van Nostrand, Reinhold, Co., 1961).

3. A. Ray McCord, "Improving Productivity—A Way of Life at TI,"*Assembly Engineering,* January 1980, p. 52.

4. Frederick Winslow Taylor, *The Principles of Scientific Management* (New York: Harper and Row, Publishers, Inc., 1911).

5. Paul Hersey and Kenneth Blanchard have provided an excellent discussion of early management thinking starting on page 90 in *Management of Organizational Behavior* 3rd ed. (Englewood Cliffs, N.J.: Prentice-Hall, Inc., 1977).

6. Hersey and Blanchard, in *Management,* describe the Hawthorne studies starting on page 51. The basic references for this work are F. J. Roethlisberger and W. J. Dickson, *Management and the Worker* (Cambridge: Harvard University Press, 1939); T. N. Whitehead,*The Industrial Worker,* vols. 1 and 2 (Cambridge: Harvard University Press, 1938); and Elton Mayo, *The Human Problems of an Industrial Civilization* (New York: Macmillan Publishing Co., Inc., 1933).

7. Douglass McGregor originally coined the terms "Theory X" and "Theory Y" in his book *The Human Side of Enterprise* (New York: McGraw-Hill Book Company, 1960).

8. Hersey and Blanchard provide a comprehensive treatment of situational leadership in Chapter 7 of *Management.*

9. The late professor Bud Kilpatrick, of the Universities of Delaware and Ohio State, specialized in transactional psychology. He described this insurance company example at an IBM management class in 1968, but there is no record of its publication.

10. James MacGregor Burns, *Leadership* (New York: Harper and Row, Publishers, Inc., 1978), p. 374.

11. Donald C. Pelz and Frank M. Andrews, *Scientists in Organizations: Productive Climates for Research and Development* (New York: John Wiley & Sons, Inc., 1966), p. 51.

12. Rensis Likert,*New Patterns of Management* (New York: McGraw-Hill Book Company, 1961), p. 24.

8

Identifying

Talented Professionals

Among highly motivated people, the most talented generally do the best. This assumes, of course, that their talents are directly suited to their work. Every field of specialty has a unique set of talents which provide the best chance of success, and those who have them have a special advantage. Those without these gifts can also succeed, but it will likely take greater effort. As in the following example, they might do better to find a calling which more closely matches their natural abilities.

An electrical engineer had always wanted to be a circuit designer. He must have struggled valiantly in engineering school, for he had neither the necessary mathematical talents nor the instincts of a builder. After graduation he got a job with a development laboratory and was assigned to the work he had always dreamed of. His manager worked with him for several months, but the engineer was unable to solve even the simplest design problems. After many discussions and a lot of management pressure, he was finally persuaded to quit engineering and try his hand as a salesman. Some months later he proudly came back to see his old pals at the lab, and he even thanked his previous manager for urging him to change his career. He was a born salesman and had been wasting his talents in a vain attempt to be a circuit designer.

Gifted professionals can generally succeed in a wide variety of jobs as long as their talents are reasonably consistent with the special needs of their work. As John Gardner has pointed out, however, finding such a fit is not as hard as it might seem, for "gifted individuals generally have many talents rather than a single talent. If the individual is promising in one line, the best guess is that he will be promising in a number of lines. . . .''[1] The key is to identify the most talented people and put them in jobs that interest them. Their development is then best insured by keeping their work continually challenging. The Peter principle says that employees tend to rise to their level of incompetence, but James Healey has proposed the far more important

Paul principle: "For every employee who rises above his level of competence, there are several whose talents are not utilized."[2]

THE IMPORTANCE OF TALENT

Talented people are the organization's most important asset. They originate the creative ideas, solve the key problems, and produce the most successful products. The enormous difference between the truly talented and the average employee was demonstrated by a limited experiment with twelve programmers.[3] Each was given two identical specifications and told to produce a running program for each. Everyone was to use the same programming language and tools, and the results were carefully measured. Even though the programs were to perform identical calculations, the variation between the best and the worst was as much as twenty-eight times, as shown in Table 8.1. Since the programmers' education and experience did not correlate with these results, the unmistakable conclusion is that some of these programmers were just more talented than the others.

TABLE 8.1   Relative Test Results

	ALGEBRA	MAZE
Program size	6:1	5:1
Program run time	5:1	13:1
Programming hours	16:1	25:1
Debugging hours	28:1	26:1

Although this was a limited experiment in only one technical field, there is little question that such wide performance variations occur quite generally. Some professionals effortlessly accomplish exceptional work, while their less fortunate peers struggle to produce mediocre results. On reflection, however, this should not be surprising. We all expect wide variation between great artists and championship athletes. World-class runners, prize-winning skiers, and great composers, for example, all have made great personal efforts to achieve championship rank, but they all generally started with superior natural talents. The distinction may not seem as obvious as in art or athletics, but outstanding performance in circuit design, computer programming, theoretical physics, and mathematics depends just as heavily on talent.

THE AVAILABILITY OF TALENT

The ability to attract and develop talent is fundamental to organizational survival, and Peter Drucker attributes the problems of the American railroads to their failings in this regard: "Before World War I able graduates of American engineering schools looked for a railroad career. From the end of World War I on, for whatever reason, the railroads no longer appealed to young engineering graduates or to any educated young people."[4]

In every organization the limited supply of talent is clearly apparent to any manager who seeks candidates for an important assignment. An organization can only address this problem by attracting more and better engineers and scientists or by better utilizing those it already has. It is enormously difficult for an organization to make itself more attractive to the best people, however, because the most stimulating technical environments are most attractive; and this environment results from the caliber and reputation of the people who are already there. This means that the best groups attract the best people and thus become even more attractive. To break this vicious cycle, every technical organization must both search for talent and make the very best use of the talents it already has.

THE CHARACTERISTICS OF TECHNICALLY TALENTED PEOPLE

Of all technical talents, creativity is possibly the most important. Frank Barron has studied highly creative people, and in one test of eighty accomplished artists he found they were universally attracted by complexity.[5] They had a strong preference for asymmetrical drawings rather than simple figures, and they looked for "vital or dynamic" pictures which most other people thought chaotic. This same set of tests was then given to a group of doctor of science candidates at the University of California who had been ranked by the faculty on their originality. Barron was ". . . somewhat surprised to discover that the more original scientists expressed preferences very similar to those of the artists." He concluded that "the creative response to disorder . . . is to find an elegant new order more satisfying than any that could be evoked by a simpler configuration."

Another of Barron's tests explored the relationship between originality and independence. He placed a test subject in a conference room with several people who were secretly part of the experiment. They were asked a series of simple questions, and the seating was arranged so that the subject was among the last to respond. Each was asked to look at a picture with several lines on it and to identify the line he or she believed was longest. Generally, the entire group gave the correct answer, but occasionally, at a secret signal, all the confederates gave the same incorrect response. Surprisingly, even though it was obvious which was the longest line, about 75 percent of the subjects contradicted the evidence of their own eyes and gave the same false response as the rest of the group.

At the completion of this test the subjects were then separated into two groups according to their willingness to give the correct answer and again questioned to determine their tolerance for disorder. As shown by their responses to the following questions, the more independent-minded 25 percent showed a marked preference for complexity:

1. I like to fool about with new ideas even if they turn out later to be a total waste of time. (True)
2. The best theory is the one that has the best practical applications. (False)
3. Some of my friends think that my ideas are impractical, if not a bit wild. (True)
4. The unfinished and the imperfect often have greater appeal for me than the completed and the polished. (True)
5. I must admit that I would find it hard to have for a close friend a person whose manners or appearance made him somewhat repulsive, no matter how brilliant or kind he might be. (False)
6. A person should not probe too deeply into his own and other people's feelings but take things as they are. (False)
7. Young people sometimes get rebellious ideas, but as they grow up they ought to get over them and settle down. (False)
8. Perfect balance is the essence of a good composition. (False)

As a result of this work Barron has concluded that truly creative people must be sufficiently independent minded to suffer the personal discomfort and occasional ridicule that often accompany new ideas. It takes a high degree of self-confidence to challenge the existing order and even more strength of character to risk criticism. Those who are too timid rarely think up creative ideas, and when they do, they don't have the courage to support them. Barron found, however, that highly creative people were well aware of their own feelings and understood the risks they took to support them.

W. O. Baker, who was president and then chairman of Bell Laboratories before his retirement, adds an interesting dimension to Barron's findings. He says that

> not only must technical people possess the ego that gives them the self-confidence necessary for undertaking a very difficult mission, but they must also have some humility, because nature will have the last laugh. They must, in short, recognize the intrinsic difficulties of their task and be modest about the chance of success.[6]

IDENTIFYING TECHNICALLY TALENTED PEOPLE

Several years ago IBM established a special program to focus on the development of outstanding technical people. As a first step a survey was run of their leading technical professionals to learn how better to identify future technical leaders. A total of twenty-five senior profesionals were questioned, including eighteen IBM Fellows.[7] The responses to the various questions were scored by adding the positive reactions and subtracting the negative ones. For example, if two respondents felt that salary progression was a positive indicator and three felt it was negative, salary progression would be scored as -1. The maximum score would thus be $+25$, and the minimum -25. Using this system, the net scores for the most frequently mentioned leading indicators of superior technical performance are as shown in Table 8.2.

TABLE 8.2   Early Indications of Technical Leadership

Professional Society Activities:	
Publications	9
Awards	7
Presentations	6
Offices	− 10
IBM technical Committee Activity:	
Presentations	3
Use on Technical Task Forces	19
Special Assignments	15
Technical Memos	6
Academic History:	
Projects	4
Grade Point Average	3
Honors	0
IBM History:	
Awards	5
Performance Rating	2
Salary Progression	− 1

These senior professionals clearly felt that a highly talented technical professional was best identified by the respect of his peers and managers. This was in turn shown by his frequency of selection for task forces or special assignments. Publications, awards, and presentations were judged to be important, although opinions varied widely, with some strongly dissenting views. Involvement with professional societies was not felt to be a strong indicator, although this more likely reflects the limited technical society involvement of many industrial engineers and scientists than the value of such activities.

IDENTIFYING MANAGERIAL TALENT

Although the identification of technical talent is largely a matter of finding those creative people with motivation and self-confidence, the search for managerial talent is a different matter. Here, motivation and self-confidence are also needed, but other factors are equally essential. Edwin Gee, a senior vice president of Du Pont, has listed the major reasons for the failure of research directors:[8]

1. Poor interpersonal relationships, difficulty in establishing rapport with subordinates, and pettiness. Where such problems exist, Gee feels they are inborn, ingrained, and irreversible.

2. Looking for intellectual solutions to managerial problems and not appreciating the subjective people factors.

3. Overdedication to scientific discovery without the ability to use these discoveries to effectively support the organization's objectives.

4. The lack of financial, profit, or business orientation. Such managers devote the same effort to projects that have small potential dollar payoff as they do to ones with larger potential.

5. A lack of market orientation means such directors fail to get adequate market-place feedback before dollar costs become excessive. As a result, a higher proportion of their projects become expensive marketplace failures because they were not previously stopped in the laboratory or plant.

6. Finally, many poor-performing research directors fail to establish goals, assessment programs, and a follow-up discipline.

Gee also describes those attributes of researchers which suggest that they will be good managers:

1. They are able to identify a problem, analyze it, and synthesize a solution.

2. They are willing to accept and even seek responsibility.

3. They view their current assignment as the most important single thing they have to do rather than as a step toward promotion.

4. They have good work habits, set personal goals, and plan ahead.

5. They are able to get results without upsetting people.

6. They have integrity.

7. In addition to technical talent, they have demonstrated at least some skill in such fields as marketing, finance, and employee relations.

8. Finally, the ability to make sound judgments is the key to both long-term potential and current readiness for promotion.

Harry Truman put it most succinctly when he said that a leader must act as if "the buck stops here."[9]

THE TAMED REBEL

Alon Gratch, while a doctoral candidate at Columbia University, made a psychological study of some seventy corporate leaders.[10] He ran a series of tests to identify their attitudes and to understand what he called their ego development. For this purpose, he divided them into Conformists and post-Conformists. The Conformist feels that rules are to be followed, but the post-Conformist sees them as guides which occasionally should be broken or changed. Gratch found that 95 percent of the successful executives in his study fell into the post-Conformist stage. This contrasts with the normal population which is predominantly Conformist.

Gratch further divided the post-Conformist stage into the Conscientious and the Autonomous. He found that Conscientious managers are "interested in motives, consequences, long-term goals and ideals. They are self-critical but not self-rejecting.'' Most important, such managers are conscious of their own feelings and capable of managing issues objectively in spite of personal considerations. Such managers, he found

> —are ambitious and have a need for achievement
> —have the flexibility to see people and situations from several perspectives
> —act and feel like rebels but consciously hold themselves in check

The highest level of ego development is the Autonomous and Integrated stage where, according to Gratch, people ''show a deep concern for the autonomy of others.'' None of Gratch's seventy successful executives fell into this Autonomous level. This is not surprising, because Autonomous individuals are more considerate of the concerns of others, more willing to accept problems as insoluble, and less inclined to strive valiantly for an unreachable goal. Great leaders are often great because they continue to struggle and often succeed even against apparently overwhelming odds.

THE RECOGNITION OF TALENT

From all the studies on this subject a few criteria seem to emerge as common identifiers of future leadership. It is clear that technically creative people must have the courage of their own convictions and be willing to face criticism. Similarly, future senior managers do not feel bound by the rules, and they have sufficient self-confidence to push for what they believe in. The personal courage to be different and the self-confidence to take the lone and often unpopular position are clearly basic characteristics of leaders in both management and technology.

This characteristic of talented people is the source of much of the difficulty with identification programs. All too often those who obey the rules and don't make waves are rewarded with steady advancement. The evidence suggests, however, that the most promising leaders are often the wild ducks, and that it might be wise to consciously look for talent among the ranks of the rebels.

This does not mean that every nonconformist will make a good leader. People choose to be different for many reasons, but some of them take this path because they see opportunities for improvement that the rest of us have missed. To avoid overlooking some of the organization's truly outstanding talent, the wild ducks should be reviewed to see what makes them wild.

Finally, the individual's dedication to his work is a vital parameter. Based on a twenty-year AT&T study, Ann Howard and Douglass Bray point out that the one characteristic that separated future top executives from their less successful peers was their continued willingness to work hard.[11] While no studies of the work attitudes of technical leaders have been made, there is no question that hard work is one of their common characteristics. Beyond these two simple measures of self-confidence and dedication, the only reliable guideline to future success is the opinion of the employee's peers and immediate managers.

THE IDENTIFICATION PROCESS

The first step in an identification process is to have the employee's direct manager evaluate his or her on-the-job performance and decide on his or her promotion potential. This manager than reviews these judgments with the next higher manager, who also talks with other managers to get as complete an opinion of the employee as possible. These individual judgments are made by the management team on all the people in the organization, and they are reviewed with the senior managers, who then select the most promising professionals for future development and promotion. The advantages of such an approach are as follows:

1. It is simple, inexpensive, and timely.
2. It accurately reflects current job performance and quickly eliminates those who obviously have low potential.
3. It reflects the views of those managers who can most directly influence the employee's career.
4. It is equally effective for both technical and managerial candidates.
5. Finally, as Leavitt points out, the combined judgment and wisdom of many experienced managers is usually very sound.[12]

The typical problems with such direct managerial evaluations of employee potential are the following:

1. One manager's views can seriously bias the evaluation. This risk is highest with the first-line manager, who is least experienced at making such judgments.
2. Although junior managers can usually judge a professional's readiness for promotion, they rarely appreciate the needs of higher-level positions and are not reliable judges of long-term potential.
3. Junior managers are often reluctant to identify their best people for promotion because they will likely lose them and have to find replacements.
4. All managers are busy and rarely take the time to do these evaluations unless they are required to.

Even though there are serious drawbacks, there is no completely satisfactory substitute for using line management to do the basic work of identification.

THE ASSESSMENT CENTER

The assessment center provides a practical and effective way to augment the immediate manager's judgment. It is typically used to evaluate a dozen or so high-potential young managers by exposing them to several days of tests and exercises. Their performance is observed by an assessment staff of two or three trained professionals and four or more senior management observers. The program involves a number of individual exercises and presentations as well as unstructured team assignments. Each individual's performance is rated for each exercise, and at the end, the observers and the assessment staff combine their views on each individual's potential and career planning needs. These judgments are then discussed with the individual by the assessment staff. As is natural in such programs, the ratings tend to be relative, which necessitates that some people be ranked at the bottom. To protect them from potential career damage, only limited assessment results are shared with line management, and then only with the senior location executive for each attendee.

Badawy discusses such programs and gives an excellent summary of their strengths and weaknesses:[13]

1. Several assessors are likely to do a better job than a single supervisor.
2. The use of structured evaluation criteria helps to provide a more complete judgment.
3. Participation in such programs helps the senior management observers sharpen their assessment skills.
4. The candidates generally find that the exercises provide helpful perspective on themselves and their work.
5. Being chosen for an assessment exercise builds the morale of the candidate and gives them an opportunity to show their abilities in fairly realistic situations.

Badawy, however, also points out some problems with assessment centers:

1. They can become self-fulfilling prophecies because those who do best will get the greatest opportunities for promotion.
2. A candidate who does poorly can become discouraged and lose self-confidence, thus hurting an otherwise promising career.
3. Those who are not given the opportunity to attend such programs may object.
4. The stress of assessment can be serious, particularly for those who do not perform well in a competitive environment.
5. Assessment programs are generally expensive to operate.

ASSESSMENT EXPERIENCE

IBM has run an assessment program in engineering, programming, and product planning since 1978 and has found it very helpful for identifying and developing high-potential managers. From the first several hundred participants, 96 percent felt assessment accurately measured the important qualities for management success, 92 percent were confident observer judgments were accurate, 96 percent rated it effective in measuring their personal strengths and weaknesses, and 97 percent said it would help them in their own self-improvement efforts.

Regarding career progress, 51 percent of the participants felt assessment would help them, and 33 percent said it would neither help nor hurt. Sixteen percent, however, felt their careers would be damaged by assessment. This probably explains why only 84 percent of the graduates would be willing to participate again.

Approximately one third of IBM's high-potential technical managers have been identified, in part, through this program, and even though the results are not made available to the immediate managers, subsequent promotional progress correlates well with the assessment ratings. Those rated very highly by the assessors have been promoted an average of 2.1 levels since assessment, while those with lower ratings only moved 0.8 levels. The highly and moderately rated managers moved 1.7 and 1.2 levels, respectively.

IDENTIFICATION PROGRAMS

Immediate managers play an important role in assessment because they nominate the people to attend. They know their people best, are best qualified to judge their needs and talents, and will control their future development. The first-line manager's critical role, however, is also the greatest weakness of the identification process, because they are generally so busy with their daily priorities that they can rarely take the time to do this job adequately. That is why such programs are never effective unless higher-level management gets directly involved.

This is best done by senior managers who take a strong personal interest in the program and are willing to spend their own time conducting periodic reviews with their top management team. For example, one IBM division president would spend one full day a year with each of his location managers, reviewing their high-potential employee identification and development programs. When he found a program that was not up to par, he would explain to the manager that this was a basic requirement of his or her job and that he would be back for another review in a few months. The program was always in good shape for the second review.

NOTES CHAPTER 8

1. John W. Gardner, *Excellence* (New York: Harper & Row, Publishers, Inc., 1961), p. 60.

2. M. K. Badawy, *Developing Managerial Skills in Engineers and Scientists: Succeeding as a Technical Manager* (New York: International Thompson Organization, Inc., Van Nostrand Reinhold Co., 1982), p. 274.

3. H. Sackman, W. J. Erikson, and E. E. Grant, "Exploratory Experimental Studies Comparing Online and Offline Programming Performance," *Communications of the ACM*, vol. 11, no. 1, (January 1968), pp. 3–11.

4. Peter F. Drucker, *Management, Tasks, Responsibilities, Practices* (New York: Harper & Row, Publishers, Inc., 1974), p. 109.

5. Frank Barron, "The Psychology of Imagination," *Scientific American,*" CXCIX, (September 1958) 151–166.

6. Michael F. Wolff, "Managing Large Egos," *Research Management,* July 1982, p. 7.

7. IBM Fellows are senior professionals who have demonstrated such outstanding technical ability that they are given the freedom to work on any project they choose. At any one time only about fifty IBM professionals hold five-year renewable appointments to the rank of Fellow.

8. Edwin A. Gee and Chaplin Tyler, *Managing Innovation* (New York: John Wiley & Sons, Inc., 1976), p. 172.

9. Merle Miller, *Plain Speaking: An Oral Biography of Harry S. Truman* (New York: The Putnam Publishing Group, Berkley Publishing Group, 1973).

10. Alon Gratch, "Tamed Rebels Make Good Managers," *The New York Times,* February 10, 1985, sec. 3, p. 3.

11. Ann Howard and Douglass W. Bray, "A.T. & T.: The Hopes of Middle Managers," *The New York Times,* March 21, 1982, sec. 3, p. 2.

12. Harold J. Leavitt, *Managerial Psychology, Fourth Edition* (Chicago, Ill.: University of Chicago Press, 1978), p. 100.

13. Badawy, *Developing Managerial Skills,* pp. 56–57.

9

Developing

Technical Talent

Although the most outstanding people are likely to do the best work, true excellence in any field requires a combination of talent, experience, and motivation. Even people with great natural talents must know how to capitalize on them before they can reach the first rank. It takes enormous personal effort to excel in any field, be it athletics, engineering, music, or science, but proper guidance can be enormously helpful in making these efforts most effective.

Professor Herbert Simon, who won a Nobel Prize for his pioneering work in artificial intelligence, has explained how expert knowledge is developed. Experts build a large store of remembered patterns, and chess masters, for example, can remember as many as fifty thousand or more combinations of chess pieces.[1] Simon calls this their vocabulary, and he explains that average players can only remember several hundred such patterns. According to Simon, the human brain has separate short-term and long-term memories. The long-term memory holds a large volume of essentially permanent information, but it cannot save or retrieve it very quickly. Short-term memory, on the other hand, is much faster, but it can only handle four to six ''chunks'' at a time.

Simon describes a simple experiment which illustrates the expert's tremendous advantage over the novice. Several subjects are shown a chess board of a game in progress, which has twenty-five or so pieces upon it. They are told to look at this board for a few seconds and then to reproduce the positions of all the pieces from memory. Most novices can only place five or six of the pieces, but the experts can reproduce the entire board with about 90 percent accuracy. This only works with board positions from actual chess games, however, for if the pieces are placed at random, the expert does no better than the novice. The reason is that the novice needs to remember each piece individually, but the expert sees a chess game as logical groupings of pieces. Each such grouping is remembered as a single chunk of information, and since each chunk includes several pieces, only five or six chunks will often include the entire board. When the pieces are randomly placed, however, the expert now must also remember each piece individually; therefore he or she can no longer draw on this store of fifty thousand or so patterns. The expert's memory is thus not necessarily better than the novice's, it is just that he or she is remembering more powerful chunks.

All experienced professionals have such expert "vocabularies" which provide them an analytic capability far greater than the average layman. The importance of powerful symbols can be easily visualized by trying to remember several eight-place binary numbers, such as 10010110, 11000101, and 10111010. Since most people are unfamiliar with this notation, they must memorize the positions of each individual bit. This means that each binary number must take eight chunks of short-term memory, thus making it impossible for many people to remember more than one such eight-place number. When the more powerful decimal notation is used, however, these same binary numbers become 150, 197, and 186, which most people can readily remember, at least for a few moments. The use of more powerful information chunks reduces the load on short-term memory, allows experts to deal with more information at one time, and thus permits them to think in far more complex and sophisticated terms.

As they accumulate a large store of knowledge in their special field, experts are also increasing the power of the symbols they work and think with. All this takes a great deal of time and effort, as shown by the studies of the psychologist John R. Hayes of Carnegie-Mellon University. He examined the careers of successful artists and found that none of them produced a world-class work until they had spent at least ten years in their chosen medium.[2] Although artists are not scientists, their fields are similar in that they require special skills and a large store of relevant knowledge. With the increasing sophistication of science and engineering, it is progressively more difficult for anyone to become a first-class expert without taking the time to learn a large store of information about his or her chosen field. Although many people are able to do this on their own, a structured development program can help the promising professional spend this preparatory time to best advantage.

PROFESSIONAL DEVELOPMENT

No one questions the athlete's need for a trainer, but the corresponding needs of technical professionals are not as clearly recognized. Young engineers and scientists are eager to learn and willing to work hard, but they rarely have the perspective to efficiently direct their energies. A structured development program which is based on each individual's needs and career plans can help them select those assignments which will build their skills and give them the perspective to avoid dead-end jobs.

In addition to assisting the professionals, such programs also help make the organization more attractive to talented people. The best engineers and scientists are properly concerned about their career development and will be more interested in an organization that shows equal concern. Professional development programs also help to insure an adequate supply of qualified candidates for the key positions. Since there is always a shortage of good people, this can be enormously valuable.

Du Pont, as part of its recruiting effort, has a corporate-wide professional development program which is administered by its Engineering Department. Of some three hundred to four hundred professionals covered, approximately seventy-five new college recruits are enrolled in this program each year. In line with their interests, these young professionals are rotated through a series of two-year assignments across a range of technical activities. The full-time headquarters staff participate in performance reviews, insure that the assignment continues to be appropriate for the individual, and arrange for new assignments. They report no difficulty in finding these assignments and believe the program has helped both to attract and retain good people while providing top-notch engineering talent to the company's operations. The professionals who have gone through the program have typically done well, both in their initial assignments and in their future promotional progress.

CAREER MOVES

The typical technical professional has many latent talents, but only a few of them can be developed in any single assignment. While it would be impractical to attempt to capitalize on all the potential talents of any engineer or scientist, it is also clear that the most productive professionals have competence in several areas. This suggests that the best people should be given the opportunity to broaden their backgrounds, and this can best be done through multiple career moves.

Managers are always reluctant to let their best people go, but sometimes professionals are reluctant to move as well. When they get comfortable in one specialty, they often cling to its safety and resist management pressure to move. William Cohen describes such a case with Mickey, an aeronautical engineer, who became a specialist in reciprocating aircraft engines during World War II.[3] He stayed on with the same company after the war and over the next several years was given several opportunities to attend a six-month course on the new jet engine technology. He always claimed to be too busy, however, so he ended up staying with the old reciprocating engine technology and never did switch to jets. Despite his acknowledged talents, he ended up as the lone advisory staff consultant who handled the few remaining problems that came up with the old World War II vintage engines.

Professional development programs help to identify people like Mickey so that management can prod them into more promising career paths. Some people are reluctant to accept the challenge and stimulation of new technical assignments, but this is often exactly what is needed to maintain their professional development.

Thomas J. Watson, Jr., once said that "men who have accomplished great deeds in large organizations might have done less if they had been challenged with less."[4]

TECHNICAL DEVELOPMENT NEEDS

As part of IBM's focus on the career development of its outstanding technical professionals, twenty-five of their most senior engineers, scientists, and programmers were asked what experiences would have been most helpful to them in their career.[5] As shown in Table 9.1, some experiences were supported by a clear majority, even though there was no general consensus. The wide divergence of opinion is shown by the fact that eleven were positive about research experience with two negatives; for assistantships, ten were in favor, and three against. The strongest divergence of opinion concerned division and corporate staff positions with nine in favor and four against. The one thing the responses of these twenty-five senior professionals all demonstrated was the wide range of potential career paths which can lead to technical success.

TABLE 9.1   Valuable Technical Development Experiences

Product development	14
Advanced technology	14
Management	13
An academic sabbatical	10
Manufacturing	9
Research	9
A technical assistantship	7
Corporate or division staff	5

The one area of most general agreement concerned the value of identification and development programs in assisting the careers of promising technical professionals. Two respondents said they had done it on their own and felt everyone else should as well, but twenty-three of the twenty-five believed that early counseling and support would have helped them.

The most surprising finding of this study was the widely shared opinion that promising technical professionals should be given management experience. Sixteen of the twenty-five felt that management experience was important, while three felt it would have a negative effect on a promising professional's career, and six voiced no opinion. Even those technologists who had no continuing interest in a management career felt that early experience as a manager had better equipped them to deal with their superiors and had helped prepare them to lead their current small technical teams. With some exceptions, these technical leaders were currently managers of small advanced technology groups, and they had found that people-management skills were important to them.

TECHNICAL BREADTH

From his extensive studies Pelz concluded that the initial focus in developing scientists and engineers should be on building a deep understanding in one primary field of specialty. He says that "the younger Ph.D. should remain in one problem or research area, but learn as much as he can about many aspects of this area; he should not limit himself to a narrow facet."[6] Even with a high degree of concentration, it can take a lot of time for professionals to reach the limits of knowledge in their chosen topic, but until they do, they are rarely able to do leading-edge work.

Once their career foundation is established, most promising professionals should attempt to get some breadth. The rate of broadening must obviously depend on the individual, but breadth should not be delayed for long, for, to quote Pelz: ". . . the key for mature scientists lies not in the dominance of breadth over depth, but rather in the presence of both breadth and depth."[7] The reason breadth is so important was best explained by the late Abraham Maslow when he said that "to him that has only a hammer, the whole world looks like a nail."[8] The narrow technologist will spend too much of his time trying to fit the problems he faces to his known but limited set of solutions.

Breadth also provides a rich foundation for intuitive judgment. In modern technology few issues are cleanly constrained to one special field, and the available data is rarely complete or even consistent. Under such conditions, a good intuition is often the only reliable guide. Intuition, however, is best gained through hands-on experience in a variety of areas, and seasoned professionals can often sense the right answer while their less experienced colleagues are still struggling to define the problem.

Tracy Kidder described this phenomenon in his anecdote about the visit of Carl Carman, a Data General vice-president, to a computer test area. The engineers told him about a problem that had plagued them for weeks, and as Kidder says:

> The ALU was sitting outside Gallifrey's (the computer's) frame, on the extender. Gallifrey was running a low-level program. Carman said, 'Hmmmmm.' He walked over to the computer and, to the engineers' horror, he grasped the ALU board by its edges and shook it. At that instant, Gallifrey failed.[9]

The engineers then realized that their problem was in the connectors which held the chips to the ALU, so they replaced them all, and the error which had plagued them for months was gone. In a few minutes Carman, with his broad experience, could "smell" the problem that these engineers had worked for weeks to find.

Breadth helps to accelerate the pace of learning by serendipitously applying knowledge from one area to problems in another. Technical intuition is often transferable between specialties, and the engineer or scientist with experience in several subjects invariably finds they have deep similarities. Much as an experienced linguist finds each new language easier to learn, broad-gauge professionals can grasp new issues and concepts far quicker than their less experienced associates. Patrick

Winston, the director of MIT's Artificial Intelligence Laboratory, suggests why this is true when he says that "you don't learn anything unless you almost know it anyway."[10]

One of the arguments against broad exposure for engineers and scientists is that it reduces the time they can spend in their prime area of specialty. Pelz has shown, however, that they will do better work when they are involved in several activities at the same time.[11] He found that only six percent of their time need be spent away from their prime project, but there was a decided peak in performance when they were involved in four to five activities. With seventy-five research Ph.D.'s, for example, those who spent half to three quarters of their time on strictly research work were more scientifically productive than the ones who devoted full time. Even when the balance of this nonproject time was spent on nontechnical matters, the part-time researchers still did better work.[12]

CONTINUING MANAGEMENT CONTACT

Managers can also help to develop their outstanding people by managing them in a stimulating way. If they expose them to multiple challenges and provide them with a high degree of control over their own work, they will grow most quickly. By showing continuing interest in their people's work, managers also reinforce its importance and help to maintain their people's enthusiasm during the long periods of drudgery between the occasional moments of excitement. Managers must be careful, however, to handle these contacts in the right way; for if they are excessively critical or highly directive, they can cause the professional to worry about his or her opinions rather than to concentrate on the technical issues.

George Farris reports on a study of NASA scientists which compared the supervisory styles of high- and low-performing groups.[13] He found that the supervisors with the best groups had a great deal of interaction with their people and behaved more like collaborators than traditional managers. Because of this their people were also more interactive with each other and maintained a more open and informal atmosphere. In the low-performing groups, however, the supervisors appeared to be dominant figures who were unlikely to be influenced by their people. Although these managers were often highly competent, their people did not see them as helpful and thus looked outside the group for assistance. Managers are responsible for the working environment of their people, and there is overwhelming evidence that the best managers provide goals, stimulation, and guidance but let their people manage themselves.

CAREER COUNSELING

One of the technical manager's most important responsibilities is to help his or her people formulate their career plans. Since few engineers or scientists have a very good idea what they want to do, the manager's first step should be to talk with them about their interests and aspirations. Many will probably feel that a move to management is necessary for their continued advancement, but they may be reluctant to take such a step. It takes a great deal of self-confidence to direct the work of someone else, and many professionals don't feel comfortable with the personal power this entails. On the other hand, some professionals have natural leadership ability, and a move into management in their first three to five years can accelerate their long-term development. Although these questions can only be settled by employees themselves, a frank discussion with the manager can suggest experiences which will help them crystallize their thinking on this question.

Badawy suggests five major topics employees should consider as they analyze their career options:[14]

1. The basic career choice between technical specialization and management.
2. An understanding of the specific work people do in each job which seems interesting.
3. The relationship of these working roles to the professional's personal goals and interests.
4. They should understand why one role is more attractive than another and be particularly careful not to move into management or any other job solely because someone has urged them to, because it pays more, or because it carries more prestige.
5. Professionals should discuss their career plans with their family so that they can jointly understand the likely sacrifices required and be better prepared to make them if and when they are asked.

Each job choice will likely have a profound long-term effect on the professional's career, so it should be made with great care. For, as Badawy says, "you are what you do."[15]

STEPS IN TECHNICAL DEVELOPMENT

For professionals who decide on a technical career, the manager's next step is to work with them on a personal development plan. Although it is impractical to try to make such plans very far in advance, temporary staff positions or technical committee participation should be considered for every promising professional. Other than that, only a general direction should be established, with one or two short-term actions identified. Figure 9.1 shows the career path of a scientist who ultimately became an IBM Fellow. Since he had a Ph.D. before joining IBM, he moved quickly into a technical staff position. Thereafter, his assignments remained in his specialty, with some broadening staff moves and technical committee and university involvement. The design engineer's career, shown in Figure 9.2, started with several years in advanced technology before he took a leave of absence to get a Ph.D. Thereafter, he

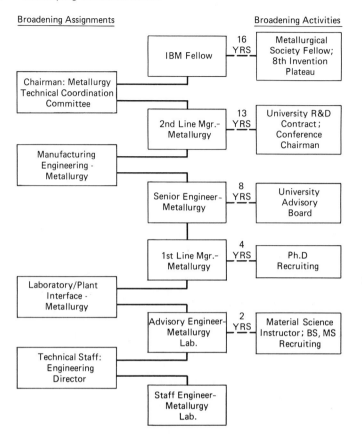

Broadening Assignments   Broadening Activities

Figure 9-1 Metallurgist's technical career roadmap. (Courtesy of IBM.)

held a number of management and technical assignments before becoming an IBM Fellow.

At the outset, promising professionals should focus on building competence in their primary field of specialty. This not only provides the technical foundation for their future career but also helps to build their professional self-confidence. Assuming they continue to demonstrate ability during this early period, the manager should then provide them with broader exposure while they remain in this current assignment. Examples of the kinds of exposures which are most helpful are

1. Participation on a laboratory professionalism committee to arrange talks and seminars on interesting technical topics.

2. A company-wide coordination assignment related to their field of specialty.

3. With further experience, they can participate in reviewing papers or chairing a session for a technical society conference.

4. They might work with a local university to arrange a joint technical program in an area of interest.

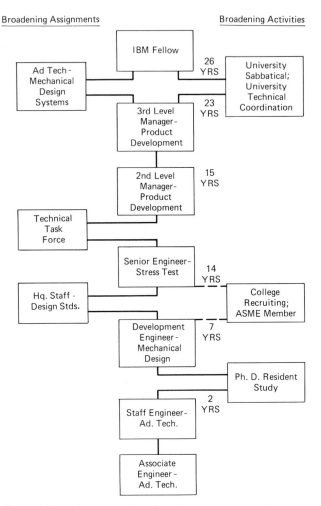

Figure 9-2   Design engineer's technical career roadmap. (Courtesy of IBM.)

5. Spending a month in a field sales office will help them to understand customer and marketing issues.

6. By participating in a short shadow program with a technical or general business executive, professionals can come to appreciate some of the key issues such executives face and better understand how a successful executive operates.

7. They should participate in occasional task forces both inside and outside their field of specialty.

There is rarely time to arrange for more than a few of these broadening activities during a professional's first few working years, but almost any such exposure can be enormously helpful.

After this initial period, broadening assignments should continue, but there should also be a move to a job outside the immediate area of specialty. Although this move should generally be temporary, the intent is to provide broader perspective on both the company and its technology. There can, of course, be no firm guideline on when to make such a move, but it is often best to take this step within the first five to ten years. If it is delayed too long, the professional will be at too high a level to be easily spared, and there will be fewer appropriate temporary positions available. Examples of the kinds of assignments which can be most helpful are the following:

1. A temporary assignment in research.
2. A teaching sabbatical at a college or university.
3. A technical staff assignment at corporate or division headquarters.
4. A one-year assignment as a technical or administrative assistant to a senior executive.
5. An educational fellowship to complete an advanced degree.

There are many potentially useful broadening assignments, but the key is to reach agreement with the professional on the areas he or she would like to explore and to establish an orderly plan to do so. The manager can both assist in implementing this plan and periodically review progress with the employee, but it must be his or her plan.

NOTES CHAPTER 9

1. Jill Larkin, John McDermott, Dorothea P. Simon, and Herbert A. Simon, "Expert and Novice Performance in Solving Physics Problems," *Science*, vol. 208, June 20, 1980, p. 1336.
2. Howard Gardner, "Science Grapples with the Creative Puzzle," *The New York Times*, May 13, 1984, Sec. 2, p. 1.
3. William A. Cohen, *Principles of Technical Management* (New York: AMACOM, a division of American Management Associations, 1980), p. 11.
4. T. J. Watson, Jr., *A Business and Its Beliefs* (New York: McGraw-Hill Book Company, 1963), p. 27.
5. This survey and the grading system used are described in Chapter 8.
6. Donald C. Pelz and Frank M. Andrews, *Scientists in Organizations: Productive Climates for Research and Development* (New York: John Wiley & Sons, Inc., 1966), p. 207.
7. Ibid.
8. Professor Joseph Weizenbaum of the MIT computer science department cited this Maslow quote in the April 4, 1982, *New York Times*.
9. Tracy Kidder, *The Soul of a New Machine* (Boston: Little, Brown & Company, 1981), p. 265.
10. Tom Alexander, "Teaching Computers the Art of Reason," *Fortune*, May 17, 1982, p. 87.

11. Pelz, *Scientists in Organizations*, p. 65.

12. Ibid. p. 56.

13. George Farris's article is included in Michael L. Tushman and William L. Moore's *Readings in the Management of Innovation* (Marshfield, Mass.: Pitman, 1982), p. 345.

14. M. K. Badawy, *Developing Managerial Skills in Engineers and Scientists: Succeeding as a Technical Manager* (New York: International Thompson Organization Inc., Van Nostrand Reinhold Co., 1982), p. 82–105.

15. Ibid., p. 87.

10

Developing
Managerial Talent

Formal management development programs aim to provide future leaders with the broad business and technical intuition they will need to progress to the top of their organizations. Peter Drucker describes a Sears Roebuck experience which shows how important this can be.[1] Shortly after World War II, Sears divided one year's M.B.A hires into three groups and put one third in large stores, one third in small stores, and one third in the headquarters mail-order department. Five years later they found that many of those who had started in the small stores were moving into store management positions, while those in the larger stores had not progressed as fast. In the mail-order department, however, the best of the trainees had left. Drucker concludes that the more complete business environment of the small stores allowed trainees to relate their work to understandable business issues and to gain an intellectual grasp of their job. They thus began to think and act more like a store manager. The trainees in the more isolated mail-order department, however, saw less, understood less, and grew more slowly. When faced with such constraints, the best soon became impatient and left for better opportunities elsewhere.

This is typical of large organizations where many jobs do not relate to such clearly necessary tasks as designing, manufacturing, servicing, or selling products. The larger the organization, the narrower the scope of each job and the harder it is for people to appreciate the value of their work. Although large companies can offer greater opportunities, the complexity of their operations often confuses and discourages the people. In smaller organizations the assignments are necessarily broader and easier to grasp; therefore, the people can more readily appreciate how their work fits in to the overall operation.

Management development programs are progressively more valuable in the larger environment because they help to counteract this organizational complexity by showing the professionals how their work relates to the broader needs of the business. Like technical development, it also makes the organization more attractive to ambitious people, reduces management hoarding of talent, more fully develops the most promising candidates, and helps to uncover high-potential people. Such programs also help to keep an organization alive and stimulated, for, in John Gardner's words, "nothing is more vital to the renewal of an organization than the system by which able people are nurtured and moved into positions where they can make their contributions."[2]

MANAGEMENT DEVELOPMENT OBJECTIVES

When technical professionals become managers, they also join the management team. This step changes their role from employee to employer and requires that they take an entirely different outlook. This point was made very effectively by a senior executive's response to a management trainee who asked why "management" had made a particular decision. He kept referring to management as "they" until the executive told him that now that he was a manager, management was no longer "they" but "we."

This is a hard lesson for many people to learn. In large organizations it is tempting to believe that some omniscient authority can make all the decisions. As they gain experience, most professionals see many things that could be improved if only some senior manager would decide to improve them. Some see this as evidence of management's ineptness, and it never occurs to them that the problems that seem so important to them are not even visible at higher levels. No all-seeing manager can possibly solve all the problems because in any large organization there are far too many issues for any one person to understand or resolve. The only practical solution is for the managers on the spot to take the responsibility for fixing their own problems. If they don't, nobody else generally can.

This sense of ownership is an essential characteristic of future executives, and the management development process attempts to couple this attitude with those hands-on experiences needed to build managers' self-confidence, so that they will act on their own. Valentine sums up such programs as a way to find out if "the manager is capable of using authority . . . to achieve improvements."[3]

STARTING THE DEVELOPMENT PROCESS

The first step in the development process is to talk to employees about their goals and objectives. Have they thought through their career, and do they understand the personal sacrifices they must make to reach an executive position? If they are not willing to work harder than everyone else they know, there is little point in working out an aggressive development plan, because they are not likely to progress very far.

If young managers are eager to learn, are doing something about their own development, and are willing to work hard, they are probably good candidates for management development. If, however, they express interest in senior management but haven't done anything to improve themselves, their chances are probably much less. They may be excellent employees, but they will not likely make it to the top rank unless they use their own time for self-improvement and demonstrate unusual drive and initiative.

Motivation is easy to spot, and with a little encouragement the best candidates will clearly stand out. Even if an employee is highly motivated, however, he or she may not be good management material. McClelland and Burnham have conducted management workshops with over five hundred managers from twenty-five different U.S. corporations to see what traits accompany high management effectiveness.[4] They found that the better managers had a stronger need for power than for being liked. If a candidate feels uncomfortable about taking an unpopular action, he or she is probably not emotionally equipped for senior management.

THE EXECUTIVE PERSONALITY

Assuming the employee is highly motivated and willing to step out of the crowd, Lee Iacocca identifies "two really important things about a candidate that you just can't learn from one short job interview. The first is whether he's lazy, and the second is whether he's got any horse sense.''[5] The ability to make sensible decisions is often a question of maturity, and McClelland and Burnham found that the better managers were more mature and less egotistical. They could deal impersonally with issues and keep their own problems in the background. They were less defensive, more willing to consult experts, and more inclined to help others. This suggests that the most promising candidates should get largely positive responses to the following questions:

1. Do they take charge and act like a leader, do people listen to their views, and are they followed?
2. Do they tactfully use their authority instead of bulling ahead regardless of suggestions and problems?
3. Are they capable of trusting personal relationships with their co-workers, and are they willing and interested in helping others?
4. Can they handle setbacks, heavy pressure, and criticism without getting defensive or discouraged?
5. Can they take management direction in an open and interactive way rather than either blindly accepting or resenting authority?

Any professionals who do well with these questions are most probably excellent management material. The key, however, is not so much managers' opinion of employees as employees' understanding of themselves. If employees have important shortcomings but recognize them and are willing to work on improving themselves, they deserve management support.

Quite apart from their personality traits, promising candidates should also meet certain basic criteria before they are ready for accelerated promotion:

1. Have they demonstrated sound technical judgment, with a record of project success? Project failures are not always the professional's fault, but the best people are usually found on the most successful projects. If they don't have a winner under their belt, it is best to wait a little longer to see what they can do.
2. Do they plan their work, manage their time, and set targets and drive to meet them?
3. Do they drive beyond the confines of their job, show initiative, and treat rules as guidelines which can be changed?
4. Can they communicate?
5. Do they know when to seek help and how to do it?
6. Do they have the integrity and negotiating skill to work effectively as part of a team?
7. Are they pragmatists? Can they face the facts and sort out the operative from the theoretical issues?

Although weaknesses can be addressed through experience and counseling, professionals should understand their problems and be willing to work on them. Such discussions are hard work, but managers who are willing to make this effort can be an enormous help to their high-potential candidates.

ALTERNATING ASSIGNMENTS

The development of promising managers is best accomplished through a carefully planned sequence of line and staff assignments. The line positions build confidence and add deeper understanding, and the staff assignments provide perspective and broadened awareness. Harold Leavitt points out that management development should be "an interactive, back-and-forth process between outside educational programs and inside active experience."[6] As with technologists, however, technical managers should start with a solid grounding in their technical field. Only after they have demonstrated competence and some initial success should they be considered for broadening. Even then, most of their learning should come from within their specialty, with only brief development assignments in other areas. At least for the first ten or so years these broadening assignments should be followed immediately by a longer assignment back at home base.

It is almost always a mistake to give a young manager two broadening assignments in a row. A young engineering manager had worked on a corporate headquarters business planning staff for two years, and it was time for him to return to his home laboratory. This business planning assignment had been stimulating, however, and he now felt that an international assignment would give him valuable added exposure. When asked about his personal goals, however, he saw his future in technical management but felt he should work in Europe for two years to understand the international aspects of the corporation's business. He had thought about this for some time and had even lined up a potential assignment in Paris. His manager felt that he was wrong, however, and enlisted the help of his prior manager back in his home laboratory. After much discussion, they finally convinced him that in two more years he would be out of touch with his technical specialty and would be largely an unknown to the senior managers in the laboratory. He reluctantly decided to return, and within a few months he was put in charge of the New Product Introduction Department in the manufacturing organization. His corporate planning experience turned out to be all the exposure he needed for this important promotion.

There are so many functions in any large business that an entire career could be spent in broadening assignments. This, however, would produce superficial knowledge, and senior technical managers must have a pragmatic action orientation, which can only come from line experience. As Lee Iacocca says, managers must "know how to look for the pressure points and how to set priorities. They're the kind of guys who can say: 'Forget that, it'll take ten years. Here's what we gotta do now.' "[7]

With the rapid pace of modern technology, people who stay in staff assignments for more than a couple of years are soon out of date and hard to place in suitable line positions. One example of this was a promising young systems engineer who took an assistant's job for a division executive. He did well, and in the next two years he caught the eye of the division president and moved to a job in his office. Again, he performed with skill, and in only two years was made administrative assistant to the company president. He held this job for three years before being moved to a corporate staff position. During this time his salary and job level had been progressively increased until it was now well above the level of most laboratory managers. He had been out of technical work for so long, however, that he no longer had the knowledge to compete with technical managers at this level. His line experience was too limited to fit him for an executive role, and he could no longer take any job that would give him the experience needed for further advancement. In spite of his enormous potential, he spent the rest of his career in various middle-level headquarters staff assignments.

THE PRODUCT DEVELOPMENT EXECUTIVE

Once it seems likely that employees have executive potential, it is necessary to decide on the kind of broadening assignments which would be most valuable to them. To better understand this question, IBM asked approximately ninety technical vice presidents, laboratory directors, and product managers to identify the experiences they felt would have best prepared them for their present positions.[8] The results show general agreement on the need for product management and product development experiences, as shown in Tables 10.1 and 10.2. There were also some wide divergences, however, for smaller numbers of executives stated the importance of such

TABLE 10.1   Valuable Technical Management Experiences

Technical Area	Percent
Product or system management	92
Business planning and management	91
Hardware development	85
Hardware design and architecture	84
Software design and architecture	79
Software development	70
Hardware product planning	65
Advanced technology	59
Software product planning	52

TABLE 10.2   Ranking of Technical Work Experiences

Technical Area	Relative Rank	
	Areas Worked In	Areas Not Worked In
Product or system management	1	4
Hardware development	2	6
Business planning and management	3	1
Advanced technology	4	5
Component development	5	11
Hardward design and architecture	6	9
Software development	7	2
Software design and architecture	8	3

areas as testing, component development, product engineering, and laboratory support. When these executives were asked about the relative value of areas where they had not worked, those without business planning experience uniformly judged it to be important, with software development a close second. Another set of questions explored the value of exposure to different parts of the organization, with 85 percent rating an assignment in more than one division as valuable, 83 percent stating that work in more than one location was important, and 60 percent judging an assignment on corporate or group staff as worthwhile.

The survey also explored the value of nondevelopment experiences, as shown in Table 10.3. Here, marketing was generally viewed as important, while those who had worked in manufacturing ranked it as even more so. Those who had not worked in business planning, however, uniformly ranked it most valuable. Even though manufacturing, marketing, and business planning were judged to be the most important areas for outside experience, only 19 percent, 17 percent, and 15 percent of the executives, respectively, had such backgrounds. There was, however, general agreement on the value of broad career exposure as preparation for a technical executive position, as shown in the idealized career path for a laboratory director in Figure 10.1.

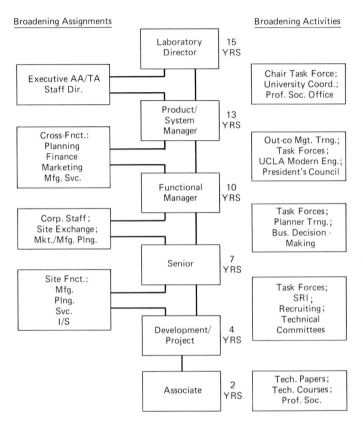

Figure 10-1 Laboratory director's career roadmap. (Courtesy of IBM.)

TABLE 10.3   Rankings of Nondevelopment Experiences

Function	Relative Rank	
	Areas Worked In	Areas Not Worked In
Business planning	3	1
Marketing	2	2
Manufacturing	1	3
Finance	5	4
Field Service	4	5

THE MANUFACTURING EXECUTIVE

A similar study, made of thirty-six IBM manufacturing executives, is shown in Table 10.4.[9] Although this group gave somewhat different priorities, they also agreed on the importance of breadth. Unlike the development executives, however, they did not view marketing as particularly valuable, although development experience was viewed as important. Business and financial backgrounds continued to get high ranking, though few actually had such exposure.

Since this study was conducted a number of years ago, it does not reflect the needs of modern high technology manufacturing. The recent focus on scientific specialization, cross-disciplinary integration, and financially oriented general management would likely change the opinions considerably.

TABLE 10.4   Manufacturing Experience Ratings

Area	Percent Extremely Valuable	Percent Actual Experience
Manufacturing planning	100%	50%
Industrial engineering	91	45
Finance	91	4
Business planning	91	19
New products (mfg.)	78	14
Production control	74	22
Manufacturing engineering	67	4
Direct manufacturing	58	50
Information systems	56	9

THE DEVELOPMENT PLAN

After defining the professionals' high-priority development needs, the next step is to formulate a development plan. This should be done quite early, because high-potential future executives need exposure to so many areas that time is the primary development constraint. Although no particular format is important, the plan should be documented and clearly spell out who will be responsible for each step. The first development question to resolve is the timing of professionals' move to a next assignment. While every case must be considered on its own, some of the key considerations are as follows:

1. They should not move until they have established a firm grounding in their basic discipline.
2. If they do not have a successful project under their belt, they should stay in the

laboratory until they have gained the reputation and self-confidence from at least one success.

3. Nonmanagement professionals who have three or more years experience and a good record of success should be given their first management assignment in the laboratory.

4. After they have demonstrated their ability to manage people, temporary broadening moves to headquarters or other laboratory and manufacturing functions should be considered.

High-potential technical managers should make their first broadening moves within five to ten years of starting work. These first years set the critical foundation for their entire career, and professionals should not be moved until they have demonstrated their competence as a first-line technical manager. Once they have, however, they should be moved quickly, since there is not a great deal of time. The most successful senior managers have generally reached their first executive positions before the age of forty, so it is important to emphasize broadening developmental experiences early in their career.

TEMPORARY ASSIGNMENTS

While professionals are in their early foundation-building phase in the laboratory, they should be given many of the same exposures as technical professionals. After they move into management, however, their broadening exposures should be focused more directly on management topics. Some examples of valuable short experiences are the following:

1. Short management education courses can provide useful perspectives as well as exposure to people with a wide variety of backgrounds.

2. Executive shadow programs give a brief snapshot of a technical executive's work and also help to provide the promising young manager with added visibility.

3. Technical task force assignments are particularly valuable developmental experiences, so they should be reserved for the best people.

4. Most technical organizations have a variety of committees and coordination groups for such topics as standards, patent reviews, education, and awards. By rotating these assignments among the promising future executives, they will better appreciate a broad range of laboratory activities.

After their initial career foundation is established, high-potential managers should be moved to a new assignment at least every two or three years. As illustrated by the case of one programming manager, this can involve quite a lot of effort on the part of several executives. This manager had worked in the laboratory for ten years, and he was increasingly concerned about his chances of reaching a senior management position. He had taken some courses for his M.B.A. at night school and felt that he was ready for a temporary assignment on the corporate financial staff. He discussed this with his immediate manager, but nothing seemed to happen; so he raised the point with an executive observer when he attended a management assessment program. This executive called the programming manager's laboratory director, and they both agreed to arrange such a move. The executive contacted several headquarters associates and finally located an appropriate job. The laboratory director then made the final arrangements, and the programming manager had his temporary assignment with the corporate finance and planning staff.

Although this assignment was arranged fairly easily, it took the executive and the lab director several months and dozens of phone calls to find the right assignment and make the final arrangements for the programming manager's temporary move. Since a manager can expect to spend a couple of hours a week over a period of several months arranging for one such assignment, few managers can afford to make such an effort for more than two or three promising candidates each year. In this case the results were well worth the effort. The programming manager was rapidly moved to a technical executive position and became a firm believer in management development.

MANAGEMENT DEVELOPMENT REVIEWS

Since most working-level managers have to defer almost everything which has not yet reached crisis proportions, people development programs must be made sufficiently important to get their attention. This can only be done if a senior executive is interested enough in the subject to get personally involved. Without such high-level commitment, no bureaucratic process can possibly make the lower-level managers take this subject seriously. Thus, the most effective way to make such programs work is for senior executives to hold periodic one-on-one reviews with each of their department heads. These sessions should focus exclusively on people development, with a specific discussion of each manager and key technical professional. The topics which should be covered are as follows:

1. The management candidates for early promotion should be identified with their likely next positions. Potential replacements for the department manager should also be identified, together with their readiness for the job.
2. Candidates for temporary headquarters assignments should be named with suggested staff areas and availability dates.
3. The departmental promotion summary should show the movement of people between functions as well as within the organization. The goals for interfunctional movement should be reviewed, together with a comparison of actual performance with prior goals.

4. The key management positions are identified and reasons given for any that are not occupied by high-potential managers. A key management position is one which provides important background for future executives, significant exposure to senior management, or essential preparation for an immediate executive promotion.

5. The promotion table for each key position is reviewed, with particular focus on the candidates' readiness and the number of people on the list from other locations and divisions.

6. High-potential managers are separately reviewed, their development plan is summarized, and their promotion table entries are listed. At least some of these potential positions should be in other locations and divisions.

The key to this entire process, however, is the senior executive's personal involvement. Many managers mistakenly think that management development can be handled by the personnel department, but as Peter Drucker says, "to depend on the personnel department to do management development is basically a misunderstanding. A marriage counselor can help with a marriage, but it's your job."[10]

MANAGEMENT DEVELOPMENT SUPPORT

Since an effective management development review takes a great deal of planning, a support staff is required both to insure that it is handled properly and to take care of all the records required for adequate follow-up tracking. The typical duties of such a staff position are to

1. Schedule and attend the executive reviews

2. Insure that the key positions are identified and replacement tables prepared

3. Retain the master file of development plans and replacement tables

4. Insure that a reasonable number of high-potential management candidates are identified in each department and that each has a development plan

5. Track implementation of the development plans and provide assistance where needed

6. Keep track of replacement activity and record how often the replacement tables are used

7. Suggest candidates for promotion when requested

8. Periodically report on the management development performance of each department and suggest areas where added management attention is required

If these mechanics are not properly handled, management development will be a hit-or-miss affair. The problems this can cause are illustrated by the case of a young engineer who worked for a large oil company. When he was recruited, he had been told about their management development program to prepare promising young engineers for senior management positions. Each candidate's career was to be personally planned and reviewed, starting with a six-month assignment in headquarters. He or she would then move to an overseas location for two years' experience before reassignment to another domestic staff. This orderly progression of jobs was to be carefully tailored to the trainee's personal interests and experiences.

One day a trainee from the Middle East unexpectedly arrived at the home office. His initial two-year field assignment was over, and since no one in headquarters had communicated with him about his next move, he came back to see what was wrong. For several confusing days his file could not be found, and all the trainees soon realized that the story of a carefully orchestrated training program was pure fiction. As one remarked, "It was obvious we were so much meat."

Minor goof-ups are understandable in parts lists, production schedules, or even financial statements, but when it comes to people, a higher standard is needed. All people are special, at least in their own eyes, and they will never excuse a management that overlooks or forgets them. This is why development programs must be managed with the greatest of care and staffed with experienced senior professionals.

DEVELOPMENT CONSIDERATIONS

One problem with high-potential management development programs is that they tend to separate people into classes. Since this is clearly undesirable, an attempt is generally made to keep such programs confidential. Unfortunately, the number of people who must be involved renders this largely impractical. The other option, open disclosure, has a number of attractive advantages:

1. The program will become public knowledge anyway, so open disclosure insures that it is properly explained.
2. The program can help with recruiting, but only if it is public knowledge.
3. It is hard to discuss development plans with people who don't know why they are needed.

The disadvantages of publicizing such programs, however, are equally compelling:

1. The employees will quickly learn who is "in" and who is "out," thus creating a potential elite.
2. The professionals who have been dropped from the program will find out and be unhappy.
3. Since only a few people can be helped by such programs, public knowledge will negatively affect many more people than will be helped.

John Gardner describes this last problem with the example of a military commander who had an extremely effective way of recommending men for officer candidates school. This, however, turned out to have a devastating effect on those who were not selected. As long as they could say he was unjust, they were relatively happy, but "the commanding officer's scrupulous search for talent had deprived them of those comfortable defenses. They had no place to hide. It was now clear to all concerned that they were enlisted men because that was where they belonged."[11]

There is no simple answer which meets all objections, but probably the best compromise is to keep the existence of a formal program confidential while publicly requiring managers to have development plans for all their people. This permits open discussion of development plans, but it also means the managers will have much more work to do. If they try to work out comprehensive plans with each of their people, they will be swamped in so much paperwork that none of the plans will be adequate. On the other hand, someone who was thought to have little potential occasionally turns out to be a star when given the chance. Thus, managers should spend at least some time on the development of each of their people.

When everyone has a development plan, there is no question of an "in" and an "out" group. Although the management review process will naturally focus on the small number with highest potential, no one will be ignored. If employees complain about an inadequate development plan, managers can tell them that development is largely their responsibility; and although they will gladly help, the work is largely up to them. If employees take this challenge seriously, managers should assist them, for motivation is the key ingredient of self-development; and all employees who are willing to work at improving themselves should get their management's help.

THE PEOPLE DEVELOPMENT BUREAUCRACY

Since development programs necessarily involve many procedures, checkpoints, reviews, and forms, they can easily become bureaucratic. There are some steps which can help to minimize this, however:

1. Restrict the number of different development programs. Separate programs for young executives, females, minorities, new managers, and the various technical specialties will each have their own forms, procedures, and reviews; and this proliferation will both confuse and overburden line management.
2. Since many of the same managers are involved in each review, one staff should handle all resource programs and make sure that they are reviewed simultaneously.
3. The professional development staff should be rotated every two to three years so that they don't develop a bureaucratic mentality.

Finally, senior executives should identify the key jobs which cannot be filled without their approval and require that the proposed promotion be reviewed by the management development staff before they agree. If this is not done, the management development organization cannot be effective.

NOTES CHAPTER 10

1. Peter F. Drucker, *The Practice of Management* (New York: Harper & Row, Publishers, Inc., 1954).

2. John W. Gardner, *Excellence* (New York: Harper & Row Publishers, Inc., 1961).

3. Raymond F. Valentine, *Initiative and Managerial Power* (New York: AMACOM, a division of American Management Associations, 1973), p. 94.

4. David C. McClelland and David Burnham, "Power is the Great Motivator," *Harvard Business Review* (March–April 1976), vol. 54, no. 2, p. 101.

5. Lee Iacocca and William Novak, *Iacocca: An Autobiography* (New York: Bantam Books, Inc., 1984), p. 23.

6. Harold J. Leavitt, *Managerial Psychology, Fourth Edition* (Chicago, Ill.: University of Chicago Press, 1978), p. 249.

7. Iacocca, *Iacocca*, p. 60.

8. This study was conducted in 1980 by the IBM Corporate Engineering, Programming, and Technology Staff.

9. This study was conducted in 1977 by J. H. Motes and A. D. Wolfson of the IBM Corporate Manufacturing Staff.

10. John J. Tarrant, *Drucker: The Man Who Invented the Corporate Society* (New York: Warner Publishing, Inc., Warner Books, Inc., 1976). This quote from Peter Drucker appears on page 316.

11. Gardner, *Excellence*, p. 72.

11

The Importance

of Innovation

Theodore Levitt once said that

> creativity is thinking up new things. Innovation is doing new things. A powerful idea can kick around unused in a company for years, not because its merits are not recognized, but because nobody has assumed the responsibility for converting it from words into action. Ideas are useless unless used. The proof of their value is only in their implementation. Until then, they are in limbo.[1]

While innovation requires creativity, it also involves a great deal of hard work. The lonely inventor with a bright idea is an essential first step, but his or her efforts will be totally wasted if someone with the necessary drive and energy doesn't pick them up and turn them into a business success. Innovation is the process of turning ideas into manufacturable and marketable form, for, in Peter Drucker's words, "business has only two basic functions: marketing and innovation. Marketing and innovation produce results. All the rest are costs."[2]

Although we all know about such great laboratory advances as the transistor and the laser, it is the manufacturing innovations which have produced the major economic changes of the modern industrial age. It was a manufacturing innovation which reduced the cost of electricity light bulbs by 80 percent and made electric lighting commercially viable. It was also Henry Ford's use of high volume manufacturing methods for the Model T Ford that cut automobile prices by a factor of three and changed the face of modern industry.[3] Innovation spans every phase of technology from research through development, manufacturing, and marketing, and its prime role is to economically couple creative technology to the needs of the market place.

INDUSTRIAL INNOVATION

Today, more than ever before, a strong market position must be based on an organization's technical competence. Brian Smith has examined what the loss of this competitive race has meant to much of the industry in Great Britain.[4] He found, for example, that the British textile industry led the industrial revolution before World War II, but they then started looking to foreign suppliers for their textile machinery. This was not because the foreign machines were cheaper or had better service, but because they were more reliable, more productive, and more efficient than the British units. Smith concludes that in textiles, as in shipbuilding and motorcycles, the foreign manufacturers were simply better at designing innovative products and that this is what caused British industry to lose its leadership position.

Such dramatic changes have also happened in the United States, as demonstrated by the development of the portable transistor radio.[5] In 1956, the U.S. portable radio market was dominated by domestically manufactured 20-ounce units which cost fifty-seven dollars. This was a big improvement over the earlier 6-pound units, but the Japanese quickly introduced smaller capacitors, miniature loudspeakers, and lightweight power supplies, which resulted in compact 10-ounce portable sets. In the next three years the Japanese captured 68 percent of the U.S. portable transistor radio market.

Behind these major innovations, there were invariably a few key technical decisions which made the crucial difference. In the case of the Lockheed Electra, a fleet of seventy-two aircraft were in service in 1961, and only seven years later the Lockheed fleet had dwindled to twenty-eight, while the newer Boeing 727s numbered over four hundred.

This dramatic reversal was the result of a series of decisions made in the design of the Electra and the 727. Since the Lockheed engineers aimed for an aircraft to operate out of small local airports, they picked propellers which provided more thrust than traditional jet engines, even though this limited maximum aircraft speed. The Boeing engineers, on the other hand, conceived of the fan-jet engine which would accelerate a cylinder of cold air around a hot central jet and produce far higher takeoff thrust than had previously been possible. They also introduced wing flaps and slats for high-lift takeoff and landing and high-speed cruising. The result was an aircraft which could operate out of smaller airfields, with the speed and comfort of a jet. Even though Boeing was a late starter, its innovative 727 rapidly beat the Electra in the marketplace. By the time the last 727 was rolled out in 1984, 1832 aircraft had been produced in twenty-four years, and the 727 accounted for 37 percent of total Boeing jet aircraft production. These planes have now flown a total of 21.4 billion miles, or the equivalent of "115 round trips to the sun."[6] Although the Boeing 727 was a remarkable marketing success, its battle with the Electra was won in Boeing's laboratories and plants.

THE RISK OF FAILURE

Since a true innovative success must be both economical to manufacture and responsive to customer needs, it must necessarily combine the high risks of technology with the uncertainties of the competitive marketplace. A 1968 Booz, Allen and Hamilton study found that two thirds of all new product development funds were spent on failures and that only about two percent of new product ideas made it through development to become successful in the marketplace.[7] Bronislaw Verhage more recently reported that 40 to 80 percent of all new product developments were commercial failures.[8]

There are many reasons for research and development failure, but the one problem that shows up with most regularity is the persistent tendency of technical people to confine themselves to the laboratory and not to seek a detailed understanding of the user's needs. High technology is always risky, but the technical solution in search of a problem faces the highest risks of all. From a study of twenty-three organizations Knut Holt found that every single company had product failures and that they were all caused by either the failure to study the user's needs or the misuse of the studies that were made. He said that

> four of the firms had made no inquiries to potential users, six had made too few inquiries, two ignored the results, two had misinterpreted the answers, six were committed to preconceived designs and three failed to understand the environment to which their products would be subjected.[9]

Edwin Mansfield, a University of Pennsylvania economist, has studied the reasons behind project failures and has similarly concluded that successful product development depends more on market astuteness than on technical competence. He estimates that only from 12 to 20 percent of all R&D projects produce a marketing success, even though their technical objectives are generally met.[10] He found that when there was a close coupling between the development and marketing functions, product innovation was generally successful.

Eric A. von Hippel has examined the sources of innovative ideas in several industries and found that when the users were technically competent, they originated the bulk of the innovations.[11] As shown in Table 11.1, for example, the users in instrumentation and process equipment had their own technical experts and were responsible for every single new advance during the entire period of the study. Even after these new innovations were introduced, the users continued to originate most of the new ideas, while the manufacturers made only incremental improvements. By contrast, in polymers and chemical additives, the users did not have the technical staff or facilities to do innovative work, consequently the important advances were all made by the manufacturers.

Abernathy and Utterback referenced eight studies which each reached a similar conclusion.[12] On average, 75 percent of all the innovations reviewed by these studies came from market sources, but the highest percentage of technically driven innovations given by any single study was only 34 percent. In one study of the sources of 567 innovations, 75 percent came from a recognized need, but only 21 percent originated from a new technical opportunity.[13] The breakdown of these figures is shown in Table 11.2.

TABLE 11.1

Field of Innovation	User	Manufacturer
Instrumentation		
First of a type	100%	0%
Major improvements	82	18
Minor improvements	70	30
Process equipment		
First of a type	100	0
Major improvements	63	21
Minor improvements	20	29
Polymers		
All major since 1955	0	100
Additives		
All since 1945	0	100

TABLE 11.2

Innovation Source	Percent
Technical feasibility	21%
Market demand	45
Production need	30
Administrative change	4

REVERSE ENGINEERING

The risky nature of technical innovation has led to something called reverse engineering. This is where an organization waits for somebody else to do the expensive pioneering and then attempts to improve on or extend their work. Westinghouse is reported to have essentially followed this path with gas turbine technology. They felt that ceramic turbine blades could be superior because they could operate at higher temperatures and efficiencies than metal blades. The research costs, however, were estimated to exceed eighty million dollars for the seven year program to solve the brittleness problem. They thus decided to wait to see what GE would do. *Fortune* quotes George Mechlin, Westinghouse's vice president for R&D, as saying that

> there are really two risks in search and development. . . . One is whether the technology will succeed. The other is whether it will satisfy some market requirements. If you hang back and wait, you can be in a position where you can know the answer to both questions, and catching up can take a lot less time than the original effort.[14]

Although the Westinghouse decision may have made good business sense, planning to copy someone else's innovations is far from risk free. The fast pace of today's technologies doesn't allow much time for catching up, and once an important advance is "in the air," many organizations will be working on it. One will necessarily be first in bringing it to the market but others will be close behind with the necessary technical competence. Any organization that waits for others to do the pioneering will often not have the knowledge or talent to catch up. It is not as important to be first to announce a new advance as it is to have the technical capacity to capitalize on new ideas when their time has come.

In technology, as everywhere else, there is no free lunch. The leaders take the greatest risks and stand to reap the greatest rewards, while the followers couple lower short-term risks with loss of technological control. To keep control of its own destiny, the technical organization must maintain a skilled team of innovators in close touch with its marketplace.

NOTES CHAPTER 11

1. Thomas J. Peters and Robert H. Waterman, Jr., *In Search of Excellence: Lessons from America's Best-Run Companies* (New York: Harper & Row, Publishers, Inc., 1982), p. 206.

2. Peter Drucker, *Management, Tasks, Responsibilities, Practices* (New York: Harper & Row, Publishers, 1974), p. 61.

3. W. J. Abernathy, and J. M. Utterback, "Patterns of Industrial Innovation," in Tushman and Moore, *Readings in the Management of Innovation* (Marshfield, Mass.: Pitman, 1982), p. 97.

4. Brian Smith, "Design Management and New Product Development," *European Journal of Marketing (UK)*, vol. 15, no. 5, 1981, p. 52.

5. George R. White includes this description of the introduction of Japanese portable transistor radios and the following Lockheed Electra example in his article "Management Criteria for Effective Innovation," *IEEE Transactions on Professional Communication*, vol. PC-22, no. 2, June 1979, p. 79.

6. *The Wall Street Journal*, August 15, 1984, p. 25.

7. D. A. Guidici, "Evaluation—How Can It Aid Innovation?" *ISA Transactions*, vol. 19, no. 4, 1980, p. 33.

8. Bronislaw Verhage, Ph. Waalewijn, and A. J. vanWeele, "New Product Development

in Dutch Companies: The Idea Generation Stage,'' *European Journal of Marketing (UK)*, vol. 15, no. 5, 1981, p. 73.

9. Knut Holt, ''Idea Generation—Key to Successful Management of Change,'' International Conference of Product Research, Amsterdam, Netherlands, August 1979.

10. Tom Alexander, ''The Right Remedy for R&D Lag,''*Fortune*, January 25, 1982, p. 67.

11. Eric A. von Hippel, ''Users as Innovators,''*Technology Review*, MIT, January 1978.

12. Abernathy, ''Patterns.'' p. 97.

13. Ibid.

14. Alexander, ''The Right Remedy.'' p. 62.

12

The Innovators

Isaac Auerbach, who once taught a course in entrepreneurship at the University of Pennsylvania, says that a Class A person with a Class B idea has a better chance for success than a Class B person with a Class A idea."[1] The people involved in innovation and the roles they play are beautifully illustrated by Elting E. Morison's story of the introduction of continuous-aim firing in the United States Navy.[2] Until the end of the nineteenth century, naval gunners had to adjust their aim for the ship's roll, and if their timing was poor or the fuses burned unevenly, their shots would miss.

In 1898 British Admiral Sir Percy Scott, commander of H.M.S. Scylla, was watching gunnery practice and thinking about the problem of accuracy when he noticed one pointer trying to adjust his gun's elevating gear in time with the ship's roll. He suddenly realized that this could be the answer and had the elevating gear on all his ship's guns changed so that they could be more easily raised and depressed. His men then started making fleet gunnery records. Shortly afterward, Scott was sent to the British China station where he met Lieutenant William S. Sims of the U.S. fleet. When Sims heard about the technique of continuous-aim firing, he changed the guns on the U.S.S. Kentucky, and soon his gunners were making U.S. fleet records as well.

Sims quite logically felt that the entire U.S. Navy should adopt this method; therefore, he prepared and sent thirteen detailed reports to the Navy Department in Washington. Initially, his suggestions were ignored, but when he didn't give up, Washington argued that the U.S. equipment was as good as that of the British and that the problem must therefore be with the officers. When Sims persisted, however, they claimed that his proposal was impossible. In shore tests, they had shown that gunners could not crank the guns fast enough to compensate for the roll of ocean waves. They failed to realize, however, that at sea little power was required to adjust the guns so that they could stay stationary while the ship rolled beneath them. When none of the arguments silenced him, the Navy finally claimed that Sims had falsified the evidence. This so infuriated him that he took the extraordinary step of writing to the president of the United States. Theodore Roosevelt was so intrigued that he brought him to Washington and ultimately made him inspector of naval target practice. Morison explains the impact of this change:

> In 1899 five ships of the North Atlantic Squadron fired five minutes each at a lighthouse hulk at the conventional range of 1600 yards. After twenty-five minutes of banging away two hits had been made on the sails of the elderly vessel. Six years later one naval gunner made fifteen hits in one minute at a target 75 by 25 feet at the same range; half of them hit in the bull's-eye 50 inches square.

The key roles in this story were played by Scott, Sims, and Roosevelt. Scott was the inventor who saw the importance of adjusting the gun's elevation to compensate for the ship's roll. His creative imagination was essential, but it wasn't enough for the U.S. Navy. Sims, although not the inventor of continuous-aim firing, saw its potential and decided to champion its cause in the U.S. fleet. His dedication and obstinacy finally took him to the president of the United States, where he found a sponsor to overcome the bureaucratic resistance. These people—the inventor, the champion, and the sponsor—are critical to the success of just about every significant innovation.

NEW IDEAS

Patrick Haggerty best defined the innovative role of creative people when he said that "organizations possess neither imagination nor generate ideas."[3] The idea which starts the innovation process often appears in a sudden flash of insight. Nineteenth-century German chemist August von Stradonitz Kekulé had such a vision when he solved the problem of the molecular structure of organic chemicals. The arrangement of the oxygen, carbon, and hydrogen atoms in organic compounds was one of the great chemical mysteries, and Kekulé had worked on it for many months without success. One evening he fell asleep before the fire and dreamt of atoms dancing like snakes, and then "he saw one snake forming a loop and eating its own tail. Kekulé awoke with a start. In that instant, his imagination conjured up a hexagonal ring, each corner taken up by a carbon atom—six atoms in all."[4] Kekulé had literally dreamed up the benzene ring, the basic building block of organic chemistry.

After he had worked for many years in a vain attempt to perfect the sewing machine, a similar incident happened to Elias Howe. He fell asleep one day and dreamed he was the prisoner of a medieval tyrant.

> One morning, he was led out for execution: drums beating, the king on a dais, a huge crowd waiting by the block. As he stood there trembling, Howe looked round at his guards, each of them toted a long spear; the broad, leaf blade of every spear punctured by a hole—the hole in the sewing needle should be at the tip, not in the middle.[5]

THE INVENTOR

Although these flashes of creative genius may seem mere accidents, studies have shown that creativity is a logical and structured process.[6,7] The first step, insight, is where the germ of the problem originates. This intuitive process rarely includes any hint of the solution, and it may actually come years before the final answer. Next, the preparation, or manipulation, stage is a logical period of problem definition and analysis which generally involves exhaustive studies or experiments. In modern science and engineering, inspiration is often found by digging out prior work on a subject. This both helps to avoid repeating earlier mistakes and occasionally actually produces an answer to the problem. More often, however, such structured efforts are fruitless, and the problem is temporarily relegated to the incubation stage, where it continues to receive subconscious attention. When something next happens to trigger the inventor's imagination, however, the manipulation phase is reentered to test it out. If it doesn't work, incubation is resumed. This alternating cycle may continue many times as a host of ideas are tried and discarded. Each cycle, however, gradually increases understanding until some idea suddenly crystallizes with a seeming flash of insight.

Alexander Graham Bell's invention of the telephone is a well-known example of this incubation process.[8] He developed the theory for electrically reproducing speech while vacationing with his parents, but he could not figure out how to make an electric current change in proportion to the sound of a voice. As he told his father at the time, if he could solve this one problem, he would be able to transmit speech telegraphically.

Bell did not forget this problem, but he put it aside for about a year while he worked on the development of a harmonic telegraph. On June 2, 1875, while attempting to transmit fixed frequency telegraph signals with magnetized steel reeds, one reed was accidentally clamped to the magnet so tightly that it would not vibrate. Watson, Bell's assistant, plucked at it and it came lose with a "twang." Bell, at the other end of the telegraph line, saw his reed vibrate while he also heard a faint twang. He shouted excitedly: "What did you do then? Don't change anything. Let me see." The vibrations from Watson's plucked reed had caused an electrical current in the electromagnet to be transmitted through the wire and make Bell's reed vibrate in exactly the same way. These vibrations then reproduced the "twang" which Bell heard.

WORKING AT CREATIVITY

Illumination, the fourth creative stage, follows insight, preparation, and incubation. This is where the inventor suddenly puts the pieces together into the full-blown solution. As in Bell's case, lucky accidents often provide the trigger, but while luck is involved, it is not blind luck. Because Bell had been incubating on the problem of electrically reproducing sound, he was prepared and waiting for just such an event to suggest the final solution.

This was the case in the early days of General Motors when Charles Kettering headed G.M.'s research. He was working on the problem of engine knock and had his people put a window in a gasoline engine cylinder so that they could see the flame and possibly better understand what was going on. They found, however, that the gasoline flame was invisible, so Kettering looked around for something they could use to give it color. He found a bottle of iodine in the first-aid cabinet, and when it was put in the gasoline, the engine knock was gone. This stroke of luck led to the completely new industry of gasoline additives.[9]

Another such lucky accident happened when Dr. Alexander Fleming was examining a culture plate that had been contaminated with mold.

> As he looked at the culture under the microscope, he saw colonies of bacteria, looking like islands surrounded by clear spaces. Fleming reasoned that the mold might be preventing the spread of bacteria, and this observation led to the discovery of penicillin. A lucky discovery? Perhaps, but how many other biologists given the same culture would have dismissed the observation as irrelevant?[10]

Chance plays an important part in the creative process, but it is not just blind luck. If these accidents had happened to someone else, their significance likely would have been missed. The inventor, however, had a prepared mind with all the ingredients of the solution just waiting for some trigger to suggest the proper arrangement. If these particular accidents had not happened, these discoveries were so nearly ripe that something else would surely have triggered them just the same.

VERIFICATION

Verification is the final, and often most tedious, part of the creative process. This is where the wild and impractical ideas are culled out by extensive testing and analysis. Although an occasional intuitive insight will point directly to the full-blown solution, most often it only provides a teasing suggestion of what might work. The idea must then be developed, refined, and molded before it has practical value. Thomas Edison is reported to have unsuccessfully tried over one hundred ways to perfect one of his ideas: "When asked if he was discouraged, Edison scoffed at the idea, pointing out that he was making progress. He now knew one hundred things that didn't work."[11]

There is a fine line between invention and development. At one extreme, invention is pure illumination, and development may seem to be all verification. Although true inventions are usually characterized by some single identifiable concept, most of them must undergo extensive development before they can be economically produced and marketed. Product development work, on the other hand, often starts with a well-known concept and refines and improves upon it. During this process, however, many new ideas and novel approaches must be introduced before a significantly improved final product will result. No single concept stands out as the most crucial idea, but many smaller creative cycles have been combined to produce a superior total result.

THE NATURE OF CREATIVITY

The first step in the innovative process is thus a creative one. Creativity, however, is less well understood. In fact, it was once viewed as a magical power arising from divine inspiration. This view is now largely obsolete, due in part to the work of Harvard philosopher Nelson Goodman on Project Zero. In 1967 he was asked to study the creative process in the arts, and as he quipped at the time, "there's nothing known about that," so he called it Project Zero.[12] This turned into a seventeen year effort to examine the skills of artists, the way they worked, and what had most deeply influenced their careers. The final conclusion was that creativity is merely a way of thinking and that the seeming sudden insights were not sudden at all but were preceded by early premonitions and hints, which were then developed through an orderly and logical process.

Goodman also found that many of the artists he studied were strongly influenced by what he called an early crystallizing experience, such as when Yehudi Menuhin attended a concert at age three and then asked for a violin for his fourth birthday. This gift was the start of a lifetime of dedication by this man who became the greatest violinist of our time. Such crystallizing experiences focus the genius on his chosen career and help to build the motivation he needs to devote his life to this one subject.

STIMULATING IDEAS

Project Hindsight looked further into the creative process to see how important prior work can be in stimulating creative ideas.[13] They found that each of the eight military projects they studied depended on several prior innovations which, though separately quite modest, together reinforced each other to produce a significant total project effort. Since most of the prior innovations were made long before these projects started, the team's awareness of this prior work turned out to be critically important to their creative success.

Another way to stimulate ideas is to have a group with a common problem get together and discuss it. This is the principle of the quality circle, where a team of workers discuss common problems and suggest solutions. The enormous power of this approach was shown by Toyota's experience, where in 1980 each production worker averaged 17.8 suggestions, of which 90 percent were accepted. General Motors was slower to adopt this approach: in the same year less than one suggestion was submitted per worker, and only 31 percent of them were adopted.[14] The number of adopted suggestions per thousand workers in General Motors was thus about three hundred per year, while Toyota had over sixteen thousand. This fifty-to-one advantage in useful per-capita worker suggestions must have increased innovation in Toyota's factories and importantly influenced their performance in the U.S. automobile market.

IMAGINATION AND NERVE

Arthur C. Clarke, who is best known for his *2001: A Space Odyssey*, points out that otherwise competent professionals often make serious blunders when they project the future.[15] In one case an 1878 British parliamentary committee declared that electric lighting was "unworthy of the attention of practical or scientific men." Lord Rutherford, who won the Nobel Prize in 1908 for his "Theory of Atomic Transmutation," similarly argued that nuclear reactions could not release more energy than they consumed. He died just five years before Enrico Fermi demonstrated the first self-sustaining nuclear chain reaction at the University of Chicago.

Clarke argues that these miscalculations are due to either a failure of imagination or a failure of nerve. Failure of imagination is most likely when all the available facts point in one direction but some limitation blocks the way. Even trained observers are often unable to imagine that a single breakthrough can clear up all remaining obstacles.

One example of this occurred in the early days of computers when machine designers failed to visualize the need for vastly larger memories. When IBM designed the 360 system in the early 1960s, the maximum addressing capacity was set at sixteen million bytes of memory. This seemed so enormous at the time that one technical committee could not visualize this ever being a limitation. Memory demands have consistently exceeded available capacity, however, and the enormous advances in semiconductor technology have made vastly larger memories practical. Today, addressing capacities of billions of bytes are essential for most large commercial systems.

Failure of nerve occurs when all the facts are available but the observer is somehow unable to accept their inevitable conclusion. This is a surprising and very common fact of technical life, and it is often the prime reason for so much resistance to change. This is what led Edward R. Murrow to remark that "the obscure we see eventually. The completely obvious, it seems, takes longer."[16]

THE CHAMPION

Modesto Maidique has concluded that new ideas either find a *champion* or they die.[17] Conard Fernilius and W. H. Waldo, in a study for the National Science Foundation, also found that the successful projects invariably had champions.[18] Texas Instruments studied fifty of their completed projects and found that none of the failures had a voluntary champion. As a result, they now require every new project to be run by someone who has, in effect, volunteered for the job.[19]

Thomas A. Edison's enormous inventive genius often overshadows his impressive performance as a champion, but he was every bit as effective in this sphere as well. In the summer of 1878 he publicly declared that he would invent the electric light bulb, and he lined up the needed initial capital and started to work. In December he told his backers that he had ''just about got it.'' A couple of months went by and nothing happened until, in February, he invited his backers out to see a demonstration. They came and saw all the bulbs blow out in less than ten minutes. This happened several times during the next eighteen months, and every time the backers would say, ''That's Edison; we know he can do it.'' And, of course, he did.[20]

Champions maintain a focused drive to overcome every obstacle, and their unshakable confidence both inspires their team and maintains their momentum. Often, the champion's single-minded refusal to give up is what keeps the project moving in spite of all the doubters. Although champions don't always win, winners, it seems, always have champions.

THE SPONSOR

After the inventor and the champion, the third key person in the innovation process is the sponsor. The sponsor may not share the knowledge, skill, or conviction of either the champion or the inventor, but he or she does have imagination and nerve. At the outset, most technology projects look very promising; but when, as often happens, they run into trouble, dedicated sponsors can be invaluable. Any backer can handle the good news, but it takes courageous sponsors to stick with their original convictions when the schedules are slipping, the people are discouraged, and the budget is nearly exhausted.

RCA's David Sarnoff demonstrated his remarkable capacity as a leader and a sponsor both with color television and again at the forty-fifth anniversary celebration of his radio career in 1951. In his speech to RCA's technical elite, he challenged them to produce a magnetic tape recorder for both black-and-white and color television. This was one of the leading technical problems of the day, and few people were confident that it could be solved, at least not very quickly. Sarnoff, however, had the confidence to ask for a demonstration on his fiftieth anniversary five years later. The scientists were staggered, and many wondered if he knew what he was saying. The project, however, instantly became a top RCA priority, and all worries about failure were submerged in the drive to meet this aggressive target. Five years later when they gave Sarnoff his demonstration, he said, ''. . . I had no doubts that they could solve these problems. . . . I have often had more faith in these men than they have had in themselves.''[21]

NOTES CHAPTER 12

1. Nancy Stern, ''From Eniac to Univac,'' *IEEE Spectrum,* (December 1981), vol. 18, no. 12, p. 61.
2. Elting E. Morison, ''A Case Study of Innovation,'' *Engineering and Science Monthly,* California Institute of Technology, April 1950.

3. Patrick E. Haggerty, "The Corporation and Innovation," *Strategic Management Journal*, 2 (1981), 97–118.

4. Lee Edson, "Intuition," *Across the Board*, June 1982. p. 7.

5. Graeme Fife, letter to the editor of The New York Times, November 21, 1984.

6. W. J. Abernathy and J. M. Utterback, "Patterns of Industrial Innovation," in Tushman and Moore, *Readings in the Management of Innovation* (Marshfield, Mass.: Pitman, 1982), p. 97.

7. Michael LeBoeuf, *Imagineering: How to Profit from Your Creative Powers* (New York: McGraw-Hill Book Company, 1980), p. 56.

8. American Telephone and Telegraph Co., "The Mad Idea," in *Communicating and the Telephone*, July 1979.

9. Alfred P. Sloan, Jr., *Adventures of a White Collar Man* (New York: Doubleday & Co., Inc., 1941).

10. LeBoeuf, *Imagineering*, p. 189.

11. Ibid., p. 26.

12. Howard Gardner, "Science Grapples with the Creative Puzzle," *The New York Times*, May 13, 1984, sec. H, p. 1.

13. C. W. Sherwin and others, *First Interim Report on Project Hindsight*, U.S. Department of Defense (Washington, D.C., June 30, 1966). Reference in A. J. A. Sparrius's "Uncertainty Reducing Techniques in Technological Innovation," *IEEE Engineering Management Review*, vol. 9, no. 4 (December 1981).

14. "Putting Workers into Workmanship," *Business Week*, February 23, 1981, p. 132D.

15. Arthur C. Clarke, *Profiles of the Future* (New York: Holt, Rinehart and Winston), 1984, pp. 16 and 29.

16. LeBoeuf, *Imagineering*, p. 19.

17. Modesto A. Maidique, "Entrepreneurs, Champions, and Technological Innovation," *Sloan Management Review*, Harvard University, Winter 1980, p. 59.

18. W. Conard Fernilius and W. H. Waldo, "Contribution of Basic Research to Recent Successful Industrial Innovations," Industrial Research Institute Research Corporation, St. Louis, Mo. Prepared for the Division of Policy Research and Analysis, National Science Foundation (Washington, D.C.: September 1979).

19. Thomas J. Peters and Robert H. Waterman, Jr., *In Search of Excellence: Lessons from America's Best-Run Companies* (New York: Harper & Row, Publishers, Inc., 1982), p. 203.

20. Nancy Stern, in "Eniac to Univac," quotes from an interview she held with Robert Friedel, the director of the IEEE Center for the History of Electrical Engineering.

21. *RCA Executive Biography: David Sarnoff* (New York: RCA Corporation, 1970).

13

Team Structure

A team is a group of people who are working together towards a common end. The internal structure of a team largely governs the relationships between the members and often determines their behavior. When this internal structure is effective, the team will concentrate on its official objectives, but when the structure is stressed, performance will generally suffer. Even though each individual member has a unique role, the overall character of a cohesive team is much like a collective personality.

Teams develop codes of conduct which influence their behavior. Fred Brooks referred to this when he said that the members of a great team run a little faster and try a bit harder, and this "provides the cushion, the reserve capacity, that enables a team to cope with routine mishaps."[1]

THE CONCEPTS OF TEAM STRUCTURE

Fredrick Winslow Taylor proposed that work be divided into precisely specified tasks, each task examined in detail, and the best working methods defined for each. A worker is then told both what to do and precisely how to do it.[2] In early factories this may have been essential, but Mayo found at Hawthorne that even routine jobs can be improved if the workers are treated with respect.[3] Peter Drucker has best explained the reason why Taylor's methods are not effective: "Machines work best if they do only one task. . . [but] for any one task and any one operation, the human being is ill suited."[4] People are adaptable and intelligent, and if their work doesn't use both these traits, they quickly find it dull and uninteresting. As Drucker adds, "What is good industrial engineering for work is exceedingly poor human engineering for workers."

It is desirable to make work interesting for the people, but this is hard to do with large groups. The job must then be subdivided, each piece handled separately, and the results somehow coordinated. Some managers attempt to follow Taylor's philosophy of rigidly defining these tasks, but this is rarely practical. In addition to demotivating the people, technology is too unpredictable, and something new invariably causes the plans to change. A rigid management style also wastes the skills and talents of the people, and it consumes managers' time. If they persist in this style, they will generally be too busy to handle all the necessary details and will thus become the limit on their organization's performance.

With experience, managers learn to involve their professionals in dividing up their team assignments into their own individual tasks. This then allows the engineers and scientists to adjust their daily work according to the progress of their co-workers and thus to maximize their total performance. Superior technical teams maintain a high level of internal communications, provide each other with informal support, and readily adjust their own assignments without their manager's involvement.

TEAMWORK

One of the finest examples of teamwork I know of was on my very first development project. The contract was for a large digital communications system which was planned for U.S. Army field use by the Signal Corps. The eight engineers on the team were mostly raw recruits, but the two technicians were old hands. Once, when we burned out the last precision resistor, they saved the day. The Signal Corps was coming for a review in one week, and the early demonstration model wouldn't work without these parts. When purchasing said they couldn't get new resistors in time, the technicians found some in only half an hour. We never asked where they came from, but we learned to trust their "midnight requisition" system.

This team did whatever was needed without question or direction. Just after we finished the first system and put it under test in the basement laboratory, a hurricane struck, and floods were predicted for the weekend. Even though no one was called, everyone showed up on Saturday morning. By late afternoon, water was actually squirting up through cracks in the cement floor, and all power had to be shut off. Everyone splashed around in that cold, dark basement, moving heavy equipment onto improvised stands; but none of it was damaged.

At the end of the project, volunteers were needed to help with the environmental tests. The equipment had to operate from $-10°$ to $132°F$ while the humidity was maintained at a constant 90 percent. This wasn't too bad during the heat-up cycle, but on the way down, it actually snowed in the chamber! Since someone had to be in there with the equipment all the time, this promised to be a tough assignment. Everyone wanted to go, however, but the medical department allowed only four of the team to go into the chamber. The equipment came through the tests with flying colors and so did the people.

TEAM CREATIVITY

In an effective team, the combined intellects of the members make more total knowledge available, and each professional helps to stimulate the team to perform better than any individual could do alone.[5] One example of this was the two engineering groups from different laboratories who were to cooperate in building a computer system for retail stores. The group from the printer organization was to build a small print unit for the receipts and transaction listings, and the communications department was responsible for the rest of the check-out terminal. These separate teams were soon in violent disagreement. The printer people found that no existing mechanism would fit in the required space, meet the cost targets, or provide adequate print quality. There wasn't enough time to design a completely new unit, so they began to argue about the specifications. The terminal engineers, on the other hand, were convinced that their needs could be met because they had seen competitive terminals that had the kind of functions they wanted.

These debates grew increasingly acrimonious until finally the two groups went to their respective laboratory managers for help. These executives then got together and agreed that the best chance to solve the problem would be to form one team with the best engineers from the two groups. This new team was then told to focus on the technical and cost issues but to leave the organizational and business questions for the laboratory managers to resolve. They started out arguing about the requirements, but they soon realized that the targets were proper and started to work cooperatively on solving the problem. They next reassessed the technical assumptions of each of the groups and found that, contrary to their prior experience, the printing no longer had to be done on flat sheets of paper. Although it had always been done this way, this was not necessary for the narrow strips to be used in this terminal. Instead of the bulky mechanism to move the print head, they could now mount an existing print element on a simple swivel to print against a curved platen. This new design was not only within the cost targets but also could be quickly made from available parts.

All the knowledge required to solve this problem had already existed in these two separate groups, but as long as they were defending their preconceived positions, they were unable to think objectively about the problem. Once they were merged into a common effort, their multidisciplined skills quickly produced a creative result. The laboratory managers knew that a single group with a crisply defined technical goal was far more likely to produce an innovative solution and that once the technical issues were resolved, the business and organizational questions could be quickly cleared up as well.

TEAM SUPPORT

From his studies of technical teams, Eugene Raudsepp concluded that

the effective team honors the individualism of its members, but acts as a unit. Each member is encouraged to contribute his or her knowledge to the overall effort. This communication of experiences and trading of ideas enables members to learn more, consider a greater variety of variables, and improve the development and use of their skills. It brings out more of their latent abilities and provides an atmosphere for continuing growth and development.[6]

Team membership satisfies their need for affiliation and provides professionals a safe haven in which to develop their ideas. The lone worker must have incredible stamina to single-handedly struggle with difficult technical problems while simultaneously facing personal insecurity. In high technology the projects are generally controversial, and the advocate of change is often subjected to personal attack. The social support of a team can thus provide professionals with reassuring security while they continue their crusade.

BASIC TEAM STRUCTURES

According to Eric Berne, groups typically have three organizational structures: the official, the individual, and the private.[7] The official structure describes how things are supposed to work according to the organizational charts and the procedures manuals. Problems change so rapidly, however, that reorganizations can rarely keep pace, and most technical work is far too comlex to describe in any reasonably sized manuals. As a result, the official structure is always out of date and far too simplistic to be useful. The only people who really know what is going on are the professionals and their immediate managers. They have learned to largely ignore this official structure and to operate through a host of private understandings and agreements which make up the individual structure.

Even with the rapid pace of modern technical change, the difference between the individual and the official structures rarely causes any trouble. In modern electronics, for example, engineers have traditionally designed machines with circuits and wires, and programming has been typically considered a support function. With the rapid development of semiconductor technology, however, sophisticated microprocessors cost less than wired logic, and the engineers found they could save time and money by making their logic from processor chips and microprograms. In a space of only a few years most engineers' jobs have changed to where they now spend the bulk of their time writing and testing microprograms. This has called for new skills, new support systems, different release and change procedures, new service concepts, and a host of advanced tools and methods. The professionals themselves have had little trouble with this change, even though the official organization and procedures manuals continued for several years to treat engineering as an exclusively hardware discipline.

After the official and individual structures, the private structure concerns the social relationships between the team members. Each group generally has some informal spokesperson who speaks up when secretarial service is inadequate, purchasing is late, or supplies are exhausted. There is also a "wise man" who provides advice and counsel on personal or business problems and a social secretary who arranges for group activities. These roles are never officially stated, but they are well known just the same. This private structure makes up the personal support framework for the members, and it is what makes the group cohesive and interdependent. Each member must support and contribute to the team's private structure to earn the full benefits of membership.

STRUCTURAL CONFLICTS

The interaction between the official, the individual, and the personal organizations rarely causes much trouble because most professionals are more concerned with doing their jobs than with following procedures. Occasionally, however, an officious manager may try to work "by the book" and disrupt an otherwise smooth operation. Charlie had managed a large technical support department before his promotion to head of the headquarters engineering standards staff of half a dozen senior professionals. According to the book, every standards change was to be issued in preliminary form, reviewed by all affected parties, approved by every level of division management, and finally signed off by the staff head. These professionals knew, however, that most of these issues were far too minor to warrant all this formality, so they had long since developed the practice of reaching informal telephone agreements with their divisional associates and then issuing informal "clarifications."

Charlie, however, was accustomed to running a larger organization, and he felt most comfortable with a daily stack of mail and a full schedule of appointments. The first thing he did on assuming his new job was to read all the organization and procedure manuals and require his people to review each of their project plans with him. He was horrified to discover that none of the recent changes had any documentation to support them. He immediately instituted periodic status reviews and a rigorous follow-up system. In no time his calendar was filled with meetings, and he was happily presiding over endless reviews of every detail of his people's work. The book was now being followed precisely, but little real work was actually being done. After a few months he was quietly reassigned to a less sensitive position.

GROUP ETHICS

The behavior of team members is influenced by their position in the team's private structure, and they have a vested interest in preserving this role. When any member's position is threatened, there is an unwritten team ethic that all the members will rally round in support and so preserve the team as a social entity. Another tacit understanding requires the members to settle their own disputes without appealing for outside help. When one engineer, for example, has a dispute with a co-worker, they should settle the issue themselves or with the help of another team member. An appeal to the team's manager or an outsider is often seen as breaking this rule and can thus be counterproductive.

Although he had never really thought about these matters, one older engineer unconsciously followed this ethic when a new member took over his accustomed role of chairing the annual technical conference. He had enjoyed being the unofficial professional coordinator, and he had already started planning the next conference by the time the new member joined the group and inserted himself in the process. He complained loudly to all the other team members, but he never went to the department manager for help. The newcomer was energetic and ambitious, and he did a good job of the initial conference planning. He had, however, expected some kind of recognition for his efforts, and when he found that the other team members were not the least bit impressed, he concluded that the work was not worth the effort and quietly let his older associate reassume his traditional role.

GROUP BEHAVIOR

The three basic kinds of groups are called the work group, the process group, and the combat group.[8] The work group has no major internal conflicts, good communication between members, and a positive and friendly atmosphere. Its energies are directed towards its job, and the members subordinate their personal interests to the group's objectives. From the manager's point of view, this is ideal group behavior, and interestingly enough, it is also the ideal for the group.

Groups with internal conflicts are called process groups. A member may be disruptive, there may be a leadership challenge, or someone may violate the group's ethics. In any of these cases, the group must devote at least some of its energies to resolving the problem. This is often a completely informal process and is generally handled without resort to outside help. Since this kind of group action is rarely possible without consensus, such process problem solving can immobilize a group for long periods.

One example of this was the case of ten managers who were attending a two-week seminar on business management. Although none of them had previously worked together, they were now to listen to a series of lectures and work out a number of case studies. At the opening session one student was the first to raise a question. His rambling comments soon showed that he was more interested in talking than in getting an answer, but the discussion leader politely handled the interruption and proceeded. This student interrupted repeatedly, however, and by the end of the day he had done almost as much talking as the instructor. The other members were thoroughly disgusted with this performance, and their annoyance increased when the same behavior continued on the second day. On the third day, without any prior agreement, the members developed an effective way to handle the problem. Whenever this student raised a question, one of them would interrupt for clarification, and then the others would join in. As soon as the student was silenced, a member would ask the instructor to continue. Initially, he tried to talk over this competition, but he was competely ignored. His questions soon ceased and the group returned to normal.

Groups sense their own internal dynamics and intuitively know how to coordinate their actions to solve process problems. When operating in the process mode, task forces, discussion groups, classes, and juries quickly learn to speak with one voice against the lone miscreant. Such group pressures can be enormous, and few members can withstand them unaided for very long.

THE COMBAT GROUP

The last team classification is the combat group. Regardless of its internal problems, this group loyally closes ranks and directs all its energies to defending itself from an external attack.

An example of this involved a technical staff which was to be split between two divisions. The staff manager had opposed the split from the beginning and argued that he should keep the entire function in one division and provide service to the other. Division management, however, rejected this approach and asked an organizational consultant to recommend how the split should be made. The staff manager brought his entire management team to an all-day meeting with the consultant, but none of them said a word. The consultant was frustrated by his inability to learn anyone's views but the staff manager's, so he next met individually with some of the department's managers. Everyone, however, merely repeated what the staff manager had already said. While the consultant was sure that some of them agreed with the change, not one of them would say anything that even implied acceptance of a split. Finally, after many meetings, the consultant had learned enough about the department's operations to make his own recommendations, but nobody on the team had said anything that was counter to the staff manager's initially stated position.

This is classic combat behavior. Even though the group had previously faced serious internal conflicts, all process issues were submerged in the face of this external threat, and everyone closed ranks behind the staff manager. Leaders of strife-torn groups often find this combat behavior helpful in suppressing internal friction, and some even create threats just to consolidate their positions.

NOTES CHAPTER 13

1. F. P. Brooks, *The Mythical Man-Month* (Reading, Mass.: Addison-Wesley Publishing Co., Inc., 1975), p. 155.
2. Fredrick W. Taylor, *The Principles of Scientific Management* (New York: Harper & Row, Publishers, Inc., 1911).
3. The Hawthorne studies were discussed in Chapter 7.
4. Peter F. Drucker, *Management, Tasks, Responsibilities, Practices* (New York: Harper & Row, Publishers, Inc., 1974), p. 183.
5. A number of studies have shown that close and sustained technical interaction between professionals stimulates their innovative performance: Frank Barron, "The Psychology of Imagination," *Scientific American*, CXCIX (September 1958) 151–166; Patrick H.

Irwin and Frank W. Langham, Jr., "The Change Seekers," *Harvard Business Review*, January/February 1966; Rensis Likert, *New Patterns of Management* (New York: McGraw-Hill Book Company, 1961); Eugene Raudsepp, "Teamwork: Silent Partner in the Design Group," *IEEE Engineering Management Review*, vol. 9, no 4, (December 1981).

6. Eugene Raudsepp, "Teamwork: Silent Partner in the Design Group," *IEEE Engineering Management Review*, vol. 9, no. 4, (December 1981) p. 94.

7. Eric Berne, *The Structure and Dynamics of Organizations and Groups* (New York: Grove Press, Inc., 1966), p. 64.

8. Ibid., p. 73.

14

Managing

Innovative Teams

Many of the techniques for managing creative people carry over to teams. Managers, for example, play the most important role in determining their team's attitudes. The way managers assign the work, evaluate performance, and set the working pace will heavily influence their feelings. If managers insure that each person feels personally valued, the team is most likely to coalesce into an effective working entity. If not, however, the group is likely to split into factions with each competing for the boss's favor.

A strong and cohesive spirit greatly improves team performance. This can not be achieved, however, unless the members each feel loyal to the group and comfortable with their role within it. Loyalty makes them feel personally responsible for the team's performance, while their individuality encourages them both to differ and to contribute. This attitude is best demonstrated by team members who do what is needed without worrying about whether it is their job or complaining about doing too much.

THE NEEDS OF CREATIVE TEAMS

Pelz found that managers who tightly control the way their people work generally get significantly less creativity than those with a looser and more informal style. He points out that the major differences in performance were because "some scientists were in situations where their creative ability 'paid off' for them, but others were in situations where creative ability seemed to hurt their performance."[1] The major factors that caused this result were managers' willingness to give their people adequate control over their own work, the people's ability to influence the managers' decisions, and their facilities for communicating new ideas both within the group and with other groups. Pelz concluded that "creative ability was less likely to pay off, and may even hurt a man's performance if he was in a restrictive situation."[2]

SIGNING UP

Another factor in building an effective team is the way the team members are recruited. If they each feel they chose their job, they are more likely to keep their energy and enthusiasm through the many routine phases of the project. Tracy Kidder describes the way Tom West handled this for his Eagle computer.[3] Tom was looking for candidates who would perform under the enormous pressure of his crash program, and he wanted people who were excited by the challenge of designing and building an advanced computer. When an engineer signed up, he in effect declared: "I want to do this job, and I'll give it my heart and soul." Although signing up was not a formal process, when one of the old hands said, "Yeah, I'll do that," he had signed up. West carefully picked only the best and the most motivated of the engineers, and although the pressure was intense, they worked incredible hours and produced a very successful machine.

THE TEAM LEADER'S STYLE

George Farris and Frank Andrews have found that the way managers deal with their people makes an enormous difference in the quality of their people's work.[4] The groups they studied were separated into the most and the least innovative, and their differences were then analyzed. In the most innovative the managers personally involved themselves in the work and maintained close technical contact with their people. For the least innovative the managers were less active and more remote. Although they occasionally provided ideas and information, they were not deeply involved and had little close interaction with their groups.

   Farris and Andrews then looked more deeply to see what kind of close involvement was most effective. They found that when the manager's ability was limited, innovation was highest when the group was given the greatest freedom. When the manager was highly skilled in administration, personnel, and technology, however, the results were mixed; sometimes freedom helped, but sometimes it did not. As they said: "If you don't know what you're doing, then stay out of the way!"[5]

   This is the age-old conflict between top-down direction and bottom-up participation. As managers become more competent and their people less so, top-down direction becomes progressively more important. In the extreme, the employees end up merely carrying out their manager's instructions. At the other end of the scale, managers' technical talents are more limited and their people are highly capable; therefore they should focus on goals and objectives and leave the technical issues up to their people.

   There is, of course, no single best answer. Managers aim to get the job done, and when their people do not perform, they must step in and straighten things out.

Unfortunately, even with capable people, there are enormous pressures that drive managers toward directive behavior. At the start of a project, they know what is needed, and it is up to them to inform their people. Often, they are more experienced as well as better informed, so when the work load is heavy and the budget is tight, they may lose patience and tell their people exactly what to do. This may quickly resolve the current problem, but it also reduces their people's motivation, further limits their performance, and may even cause the manager to become more authoritarian.

The best management guideline is to follow the principles of situational leadership and focus on building the team's task and relationship maturity. Although managers may find it necessary to be directive at the outset, they should gradually provide more latitude, while staying closely involved and showing continuing interest. Highly competent managers should certainly make suggestions and ask probing questions, but they should also progressively reduce the amount of explicit instruction they provide. By urging their people to make their own decisions, asking for the data to support them, and probing their knowledge of relevant work, managers both insure their people's competent performance and build their maturity.

It is also up to the team leader to set goals, review performance, and instill a sense of urgency. Few people can perform at peak capacity unless they feel that their work is badly needed. As Farris and Andrews found: "Performance is lowest when there is little time pressure."[6] By pushing for aggressive schedules, managers not only maintain their group's energy; they also demonstrate their belief in the importance of their work.

One example of the way management pressure stimulates team performance is the case of the programming interface standard. The three different groups involved had been unable to reach agreement on their own, so when the laboratory manager learned of the disagreement, he decided to exert some pressure. He thus gave the three department heads three weeks to solve the problem. They chartered a technical group with a senior staff professional acting as the chairman. The six technical experts were drawn from the involved departments, and they devoted full time to the problem. By six o'clock on the night before the deadline, they had settled all but one of the points. The chairman had checked, and the manager insisted that the review meeting be held the next morning; therefore he told them they would have to work all night, if necessary, to finish. It was almost midnight before they reached agreement, but even though they each had to give some ground, they all agreed that the final solution was a good one. The work had been intense, and the entire team was exhausted; but the laboratory manager's deadline had been met with a good technical answer.

TEAM SYNERGISM

A group of educational exercises called survival games have been developed to demonstrate some important principles about team performance.[7] In one example in the late 1960s a group of twenty managers were asked to pretend they were on the first Apollo moon landing mission two years hence. They were given a list of forty items—such as a life raft, an oxygen bottle, and canned food—and asked to decide, in priority order, which they should take in case they were marooned. This same test had been given to the NASA astronauts in Houston, and their combined answer was to be used as the grading standard.

First, the members of the class took the test individually and turned in their answers. The group was then arbitrarily divided into two ten-person teams, and each went to a separate meeting room for one hour to produce a team answer. In one case, a team member quickly took charge and guided the group through an orderly process of establishing criteria, evaluating the items, and assigning priorities to each. By coincidence this team included all the engineers and scientists from the class, and one of them had even worked on the space program. This total process was orderly and efficient, each point was discussed and unanimously settled, and they were finished in only forty-five minutes.

The second team had no technically trained members, and none of them knew anything about the space program. Several viewed this class as a way to demonstrate their leadership skills, so they each tried to take charge. As a result, the meeting quickly degenerated into a series of arguments with no discernible order or plan. When the hour was up, they were still arguing over the final items and had to be called back into the meeting room.

When the results were compared, the technical team members had individually done quite well, but their overall team result was little better than the average of their individual scores. On the disorderly team, none of the individual scores had been very good, but the team result was better than their best individual score. What is more, it was even better than the score of the technical team, even though their individual members had not done nearly as well.

These team exercises generally produce a similar result. When strong leaders take charge, their views tend to dominate the entire process, and while they may request everyone's opinions, their views set the agenda and largely control the final result. A managed agenda and a firm chairman can be very effective in gathering facts, but they seriously inhibit both the generation of new ideas and the open communication which is needed to reach complete agreement. With an established agenda, many members feel reluctant to disrupt proceedings, and even when they have very good ideas, they will hold back out of shyness or deference to the leader. With no strong leader, open communication is fostered by the resulting equality.

A disorderly environment is a great equalizer, and although total chaos is rarely desirable, the resulting level of communication certainly is. When the team members feel strongly enough about the subject to participate, less structure and more interaction is far more likely to produce agreement on an innovative result.

CRYSTALLIZING THE TEAM

When a team is initially formed, it is generally a loosely coupled collection of individuals, but as the following example shows, there are various techniques for building such groups into cohesive units. A corporate task force was charged with recommending how to make a number of the company's communications products more compatible. These machines each used different message formats and processing rules, and although they had all used the same line signaling and addressing schemes, the content and structure of the messages was uncontrolled. As a result, each product's analysis and processing equipment had to be specially designed, and the customers were limited in how these devices could intercommunicate. This situation was undesirable, but prior agreement had been almost impossible because some of the units were intended for low-cost applications, while others were planned for sophisticated high-performance customers.

The leading communications technologists from each product area was assigned to this task force, as were several staff experts. Because of the number of organizations involved, this produced a sixteen member group which was near the limit of manageability. It was essential, however, to include knowledgeable representatives from each involved area. The task force leader was an experienced engineer from the corporate staff who had not been previously involved in this issue, so he was viewed by all the members as a neutral party.

At the opening session, Ray suggested that the work be divided into three phases, with the first phase devoted to fact finding. He would arrange for any presentations the members wanted and would schedule discussions with any requested technical or business experts. The second phase was to be a free-form period with no agenda and no chairperson. Ray would act like any other task force member except that he would arrange for the meeting facilities and refreshments, keep the discussions from getting too disorderly, and insure that every member had an equal chance to speak. When someone tried unsuccessfully to break into the conversation, for example, he would make a note and later ask for that person's comments. The third phase was to start only after all the members had agreed that the proper conclusions had been reached and were completely satisfied on all important points. Ray would then assume the more traditional leader's role for the production of the final presentation and written report. After some discussion all the task force members agreed with this approach.

The task force met for four consecutive days every few weeks and held about thirty days of meetings over the next several months. The data-gathering and free-form discussion phases were interspersed for much of this time, and only two heated arguments required Ray's intervention. Many of the members had strong and conflicting views, so the discussions were lively, and he often had to call on members who had been unable to make themselves heard. This management style crystallized the group into a coherent team within the first few days, and they quickly developed several "in" jokes and a shorthand mode of communication. Often, for example, a single word or phrase would get quick agreement or cause a general laugh.

At the outset Ray had scheduled the final report presentation to the corporate technical director, and as this time neared the members became increasingly concerned. After all the presentations and outside discussions had been completed, only two weeks remained, and the group was far from agreement. Although they urged Ray to delay the final report, he felt that the time pressure would be helpful, so he refused. Under this severe constraint, the group worked late many evenings and soon settled all of the smaller issues. The one remaining question was how to achieve compatibility between the smallest and the largest machines. The small-product people argued that compatibility was undesirable because it would require them to add more costly features. This position was unacceptable to the high-performance people, however, because their machines would either be functionally constrained or would be limited to communicating with only a few other machine types. They finally agreed to set up a subcommittee to see if an acceptable approach could be found which would balance these conflicting needs.

A four-man subgroup was put to work on this one issue while everyone else started on the final report. The subcommittee was surprised to find that a standard compatibility format for all devices was possible with only modest cost impact for the smaller machines. The larger machines could then incorporate optional additional functions, but all units would be able to communicate at least at a basic level. The entire task force accepted this conclusion, and the report was completed on time and accepted by all the product groups. Even though many of the members had initially held opposing views, the task force finished in unanimous agreement. Because of the unstructured meetings, everyone had a chance to speak and the high level of communication fostered both creativity and understanding.

COMMUNICATION

Since communication between team members is so important, it is not surprising that communication with the manager is, if anything, more important. Eugene Raudsepp, however, found that "lack of communication is one of the most frequently cited complaints against managers."[8] It is through communication with their leader that the team members learn their goals, the tasks they are to perform, and what their manager thinks of their performance. If this communication link is inadequate, the team will be in the dark, they will not be able to think objectively, and their work will not feel personally rewarding.

The essence of good communications is two-way interaction. If managers merely share information with their people, they are just talking, and there is no guarantee that their people really understand them. True understanding is rarely possible without some level of interaction. Leavitt's analogy to artillery spotting explains why this is so important:

> If an artilleryman had to fire over a hill at an invisible target, he would have to fire blind and hope that by luck one of his shells would land on the target. He would spray the area with shells and go away, never being certain whether he had or had not destroyed his objective. But by the simple addition of a spotter standing on the hilltop, the likelihood of accurate shooting can be greatly increased. The spotter can feed back to the gunner information about the effects of the gunner's own shots. "Your last shot was a hundred yards short. The second was fifty yards over." And so on. The advantage is obvious and it is precisely the advantage of two-way over one-way communication—the commu-

nicator can learn the effects of his attempts to communicate and can adjust his behavior accordingly.[9]

There is, however, one big difference between communication and artillery. When a gun misses in wartime, there is generally little lost except for some wasted ammunition, while misses in communication can both confuse and mislead. Even then, if the manager next provides accurate information, recovery may not be complete because the recipient will often be confused and not know what to believe. When this confusion is coupled with the lack of precision in normal conversation and the human predilection for interpreting what we hear in terms of our own wants and needs, miscommunication is clearly more the rule than the exception. What is worse, a manager's miscommunication can often cause serious mischief.

OPEN COMMUNICATION

James Brian Quinn has said that ''high morale occurs when team members intensely share a common goal.''[10] This clearly requires that managers not only inform their people but also share their goals and plans with them. When managers have worked out an explicit set of goals and shared them with their people, their people can translate these objectives into their own personal actions. Thoroughly informed professionals invariably have many ideas on what to do and how to do it, and leaders who honestly respect their people's views will be rewarded with an intensely loyal, cohesive, and productive team.

Open communication, however, does not mean that managers should share everything with their people. They are busy and have limited need for, or interest in, many of the topics which concern managers. Eugene Raudsepp has stated the following four basic ground rules for honest and open communication with team members:[11]

1. Is the issue important enough to require group discussion? It is much more efficient to communicate minor issues and invite comments and questions with brief notes or memos.
2. If the problem only concerns management, it will be of little interest to the team in general.
3. If the members are unable to contribute to the issue because they didn't have the necessary knowledge or skill, involving them will only embarrass them.
4. If the decision has already been made, it must be honestly presented that way. If not, group agreement will be a sham, and group disagreement will be a problem.

Open communication between managers and their team also helps to improve the communication links between the members themselves. Poor communication, on the other hand, will add to worries and cause minor issues to be blown out of proportion. As Theodore H. White has observed: "Rumors will grow in any large organization without open communication."[12]

A TECHNICAL PROPOSAL TEAM

An IBM team for a large and complex special-system bid to the federal government shows how effective open communication can be. This group had grown quickly to approximately fifty engineers and businessmen, and working space had become a serious problem. The local IBM laboratory was already overcrowded, so a dance hall was rented from the local volunteer fire department. The facilities would normally have been totally inadequate, since there were no offices and everyone had to work in one large room. It was the only space available, however, so everybody moved in for the final sixty days before the due date.

In spite of the noise and lack of privacy, this turned out to be a remarkably efficient arrangement. There was a large blackboard on a stand which was put in the middle of the room, and everyone worked at tables set around the walls. When any issue needed discussion, it was announced to all hands, and everyone involved would congregate around the blackboard. Most of the people came to the opening of every meeting, but those not involved quickly returned to their work. If people were needed, however, they could readily be called over and the point resolved.

This free and open communication came about largely by accident, but it produced a remarkably cohesive team. Everybody knew what was going on and where they fit in. The excitement and enthusiasm grew as the deadline neared, and at the last minute there were many volunteers for the final review. This was surprising because, as a result of the tight bid deadline, it had to be held at the printer's in New York City on Christmas Eve. Because of this team's effectiveness the proposal was judged so superior that IBM won the contract.

MANAGING TEAM CONFLICT

Nothing can destroy the effectiveness of a team more quickly or more completely than unresolved conflicts between the members. Inevitable differences and disagreements will crop up in any fast-paced organization, but the members themselves can generally work them out. Occasionally, however, the problems are too complex or pervasive, and a highly destructive process often ensues. Rather than face continuing unpleasantness, the disagreeing parties start to avoid each other, and this reduced contact causes a total break in communication. This temporarily reduces the unpleasantness, but it also makes it almost impossible for the parties themselves to resolve the problem.

Under these circumstances outside intervention is generally required, and Roger Fisher's basic principles for third-party conflict resolution can be helpful.[13] First, avoid early polarization. The resolution of most problems calls for compromise on both sides, and early fixed positions make the later accommodation more difficult. Win-lose situations are the hardest to resolve, so they should be tempered by showing both parties how little they have to lose and what they can both gain from reaching agreement. Wherever possible, the stakes should be reduced so that neither party feels pressed to give up too much.

Attention should also be focused on the issues rather than on personalities, motives, or blame. Information should be obtained from several sources, and all parties should be made aware of all the pertinent facts. The disagreements should be focused on verifying the data and identifying any additional information which will clarify the remaining points in contention.

Finally, no conflict between team members can be resolved by dealing with either of them separately. They must both be equally involved and must both openly accept the conclusions. Since silence is not a reliable indicator of consent, both parties should air their opinions and restate the final agreement. Often, when the entire issue cannot be resolved in a single step, some points should be deferred for later consideration. It is important, however, to end each meeting with some agreement, even if it is only on the time and agenda for the next meeting.

There are, of course, conflicts which cannot be resolved to everyone's satisfaction. This is normal in any fast-paced organization, because different people have different priorities, and each job has its own unique set of objectives. Generally, however, both sides will accept a decision that goes against them if they can see how the greater good is served, if their views have been heard, and if they are told precisely why the decision was made.

No group of active and intelligent professionals can function for very long without generating friction of some kind. Disagreement is natural, and Pelz, in a study of eighty-three technical groups, found it often actually stimulated performance.[14] When a group of professionals are personally compatible but intellectually competitive, friendly rivalry generates the highest overall group performance. When the disputes become personal, however, performance invariably suffers.

INTERGROUP CONFLICTS

The process of resolving conflicts between groups follows essentially the same rules as for conflicts between individuals except that there are a few additional considerations. Some general guidelines for intergroup conflict resolution are as follows:

1. The managers of the conflicting groups should first be urged to resolve the issues themselves.

2. When they reach an impasse, the issues should be informally explored with each manager separately, and then they are brought together not to settle the issue but to agree on a way to settle it.

3. If the managers are well informed and deeply committed to their own position, it is often helpful to form an expert subcommittee with members taken from

each department. There should, however, be a neutral chairperson, or this group will likely become polarized at the outset and make little progress.

4. To reduce the stakes, this subcommittee should address a portion of the issue, for example, by focusing on technical questions and ignoring organizational or staffing concerns.

5. In most cases, once there is an agreed technical solution, the managers can quickly resolve the remaining questions themselves.

An example of this process was the selection of a disk storage system for a new low-cost computer. The storage group had a new disk file in development, and they wanted it used both to increase its market and because they didn't have the resources for an additional project. The computer group, however, was convinced that this existing unit would be too expensive. The disagreement continued for some time with no resolution until the two managers formed a joint subcommittee and put a respected planner in charge. He was told to focus the group on finding a technically superior solution and not to dismiss them until they found it. They started by rehashing all the prior arguments, and after a couple of days they all understood everyone's point of view. By that time they realized that neither of the prior proposals would do the job, so they started looking for a different answer. They soon found they could rather easily modify an older existing machine to the performance targets. The costs would be reduced because the machine was already in production, and the tools and most of the parts were already available. An aggressive schedule was needed to meet the announcement date, and some added development resources would be needed; but everyone agreed this was the right answer. With this agreement, the managers were soon able to get the needed staffing, and the product was completed and announced on time.

NOTES CHAPTER 14

1. Donald C. Pelz and Frank M. Andrews, *Scientists in Organizations: Productive Climates for Research and Development* (New York: John Wiley & Sons, Inc., 1966), p. 171.

2. Ibid., p. 172.

3. Tracy Kidder, *The Soul of a New Machine* (Boston: Little, Brown & Company, 1981), p. 63.

4. Michael L. Tushman and William L. Moore, *Readings in the Management of Innovation* (Marshfield, Mass.: Pitman, 1982), p. 344.

5. Ibid., p. 347.

6. Ibid., p. 346.

7. The particular game described here was conducted by Dale Zand, of New York University, at the IBM Sands Point Executive School in 1968.

8. Eugene Raudsepp, "Teamwork: Silent Partner in the Design Group," *IEEE Engineering Management Review*, vol. 9, no. 4 (December 1981), p. 94.

9. Harold J. Leavitt, *Managerial Psychology, Fourth Edition* (Chicago, Ill.: University of Chicago Press, 1978), p. 122.

10. Tushman, *Readings*, p. 556.

11. Raudsepp, "Teamwork."

12. Theodore H. White, *In Search of History* (New York: Harper and Row, Publishers, Inc., 1978).

13. Roger Fisher and William Ury, *Getting to Yes* (Boston: Houghton Mifflin Company, 1981).

14. Pelz, *Scientists in Organizations*, p. 152.

15

The Innovative

Team Environment

Since an organization's innovative ability depends primarily on its people, the nature of the work environment can play a key role in its overall performance. Peters found, when he compared the most and the least successful departments in several mining companies, that the most innovative groups looked like "nothing so much as structured chaos. Buzzing, blooming environments."[1] This free-form, seemingly chaotic behavior stimulates the interaction between team members, frees them from mental constraints, and enhances creativity.

One reason that unstructured environments are so creative is that random behavior stimulates discovery. Karl E. Weick describes an experiment with flies and bees which demonstrates how this works.[2] Half a dozen bees and an equal number of flies are put in a bottle which is placed on its side with the base against a window. The bees will try to get through the base of the bottle to the light beyond and will continue this struggle until they die of exhaustion or hunger. The flies, however, randomly buzz around, and in a few minutes they have all found the opening in the neck of the bottle and escaped.

New solutions frequently involve seemingly irrational ideas. If the search is confined to the known dimensions of the problem, no one will notice the other end of the bottle, and they will continue in their fruitless direct attack. While the organization is engrossed in this valiant assault, it is rarely able to hear the wild duck who points to a new and creative solution. This, however, is exactly what makes the truly innovative organization: the tolerance to support its wild ducks and the wisdom to listen to them.

THE SKUNK WORKS

Veronica Stolte-Heiskenen did a study of fifty research laboratories to find the relationship between laboratory size and innovative performance.[3] While she found a slight correlation, it was negative. That is, the smaller organizations often produced more innovative work per capita, and some even had a greater total output than their larger counterparts. This is why many companies establish special organizations, or "skunk works," to house their most creative people. These are small informal teams that are given considerable freedom from the normal constraints of the rest of the organization. Lockheed, for example, has a six-man group in a dingy building seven miles from corporate headquarters, which has been responsible for three of their five major recent products. Ms. Heiskenen also found that an eight-man Spanish subsidiary of another company produced as many new products as the four hundred man central product development organization.

Some years ago Thomas J. Watson, Jr., emphasized IBM's need to encourage and support its "wild ducks." As a result the company set up a special Fellow program to allow engineers and scientists with proven ability to pursue their own creative ideas. There are now between fifty and sixty IBM Fellows under five-year renewable appointments housed in the various company laboratories. They each have budgets, laboratory facilities, and small technical staffs to assist them in their work.

Regardless of management's best efforts, however, the "wild ducks" in any organization always have a hard time. Established manufacturing and development groups do not readily accept outside ideas, because they are totally committed to meeting an established plan. New ideas are thus viewed as diversions, and they get brushed off without an objective review. If management does not support its most innovative people, the main-line organization will reject them, and their valuable efforts will be wasted. Project Zero found that "creative activity is only possible if one lives in a society where it is tolerated, if not encouraged."[4]

INHIBITING INNOVATION

One way managers can improve the innovative performance of their organization is to examine the inhibitors to innovation and remove them. The problems of management style and communication have already been discussed, but other important constraints are a rigid and tightly controlled organization and a strict focus on main-line projects. Productivity measures and tight business controls can also present a serious problem, because a hard-headed management attitude will generally kill new ideas before they have progressed far enough to be justified.

Facilities, while not of paramount importance, can also be a problem. When professionals have inadequate or inconvenient space, they can be easily discouraged by myriad annoying details. The lack of contiguous working quarters also seriously limits interteam communications and reduces team effectiveness. This same concern carries over to the quality of the technical support, for professionals can easily lose time and motivation when instruments are out of calibration or computer response is slow. When a dedicated team spends hours on a job that should take a few minutes, their attitude and performance are bound to suffer. Before long they begin to question why they should work so hard at their job, when management is clearly not doing theirs.

Finally, as Pelz has pointed out, a total dedication to one job will reduce the professional's performance.[5] The best professionals have cosmopolitan leanings. They want to know what is happening in both their organization and their technical field, and they need the stimulation of broad technical exposure. When management insists that its professionals work exclusively on their immediate assignment, they soon feel trapped and constrained and their performance suffers.

MAINTAINING AN INNOVATIVE ENVIRONMENT

There are many steps managers can take to establish and maintain a suitable innovative environment in their organization. For example:

1. Establish a technical resources program and take special pains to identify and help develop the most promising people.
2. Support their most creative people by providing them with both time and resources to pursue their own interests.
3. Recognize their sponsor's role by seeking out and supporting promising inventors and champions.
4. Maintain a reasonable level of change so that the groups do not become stagnant and start to resist new ideas.
5. Maintain a strong focus on technical publications, seminars, patents, and continuing professional education.
6. Set up a management communication program, including newspapers, bulletin-board notices, periodic information meetings, and other forums where the managers can interact informally with their people.
7. Provide adequate facilities to permit the professionals to work in contiguous space and make a modern equipment support available.
8. Establish a formal program for recognizing and rewarding outstanding work.

NOTES CHAPTER 15

1. Thomas J. Peters and Robert H. Waterman, Jr., *In Search of Excellence: Lessons from America's Best-Run Companies* (New York: Harper & Row, Publishers, Inc., 1982), p. 111.
2. Ibid., p. 108.

3. Thomas J. Peters, "The Rational Model Has Led Us Astray," *Planning Review*, March 1982. This paper cites the study by Veronica Stolte-Heiskenen of fifty public and private-sector research laboratories, p. 16.

4. Howard Gardner, "Science Grapples with the Creative Puzzle," *The New York Times*, May 13, 1984, sec. 2, p. 1.

5. Donald C. Pelz and Frank M. Andrews, *Scientists in Organizations: Productive Climates for Research and Development* (New York: John Wiley & Sons, Inc., 1966), pp. 56, 65.

16

Rewards and Recognition

Although the fertile imaginations of creative people are enormously valuable, they can also cause problems. This is because creative people often think in subtle ways and are even inclined to imagine difficulties where none really exist. When people aren't adequately recognized, for example, they often suspect that something is wrong and get upset. Pelz's study of the people who had left a major government laboratory found this to be the case.[1] He compared the people who had resigned with those who stayed, and from a series of interviews with previous peers, he found general agreement that they had been fully as productive, but their talents had not been as well appreciated by their management.

Consider the example of a very creative engineer who resigned in spite of his good record and his management's high opinion. They had readily agreed to his taking a one-year leave at a university to do research and teaching and quite naturally assumed he would need little supervision. This engineer, however, became increasingly concerned as his year drew to a close, because no one had seemed very interested in his future. He finally got so upset that he decided to take a job with another company, and it took a great deal of management effort to get him to change his mind.

AWARD PROGRAMS

On any project, a very few people generally make the difference between success and failure. Someone has the initial crucial idea, a champion sells the program to management, and one or two key people spearhead the implementation. Although managers invariably know who these people are, they rarely tell them how much they appreciate them. Some of them will be sufficiently self-confident not to worry, but most professionals need more direct evidence of their manager's approbation. These engineers and scientists are the life blood of the organization, and it is important to frequently reassure them that their managers recognize their personal value.

The basic idea behind recognition programs is to reward significant achievements as promptly as possible. The famous Foxboro Award was conceived late one evening when one of their scientists solved a crucial technical problem. He excitedly raced to the president's office to show what he had done, and the delighted president looked through his desk to find something he could give in recognition. As Peters says, he "found something, leaned over the desk to the scientist and said, 'Here.' In his hand was a banana."[2] This was all he could find, but it turned out to be enough. From then on, the "golden banana" pin has been awarded by Foxboro to those company engineers and scientists who are responsible for the highest technical achievements.

RECOGNITION PROGRAMS

Although recognition of the top professionals is essential, there are hundreds or even thousands of smaller contributions routinely made every day. In aggregate these little changes can have an enormous impact, but since none of them stand out, they rarely get special attention. Even these minor advances should be encouraged in some way, however, if only by a letter from the boss or a pat on the back.

Rene McPherson, who headed the Dana Corporation before he became dean of the Stanford University Business School, said that "the real key to success is helping the middle 60 percent a few steps up the ladder."[3] When a reasonably large portion of the population know their efforts are recognized, they will continue their creative work, and the organization will continue to improve.

THE IBM AWARD PLAN

The IBM award plan combines both "informal" and "formal" awards to recognize a wide spectrum of achievements. The "informal" awards range from fifty to fifteen hundred dollars and can be given at the manager's discretion. Once the manager gets the approval of his or her immediate manager, the award can even be given on the same day.

The larger awards are more formal, and divisional management can grant sums of up to $25,000 for important achievements. The IBM corporate awards range up to $100,000 or more, and they are reserved for truly unique accomplishments. These are presented at an annual gala recognition dinner where the award recipients and their spouses are joined by senior IBM executives at a three day affair equivalent to that given the most productive salesmen.

The size of these dollar awards may seem excessive, but the achievements they celebrate are equally significant. When someone comes up with an idea that is literally worth millions of dollars, an award of $100,000 is not out of line. One of the largest awards IBM has ever given is the $225,000 presented to an IBM Fellow and eight of his prior associates for conceiving and implementing Fortran, the first widely used programming language. This achievement both revolutionized computer programming and produced a valuable IBM product. IBM gives many such awards, and in the last five years over four million dollars in corporate awards have been presented to approximately one hundred fifty employees. Twelve of these awards were for $100,000 or more.

INDUSTRY AWARD PLANS

Many other companies have similar plans. Gee, for example, describes the awards a chemical company gave to the team that created a new fertilizer product. Their idea for a novel urea nitrate compound turned out to be a significant advance over the standard nitrate of soda or sulfate of ammonia formulations then used for commercial fertilizers. The urea product was an immediate success and netted a $300,000 profit in the first twelve months of commercial operation. Management decided that 4% of this amount should be divided among the five key contributors on the twenty man team:

> —Dr. A, agronomist, conceived and defined the product characteristics and marketing strategy leading to an important advance in the fertilizer mixing art, thereby laying the groundwork for the company's successful entry into a new and opportune sales field. Allocation of 30% of the award was recommended.

> —Mr. B, A's supervisor, proposed a modification of A's initial product concept thereby significantly reducing costs of manufacture and distribution and strengthening the claims of the patent subsequently issued to B and A. Allocation of 10% of the award was recommended.

> —Dr. C, research chemist, established the principles of the product synthesis, which theretofore had not been exploited commercially in the United States. Allocation of 20% of the award was recommended.

> —Mr. D, chemical engineer, scaled up C's synthesis to the piloting stage and established design criteria for a full-scale commercial plant. This design embodied novel features resulting in substantial reduction in cost and in significant quality improvement. Allocation of 30% of the award was recommended.

> —Mr. E, sales technologist, devised a facsimile mixing unit whereby the novel applications technology was demonstrated successfully to prospective customers. Allocation of 10% of the award was recommended.[4]

Following the success of the product in its first year, a total of five annual awards were planned which were expected to total $80,000 to $100,000.

Many other companies have similar award plans, and it is not unusual for them to set the award amounts in much the same way, as shown in Table 16.1.[5]

TABLE 16.1   Six Corporate Compensation Awards

Company	Award Amount	Annual Savings	Percent
United Technologies	$ 2,900	$ 19,791	14.6%
United Technologies	2,500	40,000	6.3
Western Electric	3,910	26,000	15.0
Schering Corp.	1,125	5,000	22.5
Johnson & Johnson	6,978	46,500	15.0
GAF Corporation	3,580	29,000	12.3
Total	$20,993	$166,291	12.6

AWARD GUIDELINES

To qualify for an award, the achievement should be clear, significant, worthy of special recognition, and reasonably consistent with other awards for similar achievements. Special care should also be taken when recognizing managers, since even when they play a key role, there can be the implication that the professionals do the work and the managers get the rewards. Awards should also be given in public with plenty of publicity. This follows Charlie Beacham's principle when he was Lee Iacocca's mentor at Ford: "If you want to give a man credit, put it in writing. If you want to give him hell, do it on the phone."[6]

Large team achievements require special care; and when an entire project deserves recognition, it is best done with a special event, such as a dinner or an outing. Depending on the achievement, everyone can be given a special memento, such as a wall plaque, an engraved paperweight, or a pen set. Dollar awards should not generally be given to large groups.

When a large-team success also includes several important individual contributions, it is essential to provide both types of recognition. The entire team should have a dinner and a memento, and the unique achievements should receive significant dollar awards. The two events need not be held at the same time, but they should not be too widely separated. Presentation of the dollar awards should be made at a meeting of the entire group, and the specific achievements should be described in enough detail to make their unique nature completely clear.

Finally, awards should never be given before the achievement has actually been completed. All too often, the manager will eagerly propose an award for something that is "as good as done," only to have an unforeseen snag nullify or delay the success. It is wise to wait until the achievement has been clearly demonstrated but then to be prompt and generous with the reward.

INCENTIVE PLANS

Award plans seek to meet the employees' need for recognition and thus facilitate self-actualizing performance. Incentive programs, on the other hand, are aimed at the more fundamental demands for sustenance and comfort. Even though these basic needs fall much lower in Maslow's hierarchy, all incentive systems include some element of recognition. This is because they are invariably based, at least in part, on the management's appraisal of the employee's performance. Since this is generally well known, an incentive payment thus is tangible evidence of the professional's worth to the organization.

Various types of incentive pay systems are commonly used by high-technology firms, particularly those newer organizations that need to attract and retain growing quantities of talent. In one survey of 105 firms in the Boston area, over 80 percent of those in high technology had bonus pay plans as opposed to only 33 percent of the rest.[7] These were typically cash bonus plans granted to all technical professionals based on such nonfinancial criteria as project completion. This approach was particularly prevalent in start-up firms which were not yet sufficiently profitable to use profit sharing.

Such plans appear to be both widespread and relatively popular with employees, but there is only limited evidence to support their economic value to the organization.[8] In the case of Analog Devices, for example, a two-dimensional management incentive plan was well received by the people, although there were a few complaints. No clear cause and effect relationship could be demonstrated, but sales did increase by 40 percent, and return on assets grew from 16 percent to 21 percent during the first four years of the plan.[9]

An interesting sidelight of incentive plans is that they can be used to stimulate peripheral behavior. In Raytheon, for example, a plan was introduced to motivate engineers to write papers and give talks.[10] An award of $250 plus $100 per page was given to every engineer who wrote a paper. The award was limited to a maximum of $750. Although no papers had been published in the twelve months immediately preceding the program, five papers were published and three more were started in the next three months.

Depending on the particular needs of the organization, both award and incentive programs can be highly effective.

NOTES CHAPTER 16

1. Donald C. Pelz and Frank M. Andrews, *Scientists in Organizations: Productive Climates for Research and Development* (New York: John Wiley & Sons, Inc., 1966), p. 110.

2. Thomas J. Peters and Robert H. Waterman, Jr., *In Search of Excellence, Lessons from America's Best-Run Companies* (New York: Harper and Row, Publishers, Inc., 1982), p. 70.

3. Ibid., p. 269.

4. Edwin A. Gee and Chaplin Tyler, *Managing Innovation* (New York: John Wiley & Sons, Inc., 1976), p. 204.

5. *The New York Times,* March 24, 1974.

6. Lee Iacocca and William Novak, *Iacocca: An Autobiography* (New York: Bantam Books, Inc., 1984), p. 56.

7. David B. Balkin and Louis R. Gomez-Mejia, "Compensation Practices in High-Technology Industries," *Personnel Administrator,* June 1985, p. 111.

8. Reuven Shapira and Shlomo Globerson, "An Incentive Plan for R&D Workers," *Research Management,* September–October 1983, p. 17.

9. Ray Stata and Modesto A. Maidique, "Bonus System for Balanced Strategy," *Harvard Business Review,* November–December 1980, p. 156.

10. Dan Anderson, "Getting Engineers to Write," *IEEE Transactions on Professional Communication,* vol. PC-26, no. 4 (December 1983), p. 170.

17

The Management Team

Lee Iacocca, when he took over Chrysler, found that the top management team was not working effectively together as a unit, and he decided that his "highest priority was to put that team together before it was too late."[1] The top manager and his or her immediate subordinate managers make up this management team, and they are the most important single group in the organization. They make the key operating decisions, set the priorities, and determine the quality of the working environment. Unless they can work closely together, the organization will only be a loosely coupled group of independent departments.

CONFRONTATIONAL MANAGEMENT

The operation of any organization of even moderate size necessarily involves a great many conflicts. There are never enough resources, and schedules are always tight; therefore some central group is needed to resolve issues and set priorities. Senior managers are naturally responsible for everything in their organization, but they should involve their management team in most of the issues. If they do this effectively, they can strengthen this team; but if not, the group will fragment, and the organization's energy will be dissipated in internal friction.

Lawrence and Lorsch have found that a confrontational management style leads to the most effective group performance. Of the organizations they studied, those with the highest performance used confrontation extensively, the medium-performing groups used it to a moderate degree, and the lowest performers the least.[2] The basic ground rules for confrontational management are as follows:

1. Top managers make sure that their management team is aware of all important decisions before they are made and invite their comments and reactions in advance.

2. The member of the team who advocates the proposal is held responsible for informing the other members.

3. Those in disagreement are responsible for resolving or escalating their issues.

4. All concerned parties are present when the decision is made, and they all have an opportunity to state their views.

5. When no opposition is voiced, the top manager makes sure the issue has been thoroughly explored and is well understood by everyone involved. If not, the decision is deferred until there is a healthy level of contention.

The reason confrontation is so effective is that it both exposes the organization's latent conflicts and helps to keep the discussions on a rational plane. When decisions are made in secret, the debates become political, and a feeling of distrust invariably develops between the top managers. This not only damages management's effectiveness, but it also destroys the professionals' working environment. The reason is that the professionals are entirely dependent on their manager's ability to resolve interdepartmental issues, and a lack of management trust makes such resolution difficult if not impossible.

A further advantage of confrontation is the motivation it provides to find all the facts and to understand their implications. When there is a disagreement, each party works hard to find anything which will support his or her point of view. This is why Alfred P. Sloan, the founder of General Motors, used to say that no important decision should be made unless there is some contention.[3]

MANAGEMENT ROLES

Since technical teams as a whole generally make better decisions than their members can separately, it would seem logical that management teams would behave in much the same way. This is not always the case, however, because the members of technical groups typically represent themselves; but the managers must consider their departmental constituencies. Technical people are frequently constrained by their managers on administrative or resource questions, but their technical views are usually left pretty much up to them. This is why purely professional groups that have the time to thoroughly explore an issue rarely have trouble reaching technical agreement.

On a management team, however, the members each represent their departmental constituency. Their people depend on them for support, and the managers know that their people will be deeply concerned if they do not stand up for their interests. Managers, therefore, must insist that their own department get fair treatment in all organizational trade-offs. Every department needs space, people, computer time, services, and many other resources that are in short supply. Since such zero-sum situations always have winners and losers, they can rarely be settled by consensus.

A simple experiment in group dynamics demonstrates the enormous power of a constituency in such debates. A group of sixteen people is first divided into four four-person teams, each is asked to make some simple decision like selecting the name for a new product. To give the experiment some realism, a meaningful prize is offered to the team whose selection is accepted by the entire group. It doesn't make much difference what this prize is, however, since experience shows that no one can win it. Once each team has made its separate choice, one member is selected from each group to sit on a new four-person team which will select the winner from these four initial candidates. This final team now holds its discussions in view of the entire group. Invariably, not one of the members of this new team will agree that any solution is superior to the name selected by his or her initial group. They each feel constrained to support their constituency, and this loyalty destroys their ability to make an objective selection.

TEAM COOPERATION

In the real working environment, managers face a complex array of pressures which they must resolve in order to perform. On occasion, managers must compromise their department's interests to meet the broader goals of their management. This, however, puts them in a difficult position, for if they do so too easily, their people will sense their lack of support; but if they do not work cooperatively with the other managers, their peers and superiors will see them as parochial.

Managers sometimes feel they must choose between these extremes. Those who choose loyalty to their people lose influence in the management team and soon find their departments isolated. When managers find that one department head will not objectively make the normal trade-offs needed to resolve their daily issues, they cease to cooperate with him or her, and their people generally follow suit. Then simple things like borrowing a laboratory instrument or adjusting a meeting schedule become more difficult.

On the other hand, when managers honestly try to cooperate with their peers, they can have the reverse problem. The other managers will generally see such managers as cooperative, but their people will suspect that they are trying to curry favor with the boss at their expense. Every department needs the help and support of an effective manager, and when he or she is too anxious to please the boss or doesn't have the guts to fight for the department's interests, their jobs become more difficult. When carried to extremes, such managers are even reluctant to talk openly with their people because they can't explain what they have done in terms that are acceptable to them. As a result, managers who do not fight aggressively for their groups often become distant, uncommunicative, and, eventually, totally ineffective.

Obviously, some middle ground is desirable. Managers each represent knowledgeable groups, and they should vigorously defend their group's interests in their dealings with the management team. If the manager doesn't speak up, decisions that involve the group will not be as informed, and overall performance will likely suffer. On the other hand, a manager's parochial focus on the needs of his or her own people must also be tempered by broader considerations. When a decision must run counter to their department's interests, managers' views should be respectfully heard and considered. If the decision still goes against them, the logic behind the final conclusion should be clearly explained so that they in turn can explain it to their people. The people will then see that their interests have been considered and be more likely to accept and support the final decision.

MANAGEMENT SCOPE

Jobs, as stated in the job descriptions and tables of organization, typically have a defined scope and set of responsibilities. This formal structure helps the managers to understand their relationships with each other as well as defines the actions they can take on their own. The way job scopes are defined, however, can make an enormous difference. Too precise and rigid a structure will provide little management flexibility, but responsibilities that are too loosely defined can be confusing. The managers will then be unsure of their roles and less confident of acting on their own initiative.

Their view of this question changes dramatically as managers advance higher in the organization. At the first line, they will generally expect their superiors to clear up this interdepartmental confusion by precisely specifying each manager's job. They see job overlaps as wasteful and confusing and cannot understand why the boss doesn't resolve all this mess with one simple directive. No technical leaders, however, can precisely structure their managers' jobs in a clear and unambiguous way, so the formal organization will always be out of date; and senior managers must expect their subordinates to adjust their behavior to accommodate the changing situation.

An overall set of goals and statement of responsibilities helps to provide a working framework for the managers. They must, however, learn to adjust their own roles to meet new needs and unanticipated situations. Only in this way can the management team keep pace with the rapid changes in their working environment.

TRANSPARENT MANAGEMENT

Transparent managers are those who merely pass instructions from superior to subordinate without assuming any responsibility. When, for example, their people ask them why a decision was made, they tell them that senior management has so directed. They may have an opinion on why the decision was made, but they make it clear that they are in no way responsible.

Although this is by no means the normal management attitude, senior managers often force their subordinates to behave this way. When managers are not involved in a decision that impacts their department, they will have trouble understanding it. Since most decisions involve many complex trade-offs, any managers who have not been involved won't be able to explain the logic to their people. They will thus be tempted to blame these decisions on "those idiots upstairs," particularly if they don't agree. Although they would be wise to admit they didn't understand and promise to find out, this is hard to do. The managers are thus tempted to put the blame where it really belongs: with the superiors who kept them in the dark.

Although this reaction is often quite justified, it unfortunately harms the subordinate managers far more than their superiors. By acting in this way, they demonstrate to their people that they are not part of the management team, that they do not represent senior management, and that they are powerless to protect their interests. Since motivated professionals need the help and support of an effective manager, transparent managers quickly lose the respect of their people, and this can severely limit their value to the organization.

BUILDING THE MANAGEMENT TEAM

It is not easy to weld a group of ambitious, contentious, and aggressive managers into a cooperative and effective team. It can be done, however, and the first step is to respect the managers' obligations to their own people. When a decision affects their department, they should be involved from the outset, and their views carefully weighed, even when it is known in advance that they are opposed. Any disagreement should be openly discussed, all the issues considered, and the key alternatives evaluated before a decision is made. When this is done openly, the managers will understand the issues and be better able to explain the conclusions to their people.

One advantage of this is that the managers will recognize new issues when they are raised by their people. If they were not considered during the decision making, the managers will thus be better able to reopen the discussion to insure a more complete evaluation. It is surprising how often the working professionals will see problems that their managers had not considered. Often, such a reassessment can cause a change in the plan and result in a better final result. By insuring that all affected managers are truly part of the decision making, the organization is best able to utilize the knowledge and creativity of all its people.

Although it is important to have the managers sit in on all the key decision meetings, this alone will not build an effective management team. True participation requires active involvement, and the environment must encourage debate and contention. Even experienced and capable managers are reluctant to object when everyone agrees, for it takes enormous self-confidence to voice the lone counter opinion. This, however, is often the necessary first step in preventing a serious mistake. If senior managers truly want to understand all their managers' views, they must provide an environment where everyone feels comfortable about raising questions and voicing disagreements.

The final step in this team-building process is actually to encourage the management team members to work together as a cohesive unit. One senior manager did this quite effectively when he learned that his approved department budget had to be cut by $800,000. The overall division plan was due to be submitted, and an error had just been found in the departmental allocations which produced too expensive a total plan. All the departments had to make similar cuts to bring this plan into balance. Since this senior manager's cut was only about 3 percent, he was tempted to arbitrarily reduce everybody's budget by the same percentage. His people had worked hard to put together a very comprehensive plan, however, so he was reluctant to be arbitrary.

He called his top managers together to explain the situation and emphasized the futility of an appeal. He said he was willing to make an arbitrary cut but wanted to see if his managers had any better ideas. In the ensuing discussion, they each proposed various cuts in the other departments but none of them were willing to offer up anything from their own group. The senior manager finally concluded that he would have to make the cut himself, but he offered to leave them alone for an hour to see if they could work out a better answer. None of them knew what the senior manager would cut, so they spent the next hour reassessing their priorities. They finally concluded that one major project should be completely eliminated and two others delayed, with the rest of the plan left as before. The senior manager agreed with this proposal after they explained why they had decided on this new plan.

When the entire management team works together openly and honestly, it will invariably produce the best results. These are typically some of the most capable and best informed people in the organization, and they, as a group, are best able to balance overall technical and business issues and decide on a truly sound plan of action. When they understand the decisions, believe they are right, and can defend them to their people, the professionals will know that their needs have been considered and will be better able to work energetically on the new plan.

NOTES CHAPTER 17

1. Lee Iacocca and William Novak, *Iacocca: An Autobiography* (New York: Bantam Books, Inc., 1984), p. 166.

2. Paul R. Lawrence and Jay W. Lorsch, ''Organization and Environment: Managing Differentiation and Integration,'' Graduate School of Business Administration, Harvard University, Boston, 1967, p. 73.

3. Alfred P. Sloan, Jr., *My Years with General Motors* (Garden City, New York: Doubleday & Co., Inc., 1964).

18

Integration

and Disintegration

The primary reason for establishing an organization structure is to allocate the work among the people who have to do it. If one person could do the entire job by himself or herself, no organization would be needed; but with two or more people, things become more complicated. Jay Galbraith uses the example of carpenters working on the interlocking faces of a joint to describe the kind of problems that can arise. When one carpenter does the entire job, he or she can easily decide what to do when the two parts don't fit. When two carpenters are involved, however, they must first decide how to divide the work between them, then identify the problem, and finally figure out how to fix it.[1]

People are sensitive about mistakes, and no one likes to fix someone else's problems. Team efforts thus invariably raise questions of blame, and fundamental decisions involve how the work should be divided up, how to determine if the pieces fit, what needs to be changed to correct any ensuing problems, and who should do it. The debates over these issues can become intense both because the workers each believe they did their job properly and because they don't want to be blamed for someone else's mistakes. Although in their separate functional terms, they each probably did their best, there is a problem. It is, however, not *with* them but *between* them.

When two professionals work closely together, they can usually resolve their coordination problems quickly and informally. They both understand the total job, and they are generally on good enough personal terms to want to support each other. In larger groups informal coordination can still work as long as everyone shares a common goal and understands what the entire team is doing. As job size increases, however, a point is soon reached where the work must be divided among several teams. This now changes the situation completely, because these separate teams no longer share the common bond of membership, and they are less able to settle their differences without management's help.

An example of this is a military project to design a secure voice communications system. The electronics team was charged with designing the circuits, and the mechanical engineering group was to devise a packaging structure that would withstand rugged army field conditions. Although these two teams shared the same general objectives, they did not work together very smoothly. The electronics group was preoccupied with circuit design problems and couldn't be bothered with power and space considerations, while the mechanical engineers had to know the size and weight of the power supplies before they could start their work. The situation was further complicated by the tight schedule and the need to order specially fabricated structural members early enough to meet the manufacturing schedule. The transformers were critical to this design, and they could not be specified until the circuit power requirements were known. This in turn could not be accurately estimated until the circuit designs were completed.

The relations between these two groups got progressively worse until the department manager finally decided to combine them into a single effort with one project leader. The leader of the electronics group was given this job, and he quickly realized that the mechanical engineers had a real problem. They could not possibly finish their work on time unless the electronics engineers made a reasonably accurate estimate of power consumption. The project leader knew the circuit designs weren't done, but he ordered a complete power study and then added a contingency to take care of changes. Although some later adjustments were needed, this estimate was close enough to permit the mechanical engineers to start work, and the project was finished close to its original schedule.

In many organizational conflicts each team is completely correct in its own narrow terms. The electronics people really did not know the power needs, and they were properly reluctant to make an inaccurate guess. On the other hand, the mechanical team had to start the design so that the long lead-time parts could be ordered. Making the leader of the electronics group the manager of the total project and having him balance these conflicting views turned out to be an effective way to resolve this impasse.

PROJECT MANAGEMENT

Lawrence and Lorsch have studied ten corporations in three different industries to find out just how important the project management function is to corporate success.[2] They found a close correlation between the effectiveness of the project management system and corporate profit growth. They also found that the most effective groups used a formal management process to couple the working elements of each project into an orderly and efficient whole.

The design of a new device, such as a telephone handset, illustrates some of the problems of commercial project management. Starting with the requirements phase, the development team first addresses the problems customers have reported with prior units and any information that can be obtained on the features they would find most desirable. The characteristics of the leading competitive instruments are also examined, and price and manufacturing volume targets are established. Next, the design phase starts with work in such areas as electronics, acoustics, packaging, styling, and safety. As the design progresses, serviceability must be considered, as should manufacturing costs and production tooling. The final development steps include market planning, pricing, production scheduling, and service planning.

Even for such a seemingly simple device as a telephone handset, the involvement of a great many different specialists is required at almost every development phase. One way to manage all these different efforts would be to assemble everybody into one large team. This would have the desirable advantage of minimizing the coordination problems, but it would also introduce the practical problems of recruiting. The manufacturing experts, for example, would not be needed until the design was nearly completed. Similarly, the marketing people would only be busy at the beginning when the requirements were being established and near the end during sales planning. Since every project requires a constantly changing mix of talents, full self-sufficiency would require the perpetual recruiting of needed skills. If the project manager was saddled with this chore, he or she would have little time left for anything else.

The common answer to this problem is to use specialized support departments to provide needed skills to all the projects as required. A market research group, for example, would help every project with customer preference data and market introduction planning. Styling, cost estimating, manufacturing engineering, forecasting, and pricing are also commonly handled in this way. Typically, project managers have a core team with the talents needed for the major technical work, and they obtain support from these specialist groups for everything else.

SUPPORT PROBLEMS

Specialist support departments thus play an essential part in any technical organization, but they are also subject to various problems. As they grow larger, for example, they frequently lose touch with their end users and forget that their real purpose is to help the project teams. As soon as these specialists begin to think of their specialty as an end in itself, they become much harder for the project people to deal with.

Large staffs are also popular targets for budget cutting. Since they are generally unpopular with the project groups, they invariably have trouble defending their plans. As a result, the larger a support staff becomes, the more likely it is to be understaffed and overloaded. At this point, it is often possible to divide it into several smaller staffs which can each still be large enough to smooth project work load and retain a critical mass of technical skill. These groups can then be assigned to the major development departments so that one specialized staff will be dedicated to serve each one. This permits the organization to have many of the benefits of a project structure and much of the efficiency of specialized staffs.

An example of this was the data processing department which supported a large development laboratory. The computers were run very efficiently, but everybody complained about the shortage of computer time. Terminal response finally became so bad that weekly meetings were needed to allocate the limited number of sign-ons which could be practically serviced. Since inadequate computing was now blamed for almost every problem in the laboratory, the laboratory manager decided to launch a study to see what could be done. He found that much of the work load could be handled by smaller computer facilities managed by each of the line projects. When this change was made, the development people were happier, the coordination meetings were eliminated, and the development managers each could be held responsible for their project's performance. Although these separate departmental computing facilities weren't run as efficiently as before, response time was much better, and overall departmental efficiency was significantly improved.

THE ELEMENTS OF STRUCTURE

Edward P. Hawthorne explains that the balance between specialized support groups and dedicated project teams presents a fundamental organizational conflict.[3] The dynamic and relatively flexible projects typically respond very quickly to the changing needs of technology, and they thus provide a strong source of instability in the otherwise stable administrative and support structure. The specialized support groups, on the other hand, are most concerned with advancing the state of the art, and they thus resist the periodic and disruptive crash efforts common to challenging projects.

Every organizational structure has advantages and disadvantages, and it is rare to have any one pure structure. Some dedicated project effort is always required, and there invariably are a few specialties which must be handled by dedicated support groups. At one extreme, large teams can be nearly self-sufficient. This, however, introduces the question of the maximum practical size of a working group. Pelz found in his studies that the largest teams performed best, but he did not examine groups larger than ten to fifteen engineers and scientists.[4] Since each working team is directed by a single manager, however, it is not generally wise to have teams much larger than this. To provide proper guidance and support, managers must devote a reasonable amount of time to each individual in their group, and with too many people, this is not possible.

As soon as the project team gets larger than one manager can handle, it must be split, and some division of responsibilities is required. The four common structural approaches to this problem are as follows:[5]

1. Subject Discipline—Here, all the people are grouped according to their area of specialization, such as electrical engineering, mechanical engineering, or acoustics; and project coordination is a staff responsibility.

2. Stage Phase—In this case the organization is made up of departments which each handle one project phase, such as requirements, design, test, and manufacturing; and project responsibility is moved from one department to another as the work progresses. In the interest of continuity, it is common to move the manager and some of the people along with the project at each such transition.

3. Product Type—Here, each group focuses on a specific product set, such as radios, televisions, or stereos. The people in the television development group, for example, would move relatively freely from one television project to another to fill current staffing needs. This arrangement is generally used for relatively small and short-term projects, and department managers act as the project leader for all their projects at the same time.

4. Project Type—In this case, each group is entirely dedicated to a specific project, such as the development of a computer program or of an aircraft engine. Department heads are the project managers, and all their people are dedicated to this one activity.

SPECIALIST DEPARTMENTS

Regardless of the way the organization is set up, there will always be problems in the way the work is divided between the project teams and the supporting specialist departments. Some of the advantages of using specialist support groups are the following:

1. Specialists are best managed in a department where they can work with their peers and be guided by technically competent managers. It is hard, for example, for research chemists to do competent work without a suitably equipped laboratory, a knowledgeable manager, or association with other professionals who understand their work.

2. Most specialists are only required by any given project for a relatively brief period, and when one group needs more help, another will often need less. A support department can smooth this work load more efficiently than any one project could possibly do for itself.

3. When a project gets into trouble, the support specialists are better able to blow the whistle. This invariably causes friction with line management, but it also increases the visibility of controversial issues and improves the quality of project decisions.

These advantages of specialist departments are compelling, but there are also good reasons for assigning as many of the specialists as possible directly to the project teams:

1. If they have all the resources under their control, project managers have no need to get agreement from the support-group managers, and they can thus make faster decisions.

2. Support groups make convenient scapegoats when a project gets in trouble, and it is easier to measure project managers' performance when they control all the resources they need.

3. Comprehensive project responsibility provides one of the best training grounds for future technical leaders.

4. A closely knit project team develops the esprit de corps needed to produce superior results.

Although there are no simple answers, it is generally best to retain scarce specialized skills in support departments; but once this talent becomes more widely available, the need for specialist groups should be reconsidered. In most cases it is wise to split such large support efforts and divide the skills among the projects. The key exceptions are such business control functions as pricing, accounting, cost estimating, and market forecasting, which are often kept in separately managed staffs to insure better financial control. Research, advanced technology, and various kinds of specialized tool support should also be protected, or the projects will soon divert their resources to meet the next crisis. Other than these limited exceptions, if there is any serious doubt, it is wisest to assign the responsibilities and the resources directly to the project manager.

THE INTEGRATION JOB

Although there is no best way to divide up the work between the line project organizations and the specialist support groups, there is compelling evidence that some form of project control structure is important. Badawy, for example, cites data from companies such as Shell Oil, Dow Corning, and TRW to show that matrixlike integration structures can be highly successful.[6]

The purpose of the integration function is to coordinate the many parts of the project into an effective final result. Another, and perhaps more important, reason is to provide each project with a general business focus. In any large organization, the senior executives personally set the business direction and establish overall objectives, but they must depend on others to do the direct work which generates revenue and profit. This is the role of the people in such functional areas as development, sales, manufacturing, and service. They are responsibile for delivering products and services to paying customers, and although they all work in support of the company's overall aims, they are each constrained by their functional focus. A sales team, for example, is most concerned with getting an important order, but a manufacturing team must emphasize product quality and cost. These are all vital efforts, but since they all have a functional bias, an integrator is needed to relate them to overall corporate needs. In short, the job of integrators is to run their project as if they were the company president.

THE INTEGRATOR'S ROLE

Integrators thus have three overriding concerns: customer satisfaction, profit, and competitive superiority. Their primary objective is to satisfy customers' needs in a technically superior and profitable way. This requires that they know the customer and competitive pressures as well as the technical and financial aspects of their project.

Once a project is under way it generally achieves a momentum of its own, but this is only after the initial direction has been set. These directional decisions, however, are hard to make unless senior management has given some individual the authority to make them. The integrator serves just this purpose and is empowered both to set the initial direction and to resolve the ongoing functional disputes so that the organization can work effectively towards the agreed goal. Integrators thus are the official project champion, and they are responsible for deciding what to do and seeing that it gets done.

Integrators are also responsible for project control. They insure that the project objectives will meet business needs, and they obtain the resources to do the work. They conduct project reviews, manage the control staff, and track progress. To help with these tasks, they may have line responsibility for such pivotal functions as planning, architecture, standards, or system test.

The integrator must also have the full backing of senior management. Lawrence and Lorsch cite an example where the lack of a properly supported integration responsibility caused one company to have damaging contention between its production and engineering departments.

> The informal integrators were unable to achieve effective collaboration, at least in part because their roles were not clearly defined. Therefore, their integrative attempts were often seen as inappropriate infringements on the domains of other departments.[7]

As a result, there was intense competition and damaging conflict between the production and the engineering managers.

INTEGRATION EXAMPLES

With proper management support many different kinds of integration structures can be effective. At one extreme, informal committees can provide the coordination focus, but at the other end of the scale, entire organizations may be required. Intel, for example, has about twenty-five strategic business segments, and they use a loose structure of coordination committees to make the operational decisions. Robert Noyce, one of Intel's founders, says that ''workers may have several bosses depending on the problem at hand. Instead of staff specialists for purchasing, quality control and so on, Intel has several dozen committees or councils that make decisions and enforce standards in specialized fields."[8]

The matrix structure, as used at Dow Corning, is more formal. For each of their ten major business areas, they have established a business manager who holds profit responsibility and reports to a senior corporate executive. This business manager operates through a business board whose members are drawn from the various specialist cost centers which house the working professionals. Through these boards, the business managers have both the authority and the control over the resources needed to meet their project goals.[9]

Boeing used a different structure for the development of the 747 jet aircraft. This was such a massive project that they named a special branch manager who was given responsibility for all 747 manufacturing and development. He also had a program management department reporting directly to him which coordinated the work of these two massive line organizations through a change board and a centralized information system.[10]

INTEGRATION RESPONSIBILITY

There are many ways to break a project into separate implementable parts, but the principle issue is to insure that these parts can be put back together again at the end. This is the job of integration, and there is no standard way to do it. Sometimes entire departments are devoted to coordination and control, but in other cases it can be effectively done with no formality at all. With small projects or relatively stable technologies, informal integration is often entirely adequate, but more formality is generally needed as the projects become larger, involve more disciplines, or encounter rapid technical change. While there are no universal guidelines, integration can be very expensive, so informal methods should be used wherever possible.

One way to see if an organization has integration problems is to consider the following questions for each of the key projects:

1. Who is responsible for meeting the customer's needs?
2. Who is answerable for profitability?
3. Who is accountable for competitive superiority?

If no one can be clearly identified with each of these responsibilities and if any of them have been a source of trouble, there is undoubtedly an integration problem. When no one has been specifically assigned such roles, the senior manager over all the project elements becomes the de facto integrator. Since most large projects span engineering, manufacturing, marketing, and service, few companies have such a common manager below the company president. Company presidents undoubtedly make good integrators, but few of them can afford to dedicate the amount of time required to one single project.

STRUCTURAL PARALYSIS

Every structure has advantages and disadvantages, but they all share a common problem when the organizations become large. Here, the many different projects must all contend for the same scarce resources. One way to handle this is to use special staff oversight groups who can identify and resolve interproject issues. These staffs, however, also add to the organization structure, reduce efficiency, and require management themselves. If not properly controlled, they will grow until the cost and complexity of the organization can themselves become a problem.

Blackburn draws an interesting parallel between organizations and large biological systems.[11] He points out that the tropical rain forest develops a larger and more complex structure as it grows, and this structure requires a progressively larger share of the ecosystem's total reserves of energy. As growth progresses, this "overhead" gradually reduces net system productivity until the energy consumed by the structure equals the total capacity of the system; net productivity then reaches zero, and growth stops.

The structure of large technical organizations can follow a similar cycle. When projects become very large, they require many teams of technical people who don't individually understand the total project, know the other teams working on the job, or appreciate very many of the project-wide problems. Here, informal relationships can no longer suffice, and more formal coordination methods are needed.

The various practical coordination methods all use staffs of one kind or another to watch and direct the technical professionals. The working engineers and scientists, however, typically know their technical assignments quite well, and they begin to resent this increasing outside interference. As the number and size of these staffs grows, the professionals' resentment increases along with it, and this both reduces their initiative and makes them less willing to voluntarily adjust their work to meet the changing needs of the rest of the organization. The increasing friction between the teams then requires more management involvement and more staffs to help identify and resolve the resulting issues. At some point, as in the tropical rain forest, further structure is added solely to support and control the rest of the structure.

There is no single universal answer which resolves all these issues. Large technical projects invariably require increasing amounts of formal integration and control. A properly structured and managed integration function, however, can help to control these structural problems.

NOTES CHAPTER 18

1. Jay R. Galbraith, *Organization Design*, (Reading, Mass.: Addison-Wesley Publishing Co., Inc., 1977), p. 40.
2. Paul R. Lawrence and Jay W. Lorsch, "New Management Job: The Integrator," *Harvard Business Review*, November–December 1967, p. 142.

3. Edward P. Hawthorne, *The Management of Technology* (Maidenhead, England: McGraw-Hill Book Company (UK) Limited, 1978), p. 102.

4. Donald C. Pelz and Frank M. Andrews: *Scientists in Organizations: Productive Climates for Research and Development* (New York: John Wiley & Sons, Inc., 1966), p. 52.

5. Hawthorne, *Management of Technology* p. 104.

6. M. K. Badawy, *Developing Managerial Skills in Engineers and Scientists: Succeeding as a Technical Manager* (New York: International Thompson Organization Inc., Van Nostrand Reinhold Co., 1982), p. 217.

7. Lawrence and Lorsch, "New Management Job."

8. Steve Lohr, in his January 4, 1981 article in The New York Times, sec. 6, p. 42, "Overhauling America's Business Management," cites this quote by Robert Noyce.

9. William C. Cogan, "How the Multi-Dimensional Structure Works at Dow Corning," *Harvard Business Review on Management* (New York: Harper & Row, Publishers, Inc., 1975).

10. Galbraith, *Organization Design,* p. 195.

11. Thomas R. Blackburn, "Information and the Ecology of Scholars," *Science,* September 1973, p. 1141.

19

Managing Size

As organizations grow, their increasing complexity inhibits individual initiative and reduces the overall effectiveness of the professional people. Hage and Aiken have described several ways in which this can happen:[1]

1. With increasing size, many of the skilled professionals become grouped into specialized departments. This produces a more uniform and less stimulating technical environment.

2. Large organizations often centralize the decision-making process, which reduces communication, submerges conflict, and inhibits innovation.

3. The necessary rules, procedures, and guidelines in large organizations reduce individual initiative by constraining the people within relatively narrowly defined jobs. In such large, and often impersonal, environments, the people tend to believe that anything not explicitly in their job definition must belong to somebody else. They thus feel less responsible for resolving the problems they encounter.

4. With the growing size of the organization, the number of management levels inexorably increases as well. This adds to the communication problems, buries new ideas, conceals problems, and consequently inhibits change.

5. The high-volume focus of many large manufacturing and development organizations necessarily emphasizes predictability as a way to minimize production disruptions. This also increases resistance to change.

6. Very large organizations properly use productivity as a management measure, but this leads to an emphasis on perfecting known methods and avoiding new and unproven ideas. This in turn reduces the organization's willingness to take the risks which necessarily accompany innovation.

THE PROBLEMS OF SIZE

Since managers in large organizations cannot deal with very many of their people in person, they must rely on their management team for much of their communication. If this is not handled properly, they can run into the kinds of problems that Eric faced when he took over a large department. He came to work promptly at seven-thirty every morning and was annoyed by the large number of employees who came straggling in at 9:00 A.M. or even later. His annoyance increased when he realized that some of his senior managers were equally tardy. He brought this issue up at his weekly staff meeting, but his managers did not think the problem was very important. They argued that they worked long hours and were entitled to come in a bit later to compensate. The prior department head had also been in the habit of arriving late, and the managers didn't see where it had caused any problems. While Eric did not disagree with occasional lateness, he also knew that sloppy habits like this tended to get out of hand and that some working-hour discipline was necessary. After a heated discussion, he lost his temper and insisted that the managers get to work by the regular 8:00 A.M. starting time and make sure their people did so as well. To make sure this was done, he had the laboratory security guards count the late arrivers every day and the punctuality problem was soon resolved.

There is no question that tardiness is undesirable, but it is an issue which should be handled by first-line managers. Although Eric's concern was proper, he should not have lost his temper and given a direct order. By doing so, he relieved his managers of their responsibility for punctuality. They could now tell their people to come to work on time because the boss said so. Although this transparent behavior solved the direct punctuality problem, it made Eric appear to be a bureaucratic administrator and damaged his long-term effectiveness.

In well-run organizations very few people straggle in late. When they are busy and challenged by their work, punctuality is not a problem. In an organization with serious attendance problems, the first-level management is typically not properly supervising their people and keeping them busy. Some employees then start to slack off, lose interest in their job, and become attendance problems. When an employee exhibits such behavior, the manager should find out if this loss of job interest is due to poor supervision or if the employee has other and possibly deeper problems which need attention. If Eric had taken the time to explain his concerns and convince his managers of the symbolic importance of punctuality, they would have been better able to enforce it, not as a directive from the boss, but as something they personally believed in.

INDIRECT COMMUNICATION

Whenever senior managers communicate through their management team, there is always the chance for misunderstandings. Not only is there a problem when their people disagree with them, but there is also often real confusion about what they want. Unless senior managers make a very special effort, their pronouncements will generally be confusing, and frequently their people will be reluctant to ask for clarification. When they make a simple request, therefore, there will be several different opinions about what they are really after. The people will then discuss these ideas among themselves, and pretty soon some of them will take on the character of established fact. These rumors are started by the people trying to logically deduce what the boss has in mind, but they are often based on no more than the individual hopes and fears of the people who thought them up.

As a result, one of the greatest problems in large organizations is the people's propensity to misunderstand their senior manager. The larger the organization, the more senior managers' desires will be modified by the chain of command. If they show concern, their people will amplify it, and when they become angry, the people's reactions may approach panic. When top managers' suggestions are amplified by each management level, there is a great risk that their working-level people will spend a large part of their time responding to their casual questions and not really devoting themselves to the truly essential work of the organization.

Unfortunately, this management communication problem is not consistent. Senior managers' instructions, although frequently amplified, can also be attenuated. When their people don't know precisely what senior managers want, rather than make a mistake the people will often hold back and wait for clarification. Experienced professionals know that they are likely to get into trouble when they blindly follow some remote manager's instructions, so they generally take some of the simpler actions; and if real work is required, they stop and wait for further developments. Unless the manager follows up, the professional have so much to do that they will soon forget all about it, and nothing will end up being done.

SPAN OF CONTROL

Beyond about one hundred professionals, a controlling management style is no longer practical. Although this limit depends to some degree on the manager and the kind of work being done, everyone has some limit beyond which he or she can no longer personally make all the decisions. If managers try to exceed this point, they must work incredible hours and acquire a growing staff to track progress and enforce instructions. Even then, they will likely be a serious bottleneck.

In organizations much larger than about one hundred people, therefore, senior managers must rely on their management team to deal directly with the technical professionals. They are now the conduit through which senior managers learn about problems and by which they issue goals and directions. This kind of management, however, involves more than just communication, for here senior managers are too busy to handle many of the decisions that must be made, and they must increasingly delegate responsibilities to their subordinates as well. Then, instead of supervising work, they become more concerned with their managers' goals, performance, and style.

The first step from direct personal control is difficult for most technical managers. Up to this point, their technical knowledge has been their prime talent and the basis for much of their success. Beyond the first level, however, managers must guide their managers and depend more on leadership ability than on technical skill.

INDIRECT MANAGEMENT

This means that managers' leadership style must change as they move up in the organization. First-level managers, for example, work directly with the engineers and scientists and are intimately aware of each of their work assignments and how well they are handling them. Such managers suggest new ways to attack their most difficult problems and praise their achievements. They also know who needs help and who is doing well enough on his or her own.

At the next higher level, second-line managers should focus on how well their first-line managers are handling their people. They are now more concerned with making sure that goals are being pursued, and they have less time to focus on the direct technical work of the professionals. Second-line managers may give some specific instructions, but it is the first-level managers who must see that they are carried out. This difference is fundamental, because the first-level managers must thoroughly understand what the second-level managers want in order to properly direct their people. These second-level managers are doing what is called indirect management, because they are managing through other managers.

Indirect management can cause particularly severe problems in advanced technology because most of the jobs involve many complex technical questions which cannot possibly be anticipated in advance. At each step, new knowledge is gained and new circumstances arise which must be considered before proceeding. When the senior managers are unwilling to delegate much of the technical decision making, the first-level managers, who have the best technical knowledge, can't take action on their own. Since this can cause unacceptable delays and confusion, the most successful management style is for the senior managers to focus on insuring good first-line management understanding of what is wanted and why. When conditions change, they can then make timely decisions themselves without running upstairs for new instructions.

This need for communication becomes progressively more important with each successive management level. The higher managers advance in their organization, the further removed they are from the technical issues, and the more effort they must devote to translating their broader business goals into directions their technical people can understand. When the technical people do not truly appreciate these goals, serious problems often ensue. An example of this came up during the original design of the RCA Spectra 70 computer series in the early 1960s. General David Sarnoff had called for compatibility with the IBM 360 machines, but his people did not fully appreciate his intentions.[2,3] As a result, the finished machines had a few ''improvements'' over the IBM designs, and each of these differences required modifications in the customer's 360 programs before they could run on the new RCA systems. It was thus more difficult for IBM customers to get their programs to run, so the machines were much harder to sell. As a result, these machines were not the success they could have been if Sarnoff's objective of full compatibility had been achieved.

Although fully compatible designs are a technical challenge, they are far from impossible. The RCA engineers could have made their machines fully compatible if they had realized this was the company's objective. Since they did not truly understand Sarnoff's priorities, however, they followed their natural instincts to produce an improved design. Designers have their own views on what makes a better machine, and they are always tempted to make an instruction a little more elegant, to improve the I/O and channel commands, or to make any of the hundreds of changes which are always possible when redesigning an existing system. Any single change destroys full compatibility, however, and although the Spectra 70's "architectural improvements" may have been technically better, they cost RCA the business success Sarnoff had envisioned. It was not until Gene Amdahl produced his fully IBM compatible machines a decade later that the full implications of Sarnoff's concept were demonstrated.

There is always the risk of disaster when engineers and scientists don't understand the business objectives of their management. An objective which is obvious to an executive may never occur to technical professionals. Their intent is an outstanding technical job, and although that is always desirable, there is often a problem in defining the exact criteria for "good." As in the case of the Spectra 70, a seemingly better technical answer can sometimes lead to a business disaster. When they are fully informed, the people can avoid such mistakes, but this requires that management communicate their real objectives in terms they can understand.

INDIRECT LEADERSHIP

When Napoleon was asked how he made his army cross the Alps to defeat Italy, he replied: "One does not *make* a French army cross the Alps; one *leads* it across.⁴ This, of course, is the key to indirect management: to lead rather than direct. When managers of large organizations know what they want done, they must convince their people of the importance of their goals before they can expect to get a great deal accomplished.

Even when managers know what they want done, however, it often takes a great deal of effort to convince their people that they are right. Tom, the manager of a large development group, did not understand this. His people were developing a new programming system, and he knew from experience that performance was undoubtedly going to be a problem. Simulation models had previously been used very successfully to predict programming systems' performance, so he told the development manager to set up a simulation group. After the development manager did, Tom even followed up to make sure it was properly staffed with competent people. After this was done, he felt reassured that the performance issue would be properly handled and turned his attention to other matters.

About a year and a half later, however, this new programming system was ready for test, and its performance was found to be unacceptable. It turned out that the simulation model had been built as Tom had directed, but the system designers had not bothered to use it. Tom had correctly foreseen the problem and had even known how to solve it, but he had failed to convince the design managers that the model would be useful to them. As a result, they did not use it to analyze the performance implications of their designs and did not have any idea how bad performance would be.

When senior managers want to get something complex done, they must convince their subordinate managers of its importance. If they don't and they are unable to stay personally in touch with their subordinate managers' work, their subordinate managers are not likely to do what they want. When senior managers do convince them, however, subordinate managers can properly direct their people, track their progress, and take timely corrective action when things go wrong.

LEADERSHIP PRIORITIES

When dealing with a specific issue, senior managers' actions are usually fairly clear-cut, but when they try to set some new direction, they will almost always be misunderstood. They should stick to goals and objectives and focus increasingly more on what, when, why, and who and progressively less on how.

The case of a vice president shows how effective this can be. In reviewing the results of a customer survey, he became concerned about some of the problems with his company's products. The project manager agreed to do something about them, but he did not have any specific plans. When he was pressed, however, he promised to look into the problems in the next week or so. The vice president still did not feel he was taking the problems seriously enough, so he insisted that the project manager produce an action plan and bring it back to him for review within one week. He didn't tell him which problems to address or how to solve them, but he did insist on immediate and aggressive action. The project manager put his people right to work, and a week later, they had a suitably responsive plan.

NOTES CHAPTER 19

1. Jeffrey Pfeffer, *Organizations and Organization Theory* (Marshfield, Mass.: Pitman, 1982), p. 272.

2. In a private conversation General David Sarnoff is reported to have complained that the Spectra 70 engineers did not have the same kind of standards discipline as the early radio

and television engineers, so that they had not been able to make a truly IBM compatible series of computers.

3. Katharine Fishman, *The Computer Establishment* (New York: Harper & Row, Publishers, Inc., 1981), p. 182.

4. Arnold Brown and Edith Weiner, *Supermanaging* (New York: McGraw-Hill Book Company, 1984), p. 189.

20

Power and Politics

While power is the ability to cause action, politics is the art of obtaining power. Power and politics are important management concerns because they form the basis for all dealings between managers. When managers need help from one another, they must figure out some way to convince the other manager to support them. Occasionally, their job will be to provide such support, they will have planned to provide it, and they will have the resources available. More generally, however, at least some of these conditions will be a problem. Official departmental missions rarely anticipate all such issues in advance, and few organizations have sufficient resources to do their own jobs, let alone provide unplanned support for someone else. Most organizations are thus reluctant to take on additional work, and managers must either use the power of their positions to force compliance or apply their political talents to getting the help they need.

THE NATURE OF POWER

Power can only be measured in relative terms, and managers generally hold significant power only over the people in their own organizations. Staff directors or project managers, however, can have broader powers if they enjoy the confidence and support of some more senior manager. As long as they are believed to actually speak for this manager, they can reflect some of his or her power in their actions.

This, in fact, is one of the most interesting aspects of power. As long as it is successfully used, the power holder will appear more powerful, and he or she can thus act with increasing assurance. In the case of reflected power, however, if staff managers overstep their license and are not supported by senior management, their power base will quickly disappear because the other managers will realize that their perceptions of their power were exaggerated. Staff heads can thus wield immense power as long as they are careful not to overstep the limits of their senior executive's support.

HOW POWER AFFECTS THE USER

Based on his research Kipnis suggests that the successful exercise of power "strengthens the power-holder's belief that he or she controls the other person."[1] In fact, when people successfully use strong or coercive tactics, they see themselves as more powerful and the person they control as less so. In an experiment, Kipnis measured the performance of two hundred business students whom he had act as managers of a small manufacturing operation. Some of them were told to behave as highly authoritarian managers and to give their "employees" no latitude in their work. The rest were instructed to behave democratically and to involve their people in the working decisions.

The specific work was a simple parts assembly in which performance could be easily measured. They found that all the employees produced roughly equivalent results regardless of the manager's style but that the managers' evaluations of their people were radically different.

> [The] authoritarian leaders routinely complained that their employees were not moti-
> vated to work hard. They also evaluated their employees' work less favorably than
> democratic leaders did. That is, the authoritarians rated their workers as less suitable for
> promotion and downplayed their skills and talents.

This is counter to almost every traditional view of management. The common conception is that people's performance is affected by managers' style and that managers' opinions of them are based on their performance. Kipnis's work implies that the primary determinant of job ratings is the manager's own behavior and that his or her style, at least for very simple tasks, does not affect workers' output. Considered another way, managers' use of their power over their people determines how well they evaluate their people, almost regardless of their performance. An authoritarian management style thus not only demotivates people, but it also actually damages them. This is because managers' opinion of their people determines their people's opportunities for advancement, and when managers' authoritarian behavior reduces this opinion, their prospects for advancement are reduced, possibly for the rest of their working careers. At the lowest working levels, there are often fairly objective performance measures, but for more senior managers, this suggests that ratings be based not so much on their groups' objective performance as on the managers' ability to identify and develop their best people.

AUTHORITY

Legitimate power is the authority officially given managers by the organization. They obtain it when they assume their job, and they lose it just as quickly. This is often hard for people to accept, for once they have held powerful jobs, they somehow begin to feel they have become powerful people. A senior manager from a small regional office was promoted to headquarters. He had grown accustomed to being the top man with a corner office and comfortable upholstered furniture. He belonged to the best clubs, the local papers reported his activities, and he was frequently recognized at social occasions. On moving to the headquarters staff, he was given a small office on an inside aisle and shared a secretary with two other staff members. Even though his position was now more important in the corporate hierarchy, he had lost his power of office and the feeling of superiority that went with it.

Legitimate power carries great weight. It includes the authority to hire and fire, set salaries, and make job assignments. Without managerial backing, people cannot be promoted, and managers are the prime source of nominations for management development opportunities. Although these formal powers are rarely expressed, they are well understood and underlie all managers' dealings with their people. No threats or even hints of threats are needed because the professionals intuitively know that their manager is the single most important person in their working lives.

BLIND OBEDIENCE

An interesting characteristic of legitimate power was demonstrated by Leavitt some years ago.[2] A series of experiments were conducted with paid volunteers to demonstrate the degree to which people will blindly accept orders from a legitimate power figure.

> [They] were asked to help as "teachers" in a teaching experiment designed to test the effects of punishment on learning. They were given an electric shocking device and told to push the shock button every time they "learner" in the next room gave a wrong answer. They were also told to increase the intensity of shock with each wrong answer, if necessary, up to a point on the shock machine scale marked with danger warnings. The "learner" in the next room was actually part of the experimental team. His job was to groan and on occasion scream in pain as the shock got stronger. He would, in late stages of the experiment, beg to be released and complain that he was suffering from a heart ailment.

Leavitt goes on to say that

> the results came as a surprise both to the researchers themselves and to many other presumably sophisticated observers. They had forecast that very few subjects would push the shock buttons all the way. In fact, about 50 percent (and somewhere around that

figure seems to hold up for many kinds of subjects) followed orders to the hilt, even while thinking that they were inflicting very severe electric shocks on a screaming middle-aged man with heart disease. ˙

The authority of position is thus very powerful, and it seems to stem more from the badge of office than from the manager's ability to hire, fire, and promote. The simple fact that managers have been put in charge somehow makes what they say right, regardless of their people's previous values and beliefs. Managers thus have an enormous responsibility for the way their people behave.

THE USE AND ABUSE OF POWER

This phenomenon of blind obedience probably explains Lord Acton's statement that "power tends to corrupt; absolute power corrupts absolutely."[3] Actually, there is compelling evidence that petty powers are even more corrupting than major ones. Rosabeth Moss Kanter cites a study of Air Force officers which showed that those with the lowest status and the least advancement potential were most authoritarian in their dealings with subordinates.[4]

The way people abuse their minor powers can be quite frightening, as Professor Zimbardo of the Stanford University psychology department showed.[5] He advertised in the local newspaper for volunteers to participate in a "prison" experiment. Early one Saturday the "prisoners" were picked up, "booked," and enclosed in a wallboard "prison" in the basement of the Stanford University psychology building. Some of the volunteers were randomly selected to act as guards and the rest were treated as inmates. Zimbardo reports that in only a few hours the "guards" started to act like real guards and the "prisoners" behaved like typical prisoners. By the end of the first day some of the guards had physically and psychologically abused some of their charges, and by the end of the second day two of the prisoners had to be released for severe psychiatric problems. In only four days of the planned ten day experiment "Warden" Zimbardo stopped the experiment because, as he said, he was "afraid of his own behavior as well as that of the others."

Kipnis points out that when people impose their will on others, they are more likely to do so again.[6] This is because the successful use of power reinforces the power holder's self-confidence and undermines that of the person being controlled. Further, those managers who have the least actual leverage are most likely to resort to threats and coercion. This, however, is often counterproductive because the power behind a threat is the fear of punishment, and the minute the punishment is applied, the power is gone. People with little power thus tend to diminish it through misuse, while the more powerful gradually increase their strength by using it effectively.

People's attitudes also adapt very quickly to their power position. Lieberman studied a large number of factory workers and found that the attitudes of foremen were quite different from those of the regular workers. Further, when employees were promoted to foreman, they soon behaved just like the other foremen.[7] When Lieberman later resurveyed the same organizations, some of the foremen had been demoted and they had rapidly reassumed the traditional attitudes of the other workers.

THE POWER OF INFORMATION

Pfeffer uses the example of computer programmers to demonstrate how knowledge can provide an important source of leverage.[8] To either use or service programs, manuals are needed, but as important as these materials are, the most frequent complaint about application programs is lack of adequate documentation. As Pfeffer points out, "this inadequate documentation makes those involved in developing the system quite powerful." The programmers hold power based on their unique knowledge, and this power is reduced the minute they produce complete and readable manuals. It is thus little wonder that they are often reluctant to do so.

Leavitt has studied the flow of information in organizations and has shown that control over the sources of information also provides considerable leverage.[9] He arranged test subjects so that they could only communicate in prescribed ways. In one case one subject was placed at the hub of the communication network, so that everyone had to work through him; but in a second case everyone was given equal access. After running a number of tests, Leavitt found that those who had control over the flow of information were invariably seen by the rest as powerful figures, and everyone else felt relatively powerless.

Managers are often the primary source of information for their people. They give assignments and evaluate performance. They are the conduit for personnel policies and salary information, and they are the contact with the organization's management team. Thus the employees must learn of changes in work plans, their own personal working situation, or modifications in the organization structure through their manager. In short, managers, in addition to their legitimate power, also have great power over the information their people receive.

THE DISTRIBUTION OF POWER

The way power is distributed in organizations has a profound effect on the way people behave. In a typical university, for example, there generally is a faculty senate which sets basic policy and approves major decisions. The debates over these issues can be long and acrimonious, and committees are frequently convened to explore the facts and develop a consensus. In corporations, on the other hand, control is typically vested in chief executives, who act under the general guidance of a board of directors. They personally hold all the official power in the organization and delegate it as they choose through the organization structure.

The university has the advantage of a wide distribution of power, which insures the involvement of many people in the decision process and provides ample opportunity for discussion and contention. Decisions are often made slowly and laboriously, but this wide involvement provides a broader base of support for the resulting actions and a more fertile environment for creative ideas. Conversely, in most corporations, the pace is generally too hectic to permit extensive committee debates, and the decision process must be geared for competitive reaction and rapid technological change. Although this centralized authority structure can generally react very quickly, it can also stifle creativity.

POWER AND POLITICAL BEHAVIOR

The level of political activity also depends on the way power is distributed in the organization. If each member of the management team has a comparable power base, issues will be widely debated, and the most controversial decisions will be completely aired. This result is generally desirable, but relatively wide and even power distribution can also result in extensive debates and an apparent lack of direction. When power is centralized in a strong leader, however, there is little room for political maneuver, contention is suppressed, and the focus is on the facts which will assist the power holder in the decision process. The leadership style and level of political activity in most organizations fluctuates between these extremes.

Political behavior is often seen by management as indirect and underhanded, and their natural reaction is to stamp it out. This can be done by simply strengthening central control and making most members of the organization relatively powerless. Although this reduces contention and submerges natural conflicts, Pfeffer notes that it only "provides the appearance of rationality and satisfies social expectations concerning order."[10] Unfortunately, the resulting neatness merely papers over the inherent conflicts in the organization without resolving them. As Pfeffer adds: ". . . most organizations operate under the guise of rationality with some elements of power and politics thrown in, and thereby manage to obtain the worst of both worlds."[11] Conflict and contention are natural in complex organizations, and they must be dealt with openly. Honest political behavior is a natural and healthy part of this process.

DISHONEST POLITICAL BEHAVIOR

Powerful people can act directly, while the powerless must either submit to them or resort to political activity. Politics provides the powerless a way to enhance their power so that they can have more influence. Although political action is often seen as manipulative and vaguely dishonest, it is perfectly appropriate for such people to privately build evidence to buttress their views and to seek supportive allies.

Unfortunately, highly political situations can also lead to unprincipled behavior. People develop strong loyalties and tend to see issues through the parochial perspectives of their own specialties. Sometimes they can even become so convinced of their position that they will make up those supporting facts that they "know" will be found in time. In presentations they will stress the points that support their own views and suppress the opposing ones. This can generally be rationalized, but it is dishonest to misrepresent facts or suppress those that are pertinent to the other side.

Another political action is managers' attempts to privately convince allies to join their causes. This again is perfectly appropriate as long as it is not carried to the point of final decision. Any attempt to have the final decision made without involving all the contending parties is dishonest politics and usually results in poorer decisions and a deterioration in the level of honesty and trust in the organization.

CLIQUES AND COALITIONS

When individuals band together to increase their power base, they form a political grouping which is called a clique. Cliques generally persist for long periods, and as Tushman says, they form the basic building blocks of political organizations.[12] When several cliques band together to affect an individual decision, this becomes a coalition, which is generally disbanded after the immediate objective is achieved.

The establishment of an engineering quality program demonstrates how this works. Corporate headquarters had issued a directive that every new product was to have higher quality than its predecessor. This policy was broadly accepted in principle, but the engineers did not agree on how to implement it. The service organization unilaterally tried to impose their own plan, but development would not go along. Something had to be done, however, so the technical staff head decided to run a workshop to see if they could work out an agreed-upon development answer. He invited representatives from each of the major development organizations, but they were unable to reach agreement. His staff, however, now understood the issues well enough to make a specific proposal. When this was completed, he met separately with the leaders of the three largest development groups to obtain their agreement, and after negotiating some changes they all accepted the proposal.

With this basic agreement, the staff head circulated his proposal to the other development groups. They were each given thirty days to respond with a position or specific examples of any problems. These managers had limited resources to do this added work, so only a few of them raised new issues. These were quickly addressed, and then these groups also fell into line. With this base of agreement across the entire development organization, the quality staff, the service department, and the other staffs all quickly agreed.

The political debates required to build a coalition can take a lot of time, but they can also produce very good decisions. As each faction builds the case to support its own position, it obtains more data and can make progressively more informed judgments. When sufficient time is allowed to hear all the positions, most groups will typically support the most logical and best supported story, and this is also most likely to be the soundest position for the overall organization as well. This process only works, however, when all concerned groups are actively involved and the process is open and public.

COMMITTEES AND TASK FORCES

The members of a properly formed coalition should be well informed and thoroughly convinced on the issues. Until this point is reached, there is always the risk that some members will change their mind when an opposing faction tries to win them over. One way to obtain this informed conviction is to use committees or task forces to study the issues and make recommendations. When the most knowledgeable people from each group are involved in the task force, they can usually win over their home departments to their final conclusions. Although an informed and aggressive task force member-ship is invariably hard to manage, it generally produces the most creative and enduring results. There is ample evidence to show that such heterogeneous groups of outspoken professionals produce far better work than uniform, well-behaved ones.[13]

Task forces, however, have limitations, as Lippitt and Mackenzie found by studying the performance of faculty committees at the University of Kansas.[14] They found that such groups were most effective when used to gain broad acceptance of an already defined decision. Although the larger groups were the hardest to control, they found that those task forces with members taken from all the involved factions were also the most likely to achieve a broad consensus. Even when some groups had little to contribute, their representation both kept them informed and helped to gain their allegiance.

One of the major risks of task forces and committees is their propensity to compromise. This may be politically desirable, but it rarely produces a superior technical result. A good principle to follow, therefore, is to use large task groups to achieve a political consensus on managerial, procedural, and strategic issues. These questions rarely have a single best answer, so the objective is to get all the concerned groups to agree with the final recommendation. When the issues are largely technical, however, smaller expert groups should explicitly focus on the technical points in question with the objective of finding a truly superior solution.

CO-OPTATION

Occasionally, one opposing group ends up not agreeing with the final conclusion. Although this may not always be a problem, sometimes it is important to gain their allegiance. Co-optation is a way to do this by having an influential member of the opposition take an important role in the new effort. When people see the issues from this different vantage point, they invariably end up contributing to the program's success. When IBM introduced PL/1, a new programming language, the Fortran user community vigorously opposed it, because they felt that IBM's Fortran support would be reduced. Lois Frampton was the chairperson of the Fortran users group at the time, and she energetically championed her constituency's interests. Her vigorous opposition, however, also demonstrated her managerial talents and made her a logical choice to head the new PL/1 user committee. Once she was convinced that this new direction made long-term technical sense, she took the job and made important contributions to early user acceptance of the PL/1 programming language.

THE BUREAUCRACY

The behavior of bureaucracies demonstrates the political behavior of powerless people. The role of the bureaucracy is to handle such routine tasks as issuing pay checks, heating the buildings, and running the cafeteria. Although these details are all essential, the senior managers can't take the time to attend to them. Each one is thus reduced to a set of rules and procedures and given to an administrative function to handle.

As Hague and Aiken point out, the routine nature of bureaucratic work eliminates uncertainty, reduces complexity, and requires less skill. This ends up making such workers fairly easy to replace and thus relatively powerless.[15] According to Rosabeth Moss Kanter such powerless people become rules-minded by "invoking organization rules and insisting on careful adherence to them.[16]

Although line management can generally win any single battle with the bureaucracy, each struggle takes a lot of effort, and few managers have the time or inclination to do so very often. The case of the programmer from the New York office shows the kind of effort which is generally required. On Friday afternoon he was told to be at a meeting in California on Monday morning. After his manager approved the trip, he went to the cashier, but the office was closed. At the finance department he learned that the cash was locked up and nothing could be done until Monday. His manager then called the chief accountant who also refused to help. By now the manager was irate, so he appealed to progressively more senior financial managers until he reached the finance vice president who had to be called out of a meeting. He was annoyed at the interruption but agreed to fix the problem. The cash was then available in fifteen minutes.

The bureaucracy has a valid role in enforcing the rules and preventing recurrent problems. The accumulation of such constraints, however, becomes a kind of organizational scar tissue which is built up in response to problems. The bureaucrats are then cast in the role of defenders against the professionals, who are the cause of all the trouble. Although all bureaucrats are not necessarily obstructionists, their focus on procedures naturally opposes them to anything which is new or different. This causes frequent contention with the line organization, which is busily doing its best to innovate.

In large technical organizations this natural conflict is weighted against the professionals because the many bureaucrats quickly learn that by banding together in cliques and coalitions they can increase their leverage. Unless steps are taken to maintain a reasonable balance of power, the rules will continue to accumulate until the engineers and scientists dissipate much of their energy fighting an increasingly powerful and highly autocratic bureaucracy.

NOTES CHAPTER 20

1. David Kipnis, "The View from the Top," *Psychology Today*, December 1984, pp. 30–34.

2. Harold J. Leavitt, *Managerial Psychology, Fourth Edition* (Chicago, Ill.: University of Chicago Press, 1978), p. 141.

3. Bergen Evans, *Dictionary of Quotations* (New York: Bonanza Books, 1968), 547:15.

4. Rosabeth Moss Kanter, *Men and Women of the Corporation* (Harper & Row, Publishers, Inc., New York: Basic Books, Inc., 1977), p. 189.

5. Thomas J. Peters and Robert H. Waterman, Jr., *In Search of Excellence: Lessons from America's Best-Run Corporations* (New York: Harper & Row, Publishers, Inc., 1982), p. 79.

6. Kipnis, "The View from the Top" p. 32.

7. Jeffrey Pfeffer, *Organizations and Organization Theory* (Marshfield, Mass.: Pitman, 1982), p. 74.

8. Ibid., p. 113.

9. Ibid., p. 130.

10. Ibid., p. 88.

11. Ibid., p. 344.

12. Michael L. Tushman and William L. Moore, *Readings in the Management of Innovation* (Marshfield, Mass.: Pitman, 1982), p. 243.

13. Ibid., p. 90.

14. Ibid., p. 173.

15. Pfeffer, *Organizations*, p. 272.

16. Kanter, *Men and Women*, p. 192.

21

Technical Assessment

Dale Zand, a professor at NYU's School of Business, objects to managers who say that "I don't want to hear your problems, I want to hear your solutions."[1] This, in Zand's view, can be catastrophic, because a major source of long-term failure is management's unwillingness to systematically search for problems.

Many managers operate according to the principles of crisis management. This effectively keeps them on top of current issues, but it rarely uncovers the organization's basic problems. When responding to a crisis, managers are allowing their priorities to be set by events rather than by their judgment, and this rarely provides an effective way to build for the future. In modern technology, problems are often symptoms of deeper ills. Managers who do not occasionally step back to think about these problems and to assess their organizations will be, according to Harold Leavitt, "buffeted by the waves instead of making on-course headway through the waves."[2]

LOOKING INSTEAD OF REACTING

The objective of the assessment process is an orderly identification of the most important problems in the organization. Peter Drucker says that to be a successful manager you should start out by asking yourself "what are the few things I can do . . . that would make a difference? If you do this, you have a chance, if you don't do it, you have no chance."[3]

One of the best ways to do assessments is to ask the professionals in the organization what they think is wrong and what should be done about it. They generally know the problems very well and can be an enormously valuable source of information. When approached in the right way, the engineers and scientists will invariably have many good ideas and be willing to suggest some practical improvement steps. As John Gardner has said, one way to insure an attitude of continuous improvement "is for the organization to encourage its internal critics."[4]

SELF-ASSESSMENT

John Gardner also made the perceptive point that "most ailing organizations have developed a functional blindness to their own defects. They are not suffering because they can't solve their problems, but because they won't see their problems."[5] It is surprising how often the people in a large organization will be well aware of the key problems but do nothing whatever about them. One reason is that they often either have a vested interest in the status quo, they don't think the problems are really that important, or they assume that they can't be changed anyway. When these problems are seen only one at a time, they seem unimportant, and it is hard for the people involved to visualize their combined impact. Force of habit also causes a blindness to the possibility of change, and a structured assessment is often needed to help break this impasse.

Dr. Arthur Anderson, a retired IBM vice president, used to say, "There is always room for improvement." He believed that every complex technical organization was necessarily out of date, because its structure, methods, and even its people could never change fast enough to keep up with the rapid pace of modern technology. He addressed this problem by having his management team periodically assess their own operations, identify their key strengths and weaknesses, and then establish improvement plans.

Such a proper self-assessment takes a great deal of work, for it must involve the key managers and examine all the organization's principal operations. The objective is to find and remove the major constraints on creativity, productivity, or quality. At the outset many people will object that they know their operations and that such a study would be a waste of time. Experience has shown, however, that the people who object the loudest generally learn the most, and they then often become the strongest supporters of the assessment process.

The most difficult single step in doing an assessment is to actually get it started. Most managers will agree in principle with the idea, but there is never a convenient time to do it. It is tempting to wait until the current crisis blows over, but it is safe to predict that there will be another one right behind it. To really do an assessment, therefore, a plan should be made, the right people assigned, and a firm starting date established.

FORMAL ASSESSMENT

A formal assessment process called organization development (OD) has been discussed extensively in the literature.[6] In OD, outside experts are used to conduct interviews, to find out what the people think is wrong and their ideas on what to do about it. Since these specialists have been trained in interview methods, they can ask questions in a nonthreatening way and often uncover the most fundamental problems. Once these problems are clearly understood, it is often far easier to produce effective solutions.

People from within the organization can also perform much this same function, but there are generally some problems. Insiders will generally be more familiar with local conditions and better able to dig into key issues, but they will also likely appear more threatening to the interviewees. Also, when a department does its own assessment, it is rarely able to dedicate people to the process; consequently they cannot develop expertise in assessment methods. As a result, in-house programs are generally not as effective as using some kind of dedicated staff. Because of their familiarity with the organization's issues, however, a specialized staff from within the company can be even more effective than outsiders.

Whether the assessment is done by a specialized group or by an ad hoc team of professionals, the process is generally handled in much the same way. Brown and Weiner suggest that management formally establish a process to define the business environment, identify reasons and opportunities for change, and carefully select the people who best understand what needs to be done.[7] Warren Bennis suggests that this start by considering three basic questions:[8]

1. How well the organization's goals are understood and accepted
2. The organization's knowledge of its technological and competitive posture
3. The precise way in which the organization learns and grows to meet the changing demands of technology

THE ASSESSMENT PROCESS

The first basic guideline for effective assessment is to have the entire management team agree with the study objectives and plan. Next, the people doing the assessment should be technically knowledgeable and sufficiently independent to be objective. It should also be an open and public process, and all the people involved should know in advance what is going on and why. If not, they will likely be confused, concerned, and reluctant to speak out. Finally, management must agree to address the problems that are identified.

If all these steps are taken and if the conclusions of the study and the resulting action plans are openly presented, the result will be a significant improvement in the attitudes of all the people involved. As in the Hawthorne studies, people like to be asked what they think and as long as some action is taken, they will think more constructively about further improvements. These attitudes can be maintained and enhanced by following up the first assessment with another one in about a year and a half. If enough time is allowed for progress to be made on the prior problems, a second study will further reinforce the improvement process.

THE IBM PROGRAMMING STUDIES

Starting in the spring of 1983, IBM conducted a series of studies of its large systems programming development organizations.[9] When these studies were initially proposed, programming management was unwilling to participate because they viewed them as a headquarters audit, and it took several extended meetings and one trial study before this suspicion could be allayed. The key to final acceptance was the absolute guarantee that the study results would only be given to local management and no report would be made to headquarters.

The preparation for the initial review took several months, during which a team of six experienced programmers developed a comprehensive plan. The programming development process was subdivided into thirteen phases and eleven attributes, and a number of questions were devised to identify the organization's status in each area. The study team then rehearsed the planned interviews to insure that the professionals would not feel threatened. A manager from the local laboratory was included as a member of the study team to act as a coordinator, to help local management select the programmers to be interviewed, and to arrange for facilities and support.

During the assessment study itself, each professional was privately interviewed by the entire review team. There had originally been some concern that this large interview group would appear threatening, but this did not turn out to be a problem. As soon as the professionals realized they were dealing with knowledgeable people, they talked freely about their work, the problems that bothered them, and where they thought improvements could be made.

Because of the practice sessions, the reviewers could keep the environment nonthreatening. While a general air of informality relaxed the participants, the objective technical focus encouraged the professionals to talk openly about their work. The only interview that was in the least constrained was one in which a programmer's manager came with him to the meeting. Although the manager did nothing wrong, his presence was clearly a constraint. Thereafter, no one in the interviewee's direct management chain participated in any interview.

In advance of each meeting, the programmers were told to make only minimal preparations. They were, however, instructed to bring any important notes and documents that were relevant. At the end of each interview, the professionals were asked what changes they would make if they were running the company. The resulting discussion was invariably informative and produced many of the best suggestions.

At the end of the study the team presented a preliminary set of findings to the location senior managers, who were occasionally surprised by some of the findings. Although they asked many questions, the study team could give specific examples for each item. The team then returned to headquarters for a month to prepare a final report and recommendations, which were then presented to this same senior management team and to each project. Local management then developed action plans to address each of the major recommendations.

The positive reception to this initial study convinced the other laboratories that this process could be useful to them, and within a year and a half, similar studies had been completed at every one of IBM's 370 systems programming locations. Nearly seven hundred of the approximately four thousand programming professionals in these eight large laboratories were interviewed and asked to suggest potential areas for improvement. The local management team then responded with action programs which resulted in significant improvements in the quality and productivity of IBM's large-systems programming development process.

ASSESSMENT EXPERIENCES

A number of key lessons were learned from these programming studies:

1. A comprehensive assessment is a major undertaking, and it cannot be done in a few days or with an ad hoc team. A halfhearted effort will not produce useful results, and it will waste the time of the managers and the professionals.
2. The schedules for the first study will invariably be optimistic. Subsequent experience showed that at least three weeks should have been allowed for the first of the IBM studies, instead of the two weeks actually planned.
3. Only technically knowledgeable and experienced interviewers should be used.
4. Thorough preparation is essential. The entire study team should spend several weeks on the introductory material, experimenting with report formats and rehearsing the interview questions. These rehearsals should focus on making the entire interview process nonthreatening to the participants.
5. People should be interviewed one at a time, and they should be unaccompanied by either their associates or their management.

After the study has been completed, several points should be considered in making the final report to local management:

1. Since every assessment uncovers problems, it is essential to recognize the organization's many strong points also. Any responsible and competent technical group is properly proud of its good work, and a uniformly negative report will not be well received.
2. Great care should be used with the wording. For example, unless every case was studied, a statement that ''inspections were never used'' will invariably cause disagreement. It is more appropriate to say, ''We saw no case where inspections were used.''
3. Although many problems may be described, the focus should be on the few that are judged to be most important.
4. It is wise to be cautious with recommendations which have not actually been demonstrated in practice. In advanced technology most seemingly good ideas have hidden pitfalls, and a study team which recommends unproven schemes

will quickly lose credibility. Such suggestions should therefore be clearly identified, and where the ideas have actually been demonstrated, this prior work should be referenced.

5. The local management team may chose to follow different action priorities than those recommended, but this should not be viewed with alarm as long as their attitude is focused on improvement. Additional emphasis on some items may be appropriate, but local management priorities are often better informed than those of the study team.

6. Progress will invariably be slower than expected. It takes a great deal of time for people to adopt new working habits, but as long as the professionals themselves are a part of the process and are motivated by a constructive improvement attitude, the assessment process will be beneficial.

7. If specific local responsibility is not assigned for the implementation and tracking of each action item, there is little chance of any significant improvement actually taking place.

8. Finally, every professional group always has much more to do than it can possibly handle, so it will invariably end up deferring some items. When senior management judges these items to be important, however, they must clearly demonstrate their priorities through emphasis on improvement plans, special focus during project reviews, management changes, or specifically enforced guidelines.

CONFIDENTIALITY

Confidentiality is the single most important prerequisite for an effective assessment. Since this process must be founded in trust, it must be done *for* the local people and not *to* them. The people who are most intimately involved should be the first to hear the results, and any reports should be designed to support and not to embarrass them. There may be differences in priorities, but the basic principle is that the local managers and professionals are as eager to improve their operations as the senior management or any headquarters staff are. The study is merely an organized way to help them do it.

If the study is seen as a headquarters attempt to expose problems, all doors will quickly close, and cooperation will cease. Although audits can be valuable in certain circumstances, their results are typically presented to senior management and call for a public response. The result is often a defensive attitude, with endless debates over procedural details. For relatively standardized operations, audits can be useful, but they are of little value in improving professional attitudes or working methods.

Some of the steps which can be taken to help maintain the proper attitude of confidentiality are the following:

1. Apply confidentiality at every level. That is, problems are treated as anonymous, while positive results are credited to the person or team responsible.

2. At each reporting stage, lower level findings are combined so that no specific project, team, or individual can be identified with a problem. Team data goes to the team, project data to the project, and lab data to the lab. No reports should be made above the laboratory or plant level unless made by the local management team themselves.

3. In spite of the need for confidentiality, it is necessary to make reports to higher management. An average of all the results can be shown, but no one project or location should be identifiable. By describing many of the positive steps each group is taking, senior management will understand what is being done, and local management's interests will be protected. The use of a rating system, however, invariably causes trouble, since some group will always come out on the bottom and management will insist on knowing who it is.

4. Each laboratory or plant will, however, want to know how it compared with everyone else. Anonymity can be preserved by delaying such reports until a reasonable number of projects have been reviewed, and then the local projects can be compared to this larger unidentified sample.

ASSESSMENT CONSIDERATIONS

There are many ways to conduct an assessment, and almost any approach will work as long as it is professionally done and line management publicly supports it. Although few people will commit to action plans before they understand the problems, local management must have a positive improvement attitude before they will accept ownership of the recommendations. Without such an attitude the problems will not be solved and the study will be a waste of time.

The first assessment is the most important because word will quickly spread of any problems or blunders. Careful planning and even rehearsals are thus essential. There also is often considerable pressure from higher management for a summary of the problems and the actions to be taken. Any leak of a critical finding, however, will invariably generate requests for executive presentations, action plans, and checkpoints. Local management will then know that the study was the source of these requests and conclude that it was really an audit.

Each assessment must be the property of the line organization. If they want to report the results to their management, the assessment team should support them. Any such report should be delayed, however, until the action plans have been formulated. Since senior management would rather hear of solutions than problems, such a delay is always worthwhile.

Finally, significant organizational improvement takes a lot of work. Unless local management is truly dedicated to the task, little will actually happen. Most managers will responsibly react to their key problems once they have been identified, but some managers are so hypnotized by their current project demands that they are either unwilling or unable to make the effort. In these cases no further progress can be made unless senior management takes steps to change their priorities.

CONTINUOUS ASSESSMENTS

As experience is gained with assessments, the process must be changed to keep pace with the organization's needs. The first assessment of any laboratory or plant is generally a learning experience for everyone involved. It is also the point at which the organization being studied is most receptive. They have accepted the fact that they have problems and have agreed to an assessment; they thus are open-minded and relatively uncritical of the process. At subsequent reviews, however, the study team needs to be progressively more disciplined with their process, or they will lose credibility. Some of their key considerations at this point are the following:

1. When a rating in an area is changed from the prior study, it should be based on specific identified differences. Management has often worked hard to make improvements and their efforts should be recognized. If not, the assessment can easily appear superficial.
2. If the technical state of the art has improved and the organization is downgraded in some area because these new methods were not adopted, the omitted techniques should be identified together with justification for their use.
3. When several projects are reviewed in an organization, the results are generally averaged for the presentation to senior location management. If some of these projects are different from those in the first review, the organization rating may look worse even though the original projects may have actually improved. If this is the case it should be carefully explained at the beginning of the senior management review. Doing this, however, without appearing overly critical of the new project is extremely difficult. One answer is to have this project manager actually make the explanation. This not only preserves the principle of confidentiality, but it also permits that project manager to explain in a positive way something that will ultimately become obvious to the other projects.

Even with the best planned assessment program, some groups are often still unable to improve. This is not because they don't want to improve but because they face some stumbling block they cannot surmount. Most projects are under intense schedule and resource pressure and have trouble devoting attention to the agreed-upon improvement programs. This often means that the committed action plans don't get done. One answer is to occasionally use the assessment specialists as a consulting team and have them actually work with some project on a specific improvement plan. If done properly, this will provide graphic evidence of the value of the new methods and convince the project members to work this way, even under crisis conditions.

In the case of one programming development effort, such consultation took several weeks of the team's time over four calendar months, but it produced a dramatic change in the development group's attitudes and working methods. The original action plan recommendation had been to conduct inspections of selected product modules based on a statistical analysis of error history. The contention was that this would permit far more efficient inspection and testing and produce a better-quality product with the available resources. Since the project members had never done this before and had a critical shipment date to make, they had not been willing to risk the time and resources required. The study gave them the incentive to try the new methods. At the conclusion, the product people really understood how effective these methods could be; they committed to improving the quality of the next product release by a factor of two.

NOTES CHAPTER 21

1. Dale Zand made these comments at a Peter Drucker conference in New York City on April 22, 1982.

2. Harold J. Leavitt, *Managerial Psychology, Fourth Edition* (Chicago, Ill.: University of Chicago Press, 1978), p. 306.

3. John J. Tarrant, *Drucker: The Man Who Invented the Corporate Society* (Warner Publishing, Inc., New York: Warner Books, Inc., 1976), p. 111.

4. John Gardner, "Renewal of Organizations," 20th Annual Meeting of the Board of Trustees, Midwest Research Institute, Kansas City, Missouri, May 3, 1965.

5. Ibid.

6. *Organizational Development: A Reconnaissance,* Conference Board Report No. 605 (New York: 1973); Edgar F. Huse, *Organization Development and Change* (St. Paul, Minn: West Publishing Company, 1975); David Rodgers, *Can Business Management Save the Cities* (New York: MacMillan Publishing Co., Inc., Free Press, 1978).

7. Arnold Brown and Edith Weiner, *Supermanaging* (New York: McGraw-Hill Book Company, 1984), p. 256.

8. Warren G. Bennis, *Changing Organizations: Essays on the Development and Evolution of Human Organization* (New York: McGraw-Hill Book Company, 1966), p. 41.

9. R. A. Radice, J. T. Harding, P. E. Munnis, and R. W. Phillips, "A Programming Process Study," *IBM Systems Journal*, vol. 24, no. 2, 1985, p. 91.

22

Structural Change

Organizations are typically designed to fight the last war. Since there is an understandable need to solve known current problems, vaguer future organizational concerns tend to be deferred. This problem is compounded by the fact that many of the organization's most important problems are hard to identify. Managers often have a vested interest in the status quo and are reluctant to admit that things are not working as they should. Although it is generally wise to follow the credo, If it ain't broke, don't fix it, managers should recognize that every organization is a trade-off between conflicting pressures; and when this balance changes, the organization should change as well.

LEADERSHIP PROBLEMS

Henry Mintzberg believes that the four basic kinds of organizational behavior are determined by their leadership situation: the Autocracy, the Political Arena, the Closed System, and the Meritocracy.[1] In the Autocracy, the leader is the driving force behind the organization and is typically its only important power figure. Autocracies behave much like a palace court, where power is measured in distance from the throne, and autocratic leaders think of themselves as embodying the organization. They typically feel no need for such details as job descriptions, operating plans, or formal procedures, and what they say goes; but often that is all that does.

    Since autocrats rarely groom successors, their departure forces the organization into Mintzberg's second phase, the Political Arena. This is a highly vulnerable period with no coherent leadership and widely dispersed power. Without direction from the top, few organizations can revise their strategies, so the Political Arena typically coalesces around the departed leader's goals and is, in effect, run by his or her ghost. This petrified structure freezes around an outdated strategy and is dangerously exposed to either marketplace or technological change.

Organizations that survive the Political Arena become either Closed Systems or Meritocracies. In the Closed System, the bureaucracy takes charge, and the nominal leader is concerned with maintaining the status quo. The focus is now on administrative management through cost controls, documented plans, and formal procedures. This growing formality inhibits innovation and exposes the organization to competitive or technological surprise. By the time the leadership becomes fully entrenched, it is generally unchangeable, except by external force.

If the technocrats beat the bureaucrats in this power struggle, the Political Arena will be succeeded by the Meritocracy, where the engineers and scientists are in charge. This organization is typically better informed and less exposed to technological surprise and the professionals' natural aversion to procedures protects it from becoming bureaucratic. Financial controls are often neglected, however, and the greatest danger is the technologist's tendency to believe that all problems have technical answers. This can lead the organization to focus on the laboratory and plant and lose touch with the marketplace.

PROBLEMS OF THE AUTOCRACY

Even though autocratic behavior is most obvious at the corporate level, it can also occur in individual departments with equally severe consequences. Some of the symptoms of an overbearing autocrat are as follows:

1. The leader is the sole spokesperson for the organization and appears to be its only source of ideas. There is generally no evidence of open disagreement, and the boss typically makes decisions in private, with little prior discussion even with those of his or her people who are most involved.
2. The leader has a low opinion of his or her people, promotions are not made from within, and no successor has been groomed.
3. Autocrats often have a small intimate circle of cronies who share in their private thoughts and plans. These people, however, are not viewed as potential successors, and they rarely hold official power.
4. The organization has no formal plans, procedures, or job descriptions.
5. There is little or no delegation of authority.
6. No reward and recognition programs exist.
7. Creativity is limited, except by the leader.

There is an enormous difference between a dynamic and forceful leader and an autocrat. The leader typically believes in himself and is not afraid to defend his convictions. Most leaders are good salesmen and enjoy converting people to their cause. Autocrats, however, typically have the reverse problem. Insecure managers will appear highly autocratic to their people simply because they are unwilling to risk the give and take of personal interaction. They will quietly prepare their position and then tell their people their final conclusions. The lack of advance notice leaves them unprepared to ask questions or disagree, so they feel compelled to quietly follow orders.

This was the case with a small department of experienced engineers. The manager was technically quite competent and spent most of his time working out design problems behind his closed office door. Every few days he would call in one of his people, ask for his work status, and give him his next assignment. While his engineers viewed him as a tyrant, the manager was actually terrified of his people and dreaded these infrequent encounters. He soon asked to be relieved of his management responsibilities so that he could return to the technical work which he really enjoyed.

It takes a great deal of self-confidence for managers to deal honestly and openly with their people. Some managers feel so humiliated when their subordinates prove them wrong that they retreat behind their comfortable shield of authority. This attitude is self-destructive, however, for managers must interact freely with their people if they are to lead them. Autocratic leadership styles, however, are developed over many years, and it is rarely possible to change them. Even when he or she is convinced of the need for change, such behaviors are often so deeply rooted in the autocrat's personality that self-improvement is enormously difficult. As John Opel, IBM's chairman, once said, "You can make a tiger roar and a kangaroo jump but don't expect a kangaroo to roar."

OTHER LEADERSHIP PROBLEMS

Not much can be done about the problems of the Political Arena or the Closed System until their lack of effective leadership is addressed. At the corporate level these changes must be initiated from the outside, but departments with these characteristics can be identified and changed rather quickly. Although there are no general guidelines, the most common solution is to find and install an energetic new leader.

The Meritocracy can operate quite effectively under a form of consensus management. This may not be as effective as having a singly dynamic leader, but it can produce outstanding results all the same. Such consensus structures can also often have serious problems, however, as shown by the following symptoms:

1. The organization becomes deeply engrossed with technology and pays progressively less attention to its customers or competition.
2. Cost controls, productivity measurements, and profit management receive little or no emphasis.
3. An excessive product focus can limit the attention given to the tools and methods needed for long-term improvements in productivity and quality.

The problems of the Meritocracy can be addressed in several ways, depending on their severity:

1. In addition to the traditional mix of technical talent, the laboratories and manufacturing plants should have some strong marketing and financial people on their top management teams.
2. Management development should be given high priority to insure that the future general managers are exposed to many facets of the business.
3. Special emphasis should be given to market awareness, including the purchase and use of competitive products, customer surveys, management participation in customer executive briefings, and short temporary assignments of key technical people with the sales organization.

THE PROBLEMS OF ORGANIZATIONAL MATURITY

Much like people, organizations exhibit problems of youth and maturity. John Aplin points out that organizations can be divided into either creative or maintenance types.[2] Creative organizations grow rapidly, are highly innovative, and undergo perpetual structural change. Organizations in the maintenance phase are more stable, have more formalized plans and procedures, and place heavy emphasis on cost management. The key words in the maintenance period are productivity and control.

Since creative leaders rarely pay much attention to formal plans, the professionals often complain about the lack of long-term direction. Management, however, typically knows exactly where it is going but has not bothered to clearly tell its people. Rapid creative growth also produces a young, self-confident management team who made it on their own and see little need to formally develop promising new managers. Since the incessant demand for talent generally outstrips any possible internal supply, formal development programs rarely seem worthwhile. The constant infusion of new blood, however, does help to keep the organization intellectually stimulated and technologically aware.

This is an exciting environment, but it has serious drawbacks as well. Since management's emphasis is largely on tactical reaction, the rapid rate of management turnover often means that problems get swept under the rug rather than solved. There is rarely the continuity to make two- or three-year changes; therefore longer-term problems gradually accumulate. Finally, such organizations have not yet been humbled by serious failures, so that the seasoned "old salts" from prior disasters are not available to balance the untempered optimism of this young and vital organization.

Typically, however, the creative phase is self-limiting. Its success inevitably leads to the maintenance phase, because its initial burst of success cannot be long sustained, and its growing size demands more discipline and control. The maintenance organization addresses these problems with a formal structure, organization charts, job descriptions, and a healthy emphasis on employee benefits and management development. Growing numbers of good people are now available for internal promotion, and stability brings formal long-term plans, product procedures, cost controls, and improved profitability.

Although the transition from the creative to the maintenance phase is natural, it is also quite traumatic. The early enthusiasm is now replaced by painstaking attention to the many problems of success. Slower growth means less opportunity for advancement, and the people now begin to worry about their careers and to resent the loss of the earlier excitement and challenge. The growing bureaucracy produces an increasingly structured organization with a new emphasis on efficiency and measurement. If this reaction swings too far, it can stifle innovation in a web of financial and business controls.

ADDRESSING CREATIVE-PHASE PROBLEMS

The creative phase can be enormously productive, and the trick is carefully to adjust to its problems while not destroying its dynamic pace and excitement. The leader should lean into the wind and place personal stress on those areas that are commonly ignored, such as management development, financial control, project coordination, formal planning, productivity measurements, and quality goals. The growing number of seasoned "old salts" should also be nurtured and heeded as an invaluable source of organizational maturity.

ADDRESSING MAINTENANCE-PHASE PROBLEMS

As in the creative organization, maintenance managers should act as a balancing force. Here, however, their focus should be on the marketplace and technological awareness. The prime maintenance threat is the organization's propensity to focus on its internal problems and risk technological or competitive surprise. Managers should thus insist on demonstrable evidence of technological superiority and competitive leadership.

In any large organization many projects will properly belong in the maintenance phase, while a few will need insulation from such tight control. Multimode structures are difficult, however, because most organizations have one dominant product which largely governs management's thinking. When this product moves from its creative phase to its maintenance phase, everything else tends to move with it. Better planning and improved financial control seem logical at any time, so more procedures and controls are applied to everyone—even those who are still in their creative phase.

One answer to this is to isolate the creative parts of such large organizations so that they can have a more suitably tailored management system. IBM did this when it set up the Independent Business Unit (IBU) with responsibility for introducing the first IBM personal computer. This IBU was given the freedom to use rules and procedures appropriate to a new business venture rather than being bound by all the constraints of the other divisions. The vehicle used to speed decision making was approval by a corporate executive review board. As a result of this flexibility, they made several innovative decisions, including the first-time development and manufacture of a major IBM machine largely through subcontractors. Marketing was done also through independent retail stores, even though IBM already had a large and highly skilled field sales force. Although several of their innovations were strongly opposed by the various staffs and operating units, this personal computer IBU was allowed to use the review board and thus bypass these objections, and the soundness of their judgment was later vindicated by the PC's success.

Largely because of its great success, this IBU ultimately had to face many of the issues that had previously been faced by the regular IBM organization. The production capacity of some of its vendors presented problems, as did the relationships with the traditional IBM sales force. Once the PC was established, these problems could be addressed, but if they had not been deferred, IBM's PC introduction might never have happened or at best would have been seriously delayed. After its initial success was assured, the initial creative phase had achieved its objectives, and IBM's personal computer IBU was folded back into IBM's standard organizational structure.

The essential difference between managing the creative and the maintenance phases is a matter of priorities. In the creative phase, the thrust must be on innovation, with major emphasis on establishing a base for sustained growth. Success will obviously bring a host of new problems, but most of them are largely irrelevant until this base has been achieved. Organizations that insist on innovating in a maintenance environment either strangle their innovations or incur enormous delays and added expense. Once the innovation has gained sufficient strength, these problems can then be solved in the maintenance environment which necessarily follows.

ORGANIZATIONAL TENURE

The stability of the maintenance organization often means that many of its groups will have been largely unchanged for a long time. When professional teams work together for extended periods, the members can become complacent and intellectually stagnant. Pelz classifies such groups as old if they have worked together for more than four to five years, and he found that the performance of such groups generally started to decline.[3] The few older teams in Pelz's study that maintained an attitude of friendly internal competition, however, remained effective, while all the others performed poorly. The optimum fell between one and five years, with groups that had been formed for less than a year lacking the internal cohesion to be fully effective.

Katz and Allen reached similar conclusions from their study of fifty project teams.[4] They determined each team's performance by asking several managers their opinions and then averaging the responses. They then correlated performance with team age and generally found an increase for the first 1.5 years, a flat period up to about five years, and then a decline. The decline was so pronounced, in fact, that the difference in performance between the 1.5 and 5-plus year groups was over 20 percent. Of the ten teams with superior performance, none had worked together for more than five years.

A further conclusion of this study is that a key reason for the performance decline of the older teams was what they called the NIH or "Not Invented Here" syndrome. This, they found, caused such groups to have minimal internal communication, not to seek external technical contacts, and to quickly reject those outside ideas that did reach them. They concluded that the NIH syndrome is most likely to develop in groups that have worked together in one field for so long that they have become the local experts. This, coupled with their limited technological exposure, leads them to believe that they have a monopoly on relevant information in their field, which further limits their curiosity and creativity.

ADDRESSING THE PROBLEMS OF TENURE

When a laboratory or manufacturing plant has had the same organizational structure for a long time, many of its professional groups will likely exhibit these problems, and a working level reorganization may be called for. In many reorganizations, the senior executive assignments are reshuffled, while the functional teams are left pretty much intact. These rearrangements may be useful in resolving some structural problems, but they can have little impact on working-level stagnation. This requires that the professional groups themselves be changed so that people have new challenges and associations.

Such a restructuring was done in a large development laboratory where the administration and support groups had been largely unchanged for over ten years. The direct development teams were increasingly vocal in their complaints about this entrenched and rigid bureaucracy, so the laboratory director decided to make a complete working-level restructuring. He asked that his senior development managers form several committees to examine each administrative and support department and see which ones could be eliminated. If they could not identify any specific project problems which would result, it would be a candidate for dissolution.

Although every single department had seemingly convincing reasons for existence, several failed this stringent test and were subsequently eliminated. The remaining functions were then logically grouped together under second- and third-level managers to produce an entirely new departmental structure. This reorganization affected almost every administrative and support group in the laboratory and almost completely disrupted the established bureaucracy. Two levels of management were eliminated, and over 20 percent of the first-level managers were reassigned. Most of these excess managers and professionals were given direct development jobs, thus improving the efficiency of the total organization while increasing the size of the direct development work force.

NOTES CHAPTER 22

1. Henry Mintzberg, *Power in and around Organizations* (Englewood Cliffs, N.J.: Prentice-Hall, Inc., 1983), p. 314.

2. John C. Aplin and Richard A. Cosier, "Managing Creative and Maintenance Organizations," *The Business Quarterly,* Spring 1980, p. 56.

3. Donald C. Pelz and Frank M. Andrews, *Scientists in Organizations: Productive Climates for Research and Development* (New York: John Wiley & Sons, Inc., 1966), p. 259.

4. Ralph Katz and Thomas J. Allen, "Investigating the Not Invented Here (NIH) Syndrome: A look at the Performance, Tenure, and Communication Patterns of 50 R and D Project Groups," *R&D Management (UK),* vol. 12, no. 1, 1982, p. 7.

23

The Change Process

Although a reorganization can change the work people are supposed to do, it will have little effect on the way they do it. When organizations need to institute challenging productivity or quality programs or adapt their working practices and procedures to technological change, a much more complex change process is called for. Here, simplistic management directives will often encounter resistance or even open hostility. Most people are creatures of habit and must be convinced of the need to change before they will willingly do so. Management's job is to lead and and direct this change process.

RESISTANCE TO CHANGE

Since people naturally want to improve things, they should embrace change, but, paradoxically, they almost universally resist it. Douglas Sherwin explains that "change is great when you are its agent; it is only bad when you are its object."[1] Edgar F. Huse further notes that change is often seen as a personal threat by those involved unless they have participated in its planning.[2]

Paul Lawrence has also written on this subject, and he describes the case where an identical change was introduced to several factory groups whose productivity was closely matched.[3] One group was merely told to make the change without any explanation. They resisted all management's efforts during the entire test period, and their output dropped by a full one third. The other two groups were involved in the change planning from the outset, and even though they had an initial small productivity drop, they rapidly recovered and ultimately reached a higher performance level than before.

Lawrence suggests that resistance to change should be treated as a symptom rather than as the problem. When there is a strong focus on overcoming resistance, the people are usually seen as obstructionists, which causes management to increase its pressure on them to conform. This further increases resistance, and as these positions become entrenched, the change becomes even harder to implement than before. Lawrence has found that this vicious cycle can best be broken by concentrating on the reasons for resistance and dealing with them one at a time.

Every change involves unknowns, and people are reluctant to take risks. Their involvement in the planning, however, allows them to better understand the change, to see why it is being made, and to learn what to expect. This reduces the unknowns and helps overcome resistance. Another way to overcome resistance is to show people how the change can help them and thus present it as an opportunity instead of a threat. When this is coupled with participation in the planning, the people will have an opportunity to make suggestions, and many of them will start to act as change agents instead of objects. An additional approach comes from the fact that resistance to change is proportional to its magnitude; if a large change can be broken into smaller steps, each step is easier to sell and to implement, and total resistance is reduced.

UNFREEZING

When the change process is well thought out and properly structured, it generally starts with an "unfreezing" phase to overcome resistance.[4] Brainwashing is an extreme example of this, which attempts to destroy the will to resist through inhuman physical and psychological treatment. A less brutal unfreezing process is used on new military recruits. They are isolated in boot camps and assigned to demanding drill instructors, who put them through a grueling series of daily drills, rugged obstacle courses, and long forced marches. At the end the survivors have become a proud and cohesive fighting unit.[5]

The unfreezing techniques of brainwashing and boot camp obviously don't apply to technical organizations, but there is still the need to overcome resistance. This can be particularly difficult in large technical groups because the most simple and direct methods tend to increase resistance. When, for example, management issues a directive to change, the people will resent the implication that they needed to be told, and they will feel more inclined to resist. If, however, management merely waits for grass-roots acceptance, nothing might happen, at least not for a very long time.

It often turns out that the working professionals are not the source of the most resistance, because they are closer to the problems and generally understand what should be done better than their managers. Typically, however, unless their immediate manager supports and encourages them, professionals cannot institute very significant changes by themselves. As a result, the greatest resistance to professional change is generally at the first-line managers' level. When they become convinced that the change will really help to get the job done, they will encourage their people, who then often welcome it as an opportunity.

On the other hand, executive statements of purpose or benchmarks of success can provide an image of what is wanted and provide the people with a comparison of their situation with the ideal. When this is coupled with education programs, pilot demonstrations, or expert consultation, the need for change is more quickly recognized, and the people are better prepared to support it.

One of the most successful of all known change programs is Alcoholics Anonymous. They wait until alcoholics are so unhappy with their own situation that they come to AA for help. Until they reach this point, AA has found that any effort on their part will be fruitless. For more typical organizational problems Leavitt suggests that managers can help to accelerate this recognition in three ways.[6] First, they can make the problems more obvious and thus help their people to recognize them more quickly. Second, they can simply point them out. Paradoxically, this often causes them to blame the problem on their manager. Finally, managers can wait for the employees to come to them for help and respond by describing the change as a potential solution to these newly recognized concerns. The assessment process described in Chapter 21 is also effective for unfreezing.

PLANNING THE CHANGE

When the unfreezing phase is completed, the people are unhappy with the current situation and ready for some improvement. This vacuum must now be filled with a plan of action and early implementation steps. If this is not done reasonably soon, the entire unfreezing phase will only have served to make the people even more aware of, and unhappy with, the current situation. Management should thus take immediate steps to select a change agent to champion the change process and to build the people's enthusiasm for improvement. Some points to consider in making this selection are the following:

1. Agents should be enthusiastic about leading the change process. Irwin and Langham point out that "enthusiasm can be contagious and people tend to perform better in an optimistic environment than in a won't-work environment."[7]
2. Agents must be both technically and politically capable of understanding the problems and ensuring that effective solutions are implemented.
3. Agents need the respect of the people they are to deal with.
4. Agents must have management's confidence and support or they will not act with the assurance needed to get wide cooperation and acceptance.

Although there is no standard way to select a change agent, it is wise to pick someone who has strong views on the subject. Gerald Salancik cites the example of Pitney-Bowes's president, who, in a 1972 feedback meeting with a group of his employees, was interrupted by a young woman who asked what the company was doing to improve female employee opportunities. She said that "eighty percent of the customer account jobs were going to women and only 13 percent of the management positions.''⁸ The president saw this challenge as an opportunity to find a leader for the company's program on women's opportunities. He promptly removed her from her current assignment and put her in charge of a special task force to study the role of women in the firm.

PARTICIPATIVE PLANNING

Once the change agent has been selected, the detailed change planning must begin. This starts by identifying the people who will be affected by the change and making sure they are at least partially involved in the process. This can often be done quite easily, but when a great many people are involved, working groups should be established with representatives from each constituency. These planning teams then consider the change implementation, identify anticipated problems, and select ways to address them. If this process is open and visible and if all concerns are thoughtfully addressed, resistance will be minimized.

IMPLEMENTING THE CHANGE

The rate of change implementation is important. Some things can be done with lightning speed, but others require a great deal of patience. Purely technical changes rarely have much effect on working habits and can therefore generally be implemented rather quickly. When the people are more directly involved, however, the pace must be more deliberate, to give them time to understand the change, to accept it, and to adapt to its direct effects on them. Since the amount of time depends on the magnitude of the change, an attempt to move too quickly will both increase resistance and delay progress.

One of the most important considerations in any change process is to provide continuing evidence of progress. This is best done by dividing the total program into a series of small and manageable stages and publicizing each one as it is completed. Changes are often started with great fanfare, but then nothing is heard for an extended period. The people have been convinced that change is needed, and now they start to worry that something has gone wrong. As Irwin and Langham point out, ''An expression of progress dispels fears, insures confidence, encourages the doubters to join the team, provides the background for further achievement.''⁹

REFREEZING

One of the most discouraging experiences managers can have is to encounter a problem that they have already solved. Unfortunately, this can happen every time a change is incompletely made. When initially implemented, most changes get plenty of attention, but after this original impetus, priorities change and the organization often reverts to its prior habits. An example of what can happen is the introduction of design inspections into the programming development process some years ago. Introductory education programs were established, and all programmers were trained on how such code reviews should be performed, the procedures to follow, and the people who should participate. Some years later, it was found that the effectiveness of these inspections had seriously deteriorated. Most of the courses had long since been dropped; and although the inspection formalities were still being observed, the professionals had taken shortcuts with the process which reduced the discipline and significantly damaged inspection effectiveness.

Some practices are so obviously helpful that they will remain in place once they have been introduced. A good scheduling discipline, for example, is such a fundamental part of technical work that professionals who have worked on well-run projects find it hard to operate any other way. Once firmly established, therefore, such practices will generally stay in place with little management attention. Although most sound practices will ultimately be retained in this same way, it often takes a great deal of time for professionals to truly understand their benefits and to incorporate them in their permanent working methods. There are, however, several ways to help with this refreezing problem:

1. If the management team that originally instituted the change is kept in place, they will be sensitive to erosion and make sure the change is retained. Unfortunately, in most technical organizations management tenure is not very predictable.

2. The organization's procedures can be modified to incorporate the change as part of the bureaucratic process. This can be very effective for administrative tasks, such as planning and estimating, where compliance can be insured by relatively straightforward rules and guidelines. For more complex technical processes, however, this is often not practical.

3. The measurement system can be used to foster new methods through awards or special bonuses. Pay incentives can be very effective, but they must necessarily be based on a single objective measure. This can be a serious drawback, however, for few complex technical tasks can be comprehensively described in this way, and people who are paid accordingly will generally ignore all other considerations to maximize this one parameter. If financial incentives are to be used, they should first be tried experimentally and should always include an element of management judgment.

4. An effective approach for complex situations is to establish a dedicated staff with the responsibility for monitoring the changed process and alerting management when it starts to deteriorate. This, for example, is the role of the quality staffs in many large corporations.

5. When the objective is to change the working methods of the professional people, education is probably the most effective refreezing mechanism. As

long as it is well done and permanently retained, education programs will provide a continuous force to support the change process.

Several of these techniques can be used in combination, but education should be part of any professional refreezing program. Knowledgeable professionals are the strongest force for improvement in any technical organization, and a sound education program will continuously motivate them to press for the best known practices and methods.

GOALS

Pfeffer cites a number of studies which demonstrate the importance of goals in the change process.[10] When people understand and accept a goal and believe they can meet it, they will generally work very hard to do so. The case of a programming manager who recently attended a quality course shows how effective this can be. He discussed what he had been taught with his people, and they all decided on the goal of delivering their next program version with no defects. This was a very challenging objective because their project was to develop improvements to a sort program which was used by several thousand customers. What is more, in spite of all their efforts, previous products like this had always contained several hundred errors. After much study, however, they decided that exhaustive testing was possible, but they found that nearly ten times the normal number of test cases and several more weeks of testing were required than the schedule had allowed for. Senior management, however, strongly supported their goal, so the schedule was extended and the testing was done as planned. After installation and a full year of use, not a single program defect was found.

This quality program worked this well because the programmers had a clear and measurable goal. They knew exactly what they were trying to do and why it was important. What is more, they really believed they could do it. It is essential that goals be reasonably close to the professionals' ability to perform, for when there is no hope of meeting a target, each day's work reinforces the existing doubts and merely adds to the feelings of discouragement.

Goals must be set very carefully, however, for when a goal requires too dramatic a change, people often have trouble knowing how to start. This is when such programs should be broken into smaller and more realistic steps, with goals for each. As progress is made and a new step is reached, the bar is raised to a new level which is nearer to the final objective. In this way each step helps to increase motivation and insure continued progress.

The immediacy of the target is also important. A distant goal will rarely motivate current action. There are so many short-term crises that a long-term objective is often deferred until it too becomes a current crisis. Unfortunately, such a hectic environment can easily lead to make-shift solutions and no sustained progress. Here again, it helps to divide a long-term program into a series of shorter steps which each have goals and measurements. This then provides the employees with a sequence of current targets which directly relate to their daily work.

Although professionals will frequently understand a goal and agree that it is desirable, they often have no idea how to meet it. This is when managers can actually damage their people's motivation by pressing for progressively better plans. Managers are often tempted to arbitrarily cut cost targets or shorten schedules in the mistaken belief that this will motivate their people to try harder. Often, however, this merely discourages them by making a difficult job seem impossible.

Although managers should set overall direction, their people should be involved in defining their own goals and breaking them into measurable steps with detailed plans. When they cannot see how to do this, managers should honestly debate the problems and search for ways to remove constraints or simplify the job. When managers work this way with their people, their people will truly believe in the importance of their goals and be dedicated to meet them.

NOTES CHAPTER 23

1. Douglas S. Sherwin, "Strategy for Winning Employee Commitment," *Harvard Business Review on Management* (New York: Harper & Row, Publishers, Inc., 1975).

2. Edgar F. Huse, *Organization Development and Change* (St. Paul, Minn.: West Publishing Company, 1975).

3. Paul R. Lawrence, "How to Deal with Resistance to Change," *Harvard Business Review*, January–February 1969, p. 4.

4. Hersey and Blanchard discuss this subject, starting on page 289, in their book *Management of Organizational Behavior: Utilizing Human Resources*, 3rd ed. (Englewood Cliffs, N.J.: Prentice-Hall, Inc., 1977).

5. Ibid., p. 293.

6. Harold J. Leavitt, *Managerial Psychology, Fourth Edition* (Chicago, Ill.: University of Chicago Press, 1978), p. 165.

7. Patrick H. Irwin and Frank W. Langham, Jr., "The Change Seekers," *Harvard Business Review*, January–February 1966, p. 75.

8. Michael L. Tushman and William L. Moore, *Readings in the Management of Innovation* (Marshfield, Mass.: Pitman, 1982), p. 217.

9. Irwin and Langham, "The Change Seekers."

10. Jeffrey Pfeffer, *Organizations and Organization Theory* (Marshfield, Mass.: Pitman, 1982), p. 51.

24

Managing

Process Change

Michael Maccoby of Harvard University has coined the term "technoservice" to describe the increasingly complex nature of many of today's high technology businesses.[1] He cites many examples of technical jobs which require both extreme competence and a high degree of responsibility. Two of his examples are the nuclear near-disaster at Three Mile Island and the collapse of Mobil Oil's Ocean Ranger drilling platform, which cost fifty lives. In both cases, the people on the scene should have had the knowledge to understand the problems and the authority to promptly take action. As both subsequent investigations showed, however, those closest to the problems did not have the requisite ability or authority to properly respond.

Fortunately, few of today's technical people are faced with such life-threatening situations. Many professionals, however, are currently involved in tasks which require both technical competence and a high degree of judgment. In these cases management should be increasingly concerned with the process by which the work is done, as opposed to merely focusing on the final results. For example, in solid logic circuit design no one can tell with certainty whether the circuit will work until it has been built, and this can take many months. Since modern integrated logic chips contain hundreds or even thousands of circuits, there are many opportunities for error, and a design process which is merely good will likely contain at least one mistake. Since any single mistake is generally irreparable, this means that the chip layout and fabrication must be repeated. To save the many months of delay this normally entails, modern designers use very disciplined methods, standardized designs, comprehensive reviews, and extensive simulations.

With relatively simple technologies, each development step can be reasonably self-contained, and a good intuition is generally an adequate management guide. With advanced processes, however, uncontrolled or ill-defined methods can cause expensive and even dangerous errors which are frequently undetectable until too late. The manager must, therefore, insure that every process step is competently handled and that the combined results are adequately tested and verified. With each advance in technology, it becomes progressively more important to insist that the job be done right the first time.

ENVIRONMENTAL DISCIPLINE

The purpose of process management is to insure the kind of disciplined environment needed for advanced work. For example, the proper conditions must be maintained in a space-walking astronaut's sealed suit or they will simply not survive. Without gravity their position must also be controlled, and special tools are needed to compensate for the lack of stability resulting from their weightlessness. Although all these elements are absolutely essential, none of them is directly related to the work the astronauts will actually do. Without this environment, however, they would be incapable of doing the job.

Many of today's newer technologies require comparable discipline in the working environment. Genetic engineering, for example, involves the use of extremely pure materials and long sequences of complex reactions. High-energy physics, high-density semiconductors, and nuclear engineering also demand equally challenging environments, and the list continues to grow. In high-technology manufacturing, for example, the loss of precise control through a temperature change, a drifting instrument calibration, or a fluctuation in the raw-material mix will inevitably cause a yield bust. In high-volume processes, it is essential to quickly correct any such deviation before yield falls and costs escalate.

In such intellectual processes as systems programming, many of the same principles apply. Here, an interface error, a lost test case, or an uncontrolled program library can cause defects to be overlooked until later in the process, when they are far more difficult and expensive to fix. Any such loss of control will increase errors, raise costs, and delay schedules. Proper attention to the principles of process management will help to control such problems by providing a precise and early understanding of what is wrong and exactly what needs to be done to bring it back under control.

THE PRINCIPLES OF PROCESS MANAGEMENT

The first step in managing a process is to make sure it is under statistical control. W. Edwards Deming, who played a large part in the Japanese industrial miracle after World War II, has said that when a process is under statistical control, quality can only be improved by changing the process. If it is not under statistical control, then no sustained improvement is possible until it is.[2]

Statistical control is possible even when a process is not completely understood. For example, most successful technical organizations are able to estimate with reasonable accuracy the time and resources required to do a job that is similar to one they have done before. This ability is readily developed when the professionals compare their prior estimates with actual experience and then make allowance for systematic errors. This, however, only means that they can predict future costs if they do the work in exactly the same way as before. To cut costs, improve quality, or shorten lead times, however, the process must be understood in enough detail to project what will happen when it is changed. This requires a deeper knowledge than merely predicting the consequences of repetition.

Process control is the key to effective process management, and Badawy describes this as involving three steps:[3]

1. Precisely measuring progress toward objectives
2. Determining the cause of deviations and how to fix them
3. Taking the necessary corrective actions

THE IMPORTANCE OF MEASUREMENTS

Lord Kelvin said, in the 1890s, that

> when you can measure what you are speaking about, and express it in numbers, you know something about it; but when you cannot measure it, when you cannot express it in numbers, your knowledge is of a meager and unsatisfactory kind; it may be the beginning of knowledge, but you have scarcely in your thoughts advanced to the stage of science.[4]

The first essential step in process management is to select the important process parameters and start to measure them. According to Mason Haire this is important because "what gets measured gets done."[5] A measurement focuses attention and sets priorities. It shows where progress is being made and clearly identifies shortcomings. This generates what Ullrich calls "normative control," for motivated people take pride in their work and want to excel.[6] When they can see how their performance measures up, they exert themselves to meet and exceed their targets. This can best be accomplished by taking measurements, analyzing them, and making adjustments. By continuing this measurement-analysis-change cycle, the understanding of the process is progressively improved, and the people can more accurately project the effects of every change.

KINDS OF MEASUREMENTS

In any sophisticated process, there is an almost infinite variety of possible parameters to measure. A formally documented process definition, however, helps to identify the important measurements by subdividing the total activity into stages which each have explicit entry and exit criteria.[7] This allows for something analogous to yield curves, which permit each process step to be tracked, deviations identified, and causes isolated.

Measurements, however, can also represent a significant added professional work load. They take time to record, to verify, and to analyze, and if the number of measurements is not limited to an essential minimum, they can become a serious work load in themselves. If not handled carefully, measurements can thus reduce the effectiveness of the process rather than improving it.

It is also often the case that many of the practical process measurements are necessarily either incomplete or misleading. The measurements that can be made of any sophisticated process generally suffer from being imprecise, unverifiable, or not timely. Every measurement is thus subject to interpretation, and sufficient history is rarely available to permit the necessary trend studies. This means that no simple measures can ever completely represent an entire process. On the other hand, no complex process can be consistently improved without taking measurements. The best available measurements must therefore be made regardless of their drawbacks, for the only way to improve the measurement process is to actually take measurements.

PROCESS ANALYSIS

Perhaps the greatest value of measurements is the insight they provide into trends and changes. They should thus be permanently recorded in a data base for later study and analysis. This historical record rapidly provides a quantitative process understanding and permits progressively better improvement goals to be set for each process stage. The importance of such measurements in a complex process was explained by Jim Picciano, the manager of IBM's Burlington, Vermont, semiconductor manufacturing plant, when he said, "You can't manage from the end of the line, you must do it in-line and take prompt action."

Measurement and analysis, however, are hard work. Most professionals and managers will readily agree that measurements are a good idea, but unless they are truly convinced of their value, they will always be too busy actually to do anything. It takes a great deal of experience before pragmatic engineers and programmers realize how quickly a statistical process analysis can focus their attention on the key problem areas. Until they have gained such experience, any schedule crises will take priority over process data. Special dedicated process groups are thus needed to do the early data gathering and analysis. These groups then assist the product people to do such work and graphically demonstrate the value of statistical process management.

THE ELEMENTS OF PROCESS MANAGEMENT

To install a process management discipline, the process itself must first be defined and documented. The key measurements are then established, data gathered and analyzed, and corrective actions implemented. For systems programming, the basic elements of such a process have been summarized in the following steps:[8]

People Management

*The professionals are the key to the programming process, and they must be intimately involved in its improvement.

*Management must focus on programming defects not as personal issues but as process problems.

Process Support

*Special process groups are established.

*Needed management and professional education is provided.

*The best tools and methods are obtained and used.

Process Methodology

*The process is formally defined.

*Goals and measurements are established.

*Statistical data is gathered and analyzed to identify problems and determine causes.

Process Control

*Management practices are established to control change.

*Periodic process assessments are planned to monitor effectiveness and identify needed improvements.

*Procedures are established to certify product quality and implement corrective actions.

PROCESS MANAGEMENT PRIORITIES

As technological processes become more complex, it becomes progressively more difficult to produce any kind of effective results. With advanced semiconductors, for example, often several hundred process steps are used to produce a single product unit. If each step has a yield of 99.9 percent, a 300-hundred-step process will only yield 75 percent good product. If the yield of only three of these steps falls to 50 percent, however, the overall process yield will drop from 75 percent to under 10 percent. This in turn will reduce output volume and raise unit product cost by seven and a half times. A sophisticated process is thus no better than its weakest link.

Management priorities must adapt to these new realities. They must recognize that advanced process technologies are built on a statistical foundation. This calls for detailed statistical records and a disciplined search for every problem cause and means to prevent it. This process discipline must also be introduced carefully or else the professionals will see it as regimentation. With care and understanding, however, they will soon realize that the discipline of a controlled environment is far different from the regimentation of their work. In sophisticated modern technologies, the need is for the creativity and flexibility of motivated individuals within a disciplined process environment.

PEOPLE IN THE PROCESS ENVIRONMENT

Initially, the greatest challenge in process management is to get the people to gather reliable data. Many of the key process parameters involve the professionals' work, and deviations can often be interpreted as personal mistakes. People are understandably sensitive about their errors, and a careless manager can easily reinforce this concern. In one case the management team held a series of department-wide meetings to emphasize the cost of errors and the need to reduce them. The measurement used was the number of fixes made. Since each fix could be attributed to an individual programmer's error, however, the people were now increasingly nervous about how this data would be used, so they started to group multiple errors into single fixes. This made it appear that fewer errors were being made when in fact the reverse was the case.

It takes great personal maturity to objectively study one's own failings and work on improvements. Any measurement of professionals' work must therefore be treated with great care, for if management criticism is based on the data they report, they will likely never make accurate reports again. Unless there is some objective way to verify results, employees who feel personally threatened cannot be expected to produce reliable data. The only answer is to keep such measurements impersonal and to treat problems as process issues. The people should be praised for gathering and using data about how they do their work, regardless of their individual error rates.

Many managers object that process data is needed to identify incompetent or lazy workers. They properly feel that poor performers should be managed firmly, and if they do not improve, they should be dismissed. Any belief that process data can be used for this purpose, however, is nonsense. In the first place, no organization has very many lazy or incompetent workers, and those they do have are generally well known to the managers. Further, as soon as the employees realize that their data will be used against them, they will either slant it or refuse to gather it in the first place. Finally, if someone is suspected of incompetence, his or her data can't be trusted in any event, so it is useless for disciplinary purposes. Data to assess people's performance must therefore be gathered independently of them.

Management's focus must be on improvement, and everyone should work to find and fix the process problems that limit performance. When people make serious mistakes, the cause is most likely their tools, their education, or the way they were managed. If they are truly incompetent, the problem should be handled outside of the process, and any public blame should be avoided. The process may cause problems, but only the people can fix them; and they will only do so when they are not personally threatened.

THE POWER OF PROCESS MANAGEMENT

One common objection to the concept of process management is that such control is only necessary when the people are not sufficiently talented. There are, of course, some people who can intuitively perform with the necessary skill and precision even without any formal structure. Unfortunately, no large organization can be entirely staffed with such talents, and even a small percentage of less-gifted people will seriously damage any sophisticated but uncontrolled process.

An intuitive process is comfortable for the professionals because it allows them great freedom. Intuition, however, will only work within very tight skill and experience constraints and then only when the organization is of moderate size and the technology is relatively simple. Even then, sustained advances in productivity or quality generally require an orderly process management framework.

With a statistically controlled and managed process, there is a firm base for improvement. The people will more readily learn new methods and better retain this knowledge in the intellectual structure which the defined process provides. Finally, a quantitative discipline also permits each professional to learn from the experiences of others.

A PROCESS MANAGEMENT EXAMPLE

The introduction of process measurement disciplines into IBM's large-systems programming organization provides a comprehensive example of how these principles work. This turned out to be a major change both because many thousands of programmers were involved and because the work spanned a number of IBM divisions and groups. The effort was started by a technical staff of experienced programmers, some of whom had successfully used such methods. They knew that programming errors were not randomly distributed and that precise development data could indicate the particular parts with the greatest risk. These high-risk areas were then targeted during the remaining inspection and test phases. The reason for this entire change effort was the significant improvement in quality and productivity which would then result.

At the start of this effort this same staff group launched the previously described programming studies.[9] The potential value of statistical data was explained at every opportunity, and several seminars were given to large audiences. While all these efforts built interest, the professionals were also suspicious that managers might use this process data in performance evaluations. The managers, of course, had no such plans; but none of them had used such methods before, and they also viewed this as a theoretical exercise rather than as an essential process task. Several groups ran some limited experiments, however, and their results soon showed that the concept worked. A number of internal papers and talks were given, and these helped to build the professionals' conviction on this subject. By this time the idea of data gathering was generally accepted, and the unfreezing process was nearly complete.

As soon as open opposition to data gathering ceased, it was next important to establish change agents in each laboratory. They would assist the projects in gathering and analyzing statistical data and building an experience data base. Resources were extremely tight, however, and headquarters wanted to insure local management's support of the program. They thus authorized added people and funding on a matching-grants basis to each laboratory on condition that laboratory management assign an equal number of their own people. After some negotiation all the laboratories agreed, and in about one year these specialists were largely in place.

The final change step was to establish a technical council so that these specialists could share their experience and discuss problems. The meeting reports were widely distributed, and statistical data gathering and analysis was progressively more widely accepted as an effective aid to managing the programming development process.

The final refreezing process will take several years, but the key elements are largely in place. First, it is already clear that because of their positive value, statistical methods will sell themselves as long as management provides suitable support. An education program has been established by IBM's Software Engineering Institute to describe the benefits of statistical methods, to show why they work for programming development, and to give the students experience on practical examples. Statistical methods are also being incorporated into the business procedures by requiring quality plans for each product and statistical data to support them. With these steps in place, statistical data gathering and analysis is well on the way to becoming an established working practice in IBM's systems programming development organizations.

SOME PROCESS LESSONS

Several critical points are illustrated by this example. First, the application of statistical principles to programming development had been demonstrated long before this change effort was started. This was essential because bright technical ideas often have hidden flaws, and when they are first used on a critical project, there are often serious problems.

Second, it is essential to allow people plenty of time to adopt new methods. Unless there is clear evidence that they work, most people are reluctant to experiment with their jobs, and they need the reassurance of other people's successes. As the number of these positive experiences grows, however, this questioning attitude will gradually change and, soon, a kind of bandwagon effect develops. In this example, the turning point was reached when the professionals stopped asking, ''Why should I gather data?'' and started to ask, ''How do I use it?''

It was at just about this time that the dedicated process staffs were put in place in the laboratories. Their role as change agents accelerated the projects' acceptance of statistical methods. They also held periodic meetings and gradually formed a kind of fraternity to pool experiences, communicate solutions to key problems, and publicize successes.

The final and most important consideration was the growing acceptance by the professionals themselves of the value of statistical methods. Although an edict could have forced them to gather data, it would have been much harder to make them use it effectively. The need was not to gather data but to have people who believed in using statistical data in their daily work.

MAKING IT HAPPEN

Even with overwhelming evidence that a new method works, it is still very hard to get people to change. Frederick Winslow Taylor reported in 1911 that a 40 percent productivity improvement could be achieved in metal machining by cooling the cutting tool with a stream of water.[10] The first factory to use these methods openly demonstrated them to their competitors, but in the next twenty years, only one actually adopted them. When Taylor investigated to see what caused this long delay, he found that the only exception was a former employee who had used these methods in the first company before he changed his job. Clearly, regardless of the kind of structured change process, one knowledgeable, experienced, and dedicated change agent can make all the difference.

Even when all the professionals and their managers agree to a change and detailed plans have been established, progress can still be painfully slow. It is essential to be patient and focus on steady, small advances toward the final goal. Eric Severeid, the well-known war correspondent, described the enormous value of short-term, immediate goals in an anecdote about his wartime experiences:

> During World War II, I and several others had to parachute from a crippled army transport plane into the mountainous jungle on the Burma–India border. It was several weeks before an armed relief expedition could reach us, and then we began a painful, plodding march "out" to civilized India. We were faced by a 140-mile trek, over mountains, in August heat and monsoon rains. In the first hour of the march I rammed a boot nail deep into one foot; by evening I had bleeding blisters the size of a 50-cent piece on both feet. Could I hobble 140 miles? Could the others, some in worse shape than I, complete such a distance? We were convinced we could not. But we could hobble to that ridge, we could make the next friendly village for the night. And that, of course, was all we had to do.[11]

NOTES CHAPTER 24

1. Michael Maccoby, "A New Way of Managing," *IEEE Spectrum*, June 1984, p. 69.
2. W. Edward Deming, "Quality, Productivity, and Competitive Position," Massachusetts Institute of Technology Center for Advanced Engineering Study, Cambridge, Mass., 1982, p. 120–130.

3. M. K. Badawy, *Developing Managerial Skills in Engineers and Scientists: Succeeding as a Technical Manager* (New York: International Thompson Organization Inc., Van Nostrand Reinhold Co., 1982), p. 289.

4. Janet R. Dunham and Elizabeth Kruesi, "The Measurement Task Area," *IEEE Computer*, November 1983, vol. 16, no. 11, p. 47.

5. Thomas J. Peters and Robert H. Waterman, Jr., *In Search of Excellence: Lessons from America's Best-Run Companies* (New York: Harper & Row, Publishers, Inc., 1982), p. 268.

6. Robert A. Ullrich, *Motivation Methods That Work* (Englewood Cliffs, N.J.: Prentice-Hall, Inc., 1981), p. 32–38.

7. R. A. Radice, N. M. Roth, A. C. O'Hara, Jr., and W. A. Ciarfella, "A Programming Process Architecture," *IBM Systems Journal*, vol. 24, no. 2 (1985), p. 79.

8. Watts S. Humphrey, "Programming Quality: Objectives and Direction," *IBM Systems Journal*, vol. 24, no. 2 (1985), p. 76.

9. See "The IBM Programming Studies" in Chapter 21.

10. Robert A. Ullrich, *Motivation Methods*, p. 4.

11. Eric Severeid, "The Best Advice I Ever Had," *Reader's Digest*, vol. 70, no. 420 (April 1957), p. 140.

Index